Science an Christianity

An Introduction to the Issues

J. B. Stump

WILEY Blackwell

This edition first published 2017
© 2017 John Wiley & Sons, Inc.

Registered Office

John Wiley & Sons Ltd, The Atrium, Southern Gate, Chichester, West Sussex, PO19 8SQ, UK

Editorial Offices

350 Main Street, Malden, MA 02148-5020, USA
9600 Garsington Road, Oxford, OX4 2DQ, UK
The Atrium, Southern Gate, Chichester, West Sussex, PO19 8SQ, UK

For details of our global editorial offices, for customer services, and for information about how to apply for permission to reuse the copyright material in this book please see our website at www.wiley.com/wiley-blackwell.

The right of J. B. Stump to be identified as the author of this work has been asserted in accordance with the UK Copyright, Designs and Patents Act 1988.

Library of Congress Cataloging-in-Publication Data

Names: Stump, J. B., author.
Title: Science and Christianity : an introduction to the issues / J.B. Stump.
Description: Hoboken : Wiley, 2016. | Includes bibliographical references and index.
Identifiers: LCCN 2016005809 (print) | LCCN 2016012955 (ebook) |
    ISBN 9781118625279 (cloth) | ISBN 9781118625248 (pbk.) | ISBN 9781118625361 (pdf) |
    ISBN 9781118625132 (epub)
Subjects: LCSH: Religion and science. | Christianity. | Theology.
Classification: LCC BL240.3 .S79 2016 (print) | LCC BL240.3 (ebook) |
    DDC 261.5/5—dc23
LC record available at http://lccn.loc.gov/2016005809

A catalogue record for this book is available from the British Library.

Cover image: GettyImages / ©Spencer Black

Set in 9/12pt Meridien LT Std by Aptara

1   2017

Contents

Acknowledgments

There are many people who have contributed to the completion of this book. The staff at Wiley-Blackwell have once again been a pleasure to work with. This project spanned a time when there was some turnover in the editor's chair from Jeff Dean to Deirdre Ilkson to Marissa Koors. I was pleased to work with all of them, as well as the very able staff who saw this project through to completion.

Almost all of the work for this book was conducted while I was a faculty member at Bethel College (Indiana). A summer research grant was helpful in writing several chapters. I was able to teach an upper-level course on science and religion to a group of high-capacity students, during which the topics for many of these chapters were explored. Thanks to the library staff who encouraged me and always went the extra mile in securing resources. Several of the chapters here were used as a class project by Prof. Jennifer Ochstein's editing class; I appreciate their careful reading and eye for detail. Huge thanks are due to Mahala Rethlake, one of the significant success stories of the Bethel philosophy department, who gave a careful editing pass and formatted the entire manuscript. My former colleagues in the religion and philosophy department remain a source of constant encouragement, stimulation, and enjoyment. Special thanks to Terry Linhart, the chair of the department, for his support and friendship through some rocky times. And I am especially grateful to Chad Meister, with whom I have spent countless hours over coffee discussing these (and many other) topics. The fact that I am no longer employed at Bethel does not take anything away from the positive experiences I had there.

The BioLogos Foundation has provided an enriching environment for me the last couple of years. Through my work there I've been fortunate to rub shoulders (both electronically and in person) with some of the leading voices in the dialogue between science and Christianity. President Deb Haarsma has been uniformly supportive (and understanding when the lines demarcating my jobs became blurry). The graciousness with which she approaches the dialogue between science and Christianity should be a model for all.

Finally, my family must be acknowledged. My parents are not academics in the professional sense, but my father, Ron Stump, started his career as a science teacher, and I am very thankful for the orientation toward the natural world he provided. My mother's side of the family did have some academics, and I'm sure that much of my penchant for introspection comes through her—Nancy (Ummel) Stump. Both sides of the family passed down their Christian heritage and provided the categories through which I was introduced to theology. I am so proud of my sons, Casey, Trevor, and Connor. I love it when they want to discuss the topics I research and write about; but I love it even more when they teach me about the things they are most interested in. My wife Christine gets her own page immediately following.

To my wife Christine
for faithfully and cheerfully
accompanying me on this journey.
I couldn't ask for a better
traveling companion.

Introduction

In the last few decades of the 20th century, a widespread scholarly interest developed in issues related to science and religion. This interest has shown no signs of abating, as conferences are organized, books written, and even university departments are now being formed. The academic field is maturing as the second generation of scholars in this field reflects on the seminal work of the founding generation. One of the implications of the maturing of the field is the need for a more fine-grained analysis of the issues. So instead of more general works on science and religion, this book introduces the relationship of science to Christianity.

Of course, there are some commonalities among religions with respect to their interactions with science, but as we get into specific doctrines it is the differences in both the sciences and in the various world religions that become important after a basic introduction to this fascinating interdisciplinary field. For example, the nature of God in Christian theism is very different from the understanding of God or gods in Hinduism or of ultimate (non)reality in some forms of Buddhism. And even within the traditional monotheistic religions which affirm the same creator God, there are significant discrepancies in understanding how God relates to the natural world and how God has revealed the divine nature to humans.

Focusing more narrowly on Christianity is not at all to suggest that it is the only relevant religion in dialogue with science. Other books should be written (and are being written) on Buddhism and science or Islam and science, etc. These religions have their own histories and methodologies and should be accorded the respect that is due them rather than trying to subsume them under a generic heading and discussion of religion, or by giving them a paragraph or two of attention in a work that is in reality discussing Christianity. It is a fact that Christianity has been the dominant religious system that has interacted with the sciences throughout history—a fact that is explored in the book.

But now I want to be clear that this book is not a work of Christian apologetics. I am not arguing for the truth of Christianity (or of any particular scientific theory, for that matter). Rather, I will attempt to present the issues as fairly and objectively as possible, discussing the strengths and weaknesses of particular interpretations. Undoubtedly there are places where my own biases shine through, but I'm not trying to advocate for specific positions.

The study of science and Christianity draws from a number of different disciplines. Besides the obvious ones of the various sciences and Christian theology, history has a prominent place in my exposition of these topics. Fundamentally, though, this is a philosophically oriented treatment of science and Christianity. Lines of demarcation are notoriously difficult to draw, but in the strict sense of the term, the scholars engaged in research in this field are not scientists (at least *qua* researchers in *this* field). That is, they are not conducting experiments or even writing up the results of empirical discoveries for journals like *Nature* or *Science*. Some scholars in this field have done those things, but those are contributions to science, not to the discipline of science and Christianity. Instead, in this discipline they are reflecting on the results of science, particularly with respect to the claims of Christian theology. Nor are the science and religion scholars playing the part of the theologian—though the lines are somewhat less distinct in this case. Again, the job of scholars in the field as I understand it is to reflect on the work of theologians as it relates to scientific discoveries. So in this sense, they are doing a *philosophy of* science and Christianity. It is in that vein that I write about the field.

Science, Christianity, and the systematic study of their interaction

The history of science's interaction with Christianity is dependent on the histories of the subjects considered individually. It is not too difficult to give a starting point to Christianity: there is little doubt that Jesus of Nazareth lived in the first third of the 1st century CE, that he was put to death by the Roman government around 30 or 33 CE, and that his disciples believed him to have resurrected from the dead. Originally, Christians were a sect of Jews who believed Jesus to be their long-awaited Messiah, but they increasingly became a distinct religious group in the 1st century as Gentiles were invited to join the movement. After 70 CE when the Romans laid siege to Jerusalem and destroyed the Jewish temple, Jews and Christians largely went their separate ways. Christians themselves suffered through periods of intense persecution from the Roman government, but within a few centuries they became the dominant religious group of the Roman Empire, and hence of what is known as Western civilization.

The birth of science is more difficult to pinpoint. The English word "science" comes from the Latin *scientia*, but this was used to refer to a wide range of knowledge, certainly outside the parameters of what we would consider science today. Closer to our conception of science is what was called "natural philosophy." Natural philosophers were those who studied the natural world, as opposed to moral philosophers, who studied ethics. The methods of natural philosophers were varied, and so in 1834 the Cambridge University professor William Whewell (1794–1866) coined the term "scientist" to distinguish the empirical approach of some researchers from the more general "natural philosophers." It is this usage that has become standard.

However, if we were to consider the relationship of Christianity with science only as it has been understood since 1834, we would be omitting much that is relevant to our study here. As far back as we have written records, human beings have been asking questions about the world around them. Perhaps beginning with the ancient Greeks, we find the attempt to give answers in terms of what we today call natural causes, as opposed to the supernatural causes invoked by mythologies and religions. In that sense we can consider the relationship between Christianity and the science (or proto-science) of providing natural explanations.

It should be acknowledged that the religion of Christianity and the practice of science are much more encompassing social practices than merely systems of beliefs. It might be argued that the rituals associated with Christianity are more important and defining for the religion as a whole than are the beliefs. Likewise increasing attention has been given since the previous generation of philosophers of science to the non-cognitive dimensions of the scientific enterprise. The relations of these social dimensions need to be explored, but our focus in this book is on the cognitive dimensions of science and Christianity. More specifically, what are the beliefs of each that intersect? What are the methods of inquiry, and how do these interact?

This kind of study has been more systematically pursued since the 1960s and 1970s. Ian Barbour is generally taken to be the godfather of the academic discipline of science and religion. His 1966 book *Issues in Science and Religion* was the starting point for a generation of scholars who began to reflect more seriously on the relationship between science and religion. Soon after Barbour, along came Arthur Peacocke and John Polkinghorne. The three of them form the triumvirate of scientist theologians who had that rare combination of knowing science from the inside along with being able to reflect upon it insightfully with respect to religion. They have been a foundational source for the science and religion scholars of today.

The significant growth of the academic discipline of science and religion in the past generation has an economic causal factor. The John Templeton Foundation gives millions of dollars each year to a wide variety of research programs in science and religion. Nearly everyone working in the field has benefited from this largesse.

Features and outline of this book

Each chapter of this book is separated into numbered sections. The numbers are keyed to the "Questions to be addressed in this chapter" box at the beginning of each chapter, and to the "Summary of main points" box at the end. These are not designed to reduce the complexity of the material into easy bullet points but to help in dividing up the content of each chapter into more manageable chunks.

There are ample boxes throughout the text that provide longer quotations from important sources, more detailed explanation of key concepts, and some pictures. It is hoped that these are enriching resources and not distracting. At the end of the text is a timeline of the historical figures discussed in the book and a glossary that provides definitions for specialized terminology. Terms included in the glossary are printed in bold font in the text. And all Scripture quotations are taken from the NRSV translation unless otherwise indicated.

Each chapter also includes a short annotated list of resources for further reading on that subject. This book loosely tracks many of the topics of *The Blackwell Companion to Science and Christianity*, which I edited with Alan Padgett in 2012. Many of the articles there provide good next steps for exploring the topics introduced here.

Chapters 1 through 3 function as a kind of unit. They deal with the ways in which science and religion (particularly Christianity) have been related, and offer some historical episodes as illustrations of these. Chapter 1 considers the extreme relationships of conflict and independence, and it is not too hard to find instances of these throughout history. But there are also nuances to these positions that ought to be considered as well. Chapters 2 and 3 present what I think are among the strongest cases historically of science and Christianity directly and substantially influencing each other. For Christianity influencing science, the best case is in the very founding of modern science; we look at the case for and against that in Chapter 2. For science influencing Christianity (at least on the largest scale), we look to the thesis of secularization: has science caused the secularization of society? This is the topic of Chapter 3. Then Chapter 4 is also historical in a sense, though dealing with the more recent history of Young Earth Creationism and the Intelligent Design movement.

Chapters 5 and 6 address foundational topics that underlie much of the dialogue about Christianity and science. Christians can't do without the Bible (Chapter 5), and most scientists feel they can't do their jobs properly without methodological naturalism (Chapter 6). We'll see in both these cases that there are methodological approaches that are profitable for the dialogue, and approaches that can stop any productive dialogue.

Chapter 7 tackles natural theology, which has been one of the chief points of interaction between science and Christianity. Besides some of the classical forms of natural theology, I look at a more popular contemporary version many call the "theology of nature." Chapter 8 covers what was often the focal point of science and religion discussions in the previous generation: cosmology—including the Big Bang, fine tuning, and the multiverse. Today, evolution has moved into the most prominent position for discussion. It is the subject of Chapter 9.

Chapters 10 and 11 focus on interaction problems. The first is how God interacts with the world, or what is often called "divine action." It is sometimes described by analogy with interaction of human minds and bodies, though some might claim such an analogy does little to clarify the situation. This human interaction problem, along with the theological implications of the soul, forms the subject of Chapter 11.

If God is understood as interacting with the world, then questions inevitably arise about why more evils aren't prevented. Especially with what we now understand as an unfathomably long history of animal pain and suffering, the problem of natural evil is particularly acute. It is addressed in Chapter 12. Many attempts at explaining natural evil appeal to a final promised state in which individuals—both human and animal—who have wrongly suffered will find ultimate fulfillment. The conclusion of the book reflects and speculates on the end times as understood from the perspective of science and from Christian theology.

I hope that each of these chapters stands on its own, but there is also a sense in which I've tried to order them so as to pull the reader along from one topic to the next. If the book accomplishes nothing other than spurring further interest in these topics of science and Christianity, I will count it a success.

CHAPTER 1

Conflict and Independence

In 1633, at the age of 70, Galileo Galilei—the famed mathematician and scientist from Pisa—was forced on threat of excommunication and possible execution to kneel before the Inquisitors of the Roman Catholic Church. He was given a prepared statement to read aloud which disavowed the work he had done the previous two decades. Of what heinous heresy was he suspected? Simply that the earth moved around the sun each year and turned on its axis every day.

When most people consider the way science and religion—or more specifically for this book, science and Christianity—have interacted, it is this story of Galileo and the Church that is taken as the paradigm. Over the centuries Christianity had developed a geocentric worldview that included the belief that the earth was immobile at the center of the universe, and all of the celestial objects circled it. This cosmological picture was primarily informed by Aristotle's physics and Ptolemy's astronomy, but the Church could also appeal to verses in the Bible that were most naturally interpreted as supporting the earth-centered cosmos. That led to some fireworks.

Today, the popular understanding is that the Galileo episode was a straightforward conflict between science and Christianity in which the Church was more concerned with protecting its tradition and authority than with discovering the truth. As might be expected, the real story is more complicated than this. We consider it further in this chapter, along with several other episodes that illustrate the complex relationship between science and Christianity.

The aim here is not to provide a full-blown history of science and Christianity, nor is it to prescribe how these two influential enterprises in society *should* interact today. More modestly, this chapter aims to illustrate and explain some of the ways that science and Christianity have in fact interacted. Before looking at these, it will be helpful to discuss a few of the classification systems that have been used to organize the topic.

Science and Christianity: An Introduction to the Issues, First Edition. By J. B. Stump.
© 2017 John Wiley & Sons, Ltd. Published 2017 by John Wiley & Sons, Ltd.

> **?**   ## Questions to be addressed in this chapter:
>
> 1. What are the ways that scholars organize the relationship between science and Christianity?
> 2. What was the conflict between Galileo and the Church?
> 3. How can science and Christianity be seen as independent forms of inquiry?
> 4. What is the Two Books metaphor?

1. Ways that science and Christianity might be related

As long as science and Christianity have been around, people have written about them and their relationship, but systematic reflection on these topics by a community of scholars is a fairly recent phenomenon. It has only been for the last generation or so that "Science and Religion" has been a distinct academic discipline with its own journals and university degree programs. The godfather of this movement has been Ian Barbour (1923–2013). His book *Issues in Science and Religion* (1966) is a thorough overview of the relevant topics, and it set the agenda for subsequent thinkers in the field. In that book and his *Myths, Models and Paradigms* (1974), he began developing a classification system for how science and religion can be related to each other. But it was his Gifford Lectures of 1989–1990 (Barbour 1990) where this typology was defended systematically.

Barbour's four categories are conflict, independence, dialogue, and integration. The first assumes that either the scientific or the religious way of acquiring knowledge is correct, and not both; thus, they are in conflict with each other. At the other end of the spectrum—the independence thesis—science and religion are completely separate and self-contained ways of knowing; as such, they operate in different spheres, and their claims neither conflict nor agree with each other. The dialogue model assumes that science and religion do impinge on each other at certain points, such as the origin of the universe, and so they ought to recognize the insights that each brings to these questions. Finally, the integration model pushes beyond mere dialogue between distinct disciplines and tries to effect a synthesis of science and religion; this can be seen in attempts to develop a **theology** of nature or in process theology where explanations are developed that draw from both the sciences and theology.

 Barbour's four-fold typology of contemporary views for how science and religion may be related

1. **Conflict:** science or religion can be victorious in their explanations, but not both
2. **Independence:** science and religion each have their own sphere of inquiry and cannot conflict
3. **Dialogue:** there is contact between science and religion at boundary questions, like the reason for the orderliness of the universe
4. **Integration:** theological doctrines and scientific theories might be integrated into one coherent model, like a theology of creation

As might be expected, other scholars reflected on Barbour's work and offered critiques and modifications to his typology. Ted Peters (1996) expanded the list of categories, identifying eight different ways that science and religion interact. Christian Berg (2004) reorganized the typology completely, believing it more useful to look at the relationship between science and religion under the dimensions of **metaphysics, epistemology**, and **ethics.** Stenmark (2012) suggested that we should first consider the kind of jobs science and Christianity do. If they are trying to do the same job, then they are in competition; if they do completely different jobs, then they are independent of each other; and if their jobs are different but they overlap to some extent, then there will be points of contact between science and religion.

After Barbour, it might be argued that the next most influential scholar in framing the discussion of how science and religion are related is John Hedley Brooke. His *Science and Religion: Some Historical Perspectives* (1991) derives from detailed historical research the many facets of how science and religion have been related. The conclusion of his work is that the relationship between science and religion cannot be described under one general heading. This has come to be known as the **Complexity thesis.** Another contemporary historian of science, Ronald Numbers, is convinced of the complexity thesis, but sees the need to provide some midscale generalizations or patterns that might prove helpful in organizing and understanding the vast data and literature on the subject. To this end, he describes five trends in the ongoing relationship between science and religion: naturalization, privatization, secularization, globalization, and radicalization (Numbers 2010).

These ways of carving up the conceptual territory at the intersection of science and religion are all helpful. Undoubtedly there are even more ways to get at other nuances of the relationship. For our purposes in this chapter, it will suffice to look more generally at the relationship by considering historical examples of conflict and independence. The next two chapters address examples of influence on each other.

2. Conflict

Today's accepted narrative arc of how historians have understood the relationship between science and Christianity begins with the **conflict thesis** of John William Draper and Andrew Dickson White. Draper's *History of the Conflict between Religion and Science* (1896), first published in 1874, and White's *A History of the Warfare of Science with Theology in Christendom* (1922), first published in 1896, set the tone for how scholars thought about science and Christianity in the first half of the 20th century. On this view, Christianity is cast in the role of the oppressive and stultifying stepmother who held back the young, reasonable, and progressive maiden of science and kept her from flowering throughout the **Middle Ages.** Then science finally broke free from the oppressive Church, or so the story goes, and steadily added to our accumulated knowledge and quality of life.

> ### 📝 John William Draper (1811–1882)
>
> A chemist and physician, Draper was one of the founders of the New York University School of Medicine. His *History of the Conflict between Religion and Science* (1896), first published in 1874, was widely read and conditioned generations of people to view science and religion as competing explanations.
>
> ### Andrew Dickson White (1832–1918)
>
> White was a professor of history and English at the University of Michigan until 1863 and then joined with Ezra Cornell to found Cornell University. White became the university's first president. He published *A History of the Warfare of Science with Theology in Christendom* (1922) in 1896, which continued Draper's interpretation.

This account found sympathetic ears during the heyday of positivism early in the 20th century, and it gained enough traction in the wider culture so that even after the demise of positivism it is still common to hear science and Christianity being pitted against each other in warlike tones. Draper's words gave voice to the feeling that many still share today:

> The history of Science is not a mere record of isolated discoveries; it is a narrative of the conflict of two contending powers, the expansive force of the human intellect on one side, and the compression arising from traditionary faith and human interests on the other. (Draper 1896, vi)

That Draper's and White's historical analyses have been severely criticized by contemporary historians of science is almost beside the point. The rhetoric of this view operates more at the level of talk show discussions, and the sensationalized story plays well within the broader culture.

Of course, even within academia it is not difficult to gather evidence from the pages of history that seems to lend support to the conflict thesis. Indeed, the marquee event of the relationship between science and Christianity appears to illustrate precisely the claim of Draper: Galileo's forced recantation before the Church. The story was introduced at the beginning of the chapter, but now let's look at it more closely.

In the early 17th century, Holland was famous for its industry of grinding glass into lenses. In 1609, Galileo heard that someone there had placed just the right lenses at either end of an enclosed tube and was thereby able to magnify threefold the image of objects seen at a distance. Galileo improved the design of what would come to be called the telescope and succeeded in achieving a magnification of twenty times. In late 1609, he pointed his telescope to the heavens and made several discoveries that challenged the picture of the universe the Church had held for centuries. He wrote up these discoveries and published them in 1610 in a pamphlet portentously titled, "The Starry Messenger: Revealing great, unusual, and remarkable spectacles" (found in Drake 1957). What did he see?

First, he saw that the moon was not a perfect sphere. The prevailing view was that all objects in the celestial realm had to be perfect spheres. But Galileo's moon appeared to have mountains and craters on its surface, just like the kind of irregularity we find in objects of the terrestrial region. Next, he reported seeing many more stars than were visible to the naked eye—ten times as many. His pamphlet included drawings of familiar constellations along with the positions of these additional stars. He also observed that the "Milky Way," which presents itself to the naked eye as a uniformly cloudy substance, is diffused into "congeries of innumerable stars grouped together in clusters" (ibid., 49). Finally, and most importantly to Galileo's mind, he saw four bright dots around the planet Jupiter. Subsequent observations showed that these were not static relative to the planet but instead orbited around Jupiter. This undermined the belief that all celestial objects orbited the earth. Whether or not Jupiter orbited the earth, here were four celestial objects—originally called "stars"—that circled another body in the heavens. Later telescopic observations would include the phases of Venus, which are predicted by the sun-centered system, and sunspots, which speak to the imperfection of another "heavenly" body.

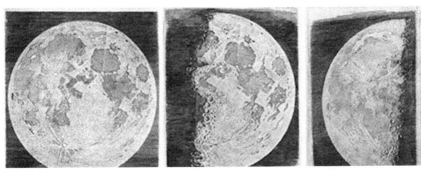

Fig. 1.1 *Three Maps of the Moon*, 1637, by Claude Mellan. These engravings show three different phases of the moon in the kind of detail made possible by the telescope. Source: Abbeville, Musée Boucher de Perthes.

The "Starry Messenger" clearly endorses the Copernican heliocentric model, but does not raise at all the theological questions that would trouble the Church. Reading the pamphlet today, it almost seems like Galileo didn't realize that his discoveries had any theological ramifications. He would soon be disabused of that idea. Over the next few years, conservative philosophers and clergy began arguing that Galileo was a heretic because he believed the earth moved while the Bible clearly indicated otherwise. Instead of engaging in a public dispute, Galileo attempted to counter these charges privately by writing long letters on the topic of the relationship of the Bible to science.

One of these letters was written in 1615 to the widow of the Grand Duke of Tuscany, Ferdinando de' Medici, one of Galileo's patrons, in whose honor Galileo named the moons of Jupiter. The letter has come to be known as the "Letter to the Grand Duchess Christina." In it Galileo argued that while the Bible indeed should be taken as infallible when understood correctly it really has very little to say about matters of astronomy. Where it does mention things like the apparent motion of the earth, we should understand this as language that was accommodated to the people of the time and place in which it was written. Perhaps that argument by itself might have placated some, but Galileo argued in further ways that seemed to undermine the authority of scripture. He said, "I think that in discussions of physical problems we ought to begin not from the authority of scriptural passages, but from sense-experiences and necessary demonstrations" (ibid., 182). This was a direct challenge to the primacy the Church enjoyed as the caretaker of knowledge in all areas of life. The Protestant Reformation was still fresh in the minds of the Catholic Church leaders, and they were not going to let something like sense experience—let alone the sense experience delivered through a tube with lenses at either end—overturn what they knew to be true by revelation.

Galileo's letters were circulated widely, and the Church hierarchy felt that they needed to put a check on the momentum Galileo's position was gaining. In March 1616, the Congregation of the Index published a decree that declared false the idea that the earth moves. Galileo was issued a personal warning by Cardinal Robert Bellarmine (with the authority of the Inquisition) that he was not to hold or defend such a theory. Galileo was a good Catholic, believing that the Church held the fate of his eternal soul in its hands. So he complied until 1623, when Cardinal Maffeo Barberini became Pope Urban VIII. Barberini had been sympathetic to Galileo, so Galileo felt free to embark on a major project related to heliocentrism.

Geocentrism   [jee-oh-**sen**-triz-um]
The doctrine that the earth is the center of the universe.

Heliocentrism   [hee-lee-oh-**sen**-triz-um]
The doctrine that the sun is the center of the universe, and later that the sun is the center of the solar system.

Geokineticism   [jee-oh-ki-**ne**-ti-siz-um]
The doctrine that the earth moves around the sun.

It is only fair to note that the objections against heliocentrism were not exclusively theological. There were significant difficulties for the accepted physics of the day created by the supposition that the earth moves. Why can't we feel it? Why aren't there constant massive winds? Why don't projectiles seem affected by the motion of the earth beneath them? Such questions show that a major overhaul to the general belief system was needed if heliocentrism was to be accepted. Galileo set out to describe a comprehensive worldview that incorporated the new empirical discoveries within the framework of a new physics and a way of understanding them theologically. In 1632, he published a book as a dialogue between three characters, entitled *Dialogue Concerning the Two Chief World Systems: Ptolemaic and Copernican* (Galilei 1967). Galileo argued that the book did not violate the warning he was given in 1616, saying that the book does not really defend the thesis that the earth moves but merely presents some favorable arguments that are ultimately inconclusive. The Inquisitors saw it otherwise, and Urban VIII did not come to Galileo's defense. Ultimately, he was convicted of the "vehement suspicion of heresy," forced to recant, and condemned to house arrest for the remainder of his life. The offending beliefs in particular were the cosmological thesis that the earth moves and the methodological principle that the Bible is not a scientific authority.

Galileo's forced recantation

"I, Galileo, son of the late Vincenzo Galilei, Florentine, aged seventy years, arraigned personally before this tribunal and kneeling before you, Most Eminent and Reverend Lord Cardinals Inquisitors-General against heretical pravity throughout the entire Christian commonwealth, having before my eyes and touching with my hands the Holy Gospels, swear that I have always believed, do believe, and by God's help will in the future believe all that is held, preached, and taught by the Holy catholic and apostolic Church. But, whereas—after an injunction had been judicially intimated to me by this Holy Office to the effect that I must altogether abandon the false opinion that the Sun is the center of the world and immovable and that the Earth is not the center of the world and moves and that I must not hold, defend, or teach in any way whatsoever, verbally or in writing, the said false doctrine, and after it had been notified to me that the said doctrine was contrary to Holy Scripture—I wrote and printed a book in which I discuss this new doctrine already condemned and adduce arguments of great cogency in its favor without presenting any solution of these, I have been pronounced by the Holy Office to be vehemently suspected of heresy, that is to say of having held and believed that the Sun is the center of the world and immovable and that the Earth is not the center and moves: Therefore, desiring to remove from the minds of your Eminences, and of all faithful Christians, this vehement suspicion justly conceived against me, with sincere heart and unfeigned faith I abjure, curse, and detest the aforesaid errors and heresies…"

Galileo recited the statement and then signed it with the following:

"I, the said Galileo Galilei, have abjured, sworn, promised, and abound myself as above; and in witness of the truth thereof I have with my own hand subscribed the present document of my abjuration and recited it word for word at Rome, in the convent of the Minerva, this twenty-second day of June, 1633." (Santillana 1955, 312–313)

The scientific conclusion that the earth moves was certainly jarring to the mindset of 17th-century Christians. But perhaps more unsettling was the latter half of the charge—that the Bible should not be used as a scientific authority. It may be anachronistic to say "scientific" here, as our conception of science today is much narrower than the **natural philosophy** of the 17th century. Of course, the Bible does not contain mathematical formulas and discourses on atomic structures. But does it contain references to the natural world that are to be taken as infallible? When Joshua says that the sun stood still (Joshua 10) or the Psalmist that the Lord set the earth on its foundation and it can never be moved (Psalm 104), do these statements have implications for scientific theories? If so, there would definitely be conflict between the science of Galileo and the theology of orthodox Christianity. But the conflict goes deeper than that.

Galileo thought he was mitigating the potential conflict between his scientific theories and the Bible by adopting a hermeneutic strategy that asserts an independence of the two. In his "Letter to the Grand Duchess Christina" he stated, "the intention of the Holy Ghost [in the role of the Bible's author] is to teach us how one goes to heaven, not how heaven goes" (Drake 1957, 186). In reality, Galileo's attempt to pull the rug out from under the conflict only intensified it. The problem resulted not because he claimed that some things in the Bible were not to be taken so literally. That is a practice that had been accepted by the Church since its inception. For example, when God is described as a rock (2 Samuel 22), no one argues for a literal interpretation. The real source of conflict between science and Christianity in this episode was that Galileo, a scientist with only lay standing in the Church, was attempting to instruct others on how the Bible should be interpreted. That was the job of the Church leaders. And that was why Galileo was a threat and had to be reprimanded.

3. Independence

At other times in the history of science and Christianity, the two sides seemed content to go about their own business without interfering with each other. Some people have tried to make this approach normative for all interactions between science and Christianity. Just as Galileo said, science is trying to figure out how the world works, while the Bible—and Christianity more generally—is concerned primarily with the salvation of souls. These are independent practices and should be kept as such. Even White's *Warfare* book seems to recognize to some extent a legitimate place for religion, so long as it doesn't try to interfere with science. In the introduction to his work he states his thesis to be:

> In all modern history, interference with science in the supposed interest of religion, no matter how conscientious such interference may have been, has resulted in the direst evils both to religion and to science, and invariably; and, on the other hand, all untrammeled scientific investigation, no matter how dangerous to religion some of its stages may have seemed for the time to be, has invariably resulted in the highest good both of religion and of science. (White 1922, viii)

White seems to say that if we just let science go about its business without interference from religion, then both science and religion will benefit. Such an approach is quite different from some of the anti-religion voices of today who call for the abolishment of religion. White claimed that the motivation for founding Cornell University was not to abolish religion but to separate it from the sectarian motivations that were too conspicuous in the other major American universities. He didn't want to have to consider, when hiring a professor of mathematics or language or chemistry, which religious sect to which he or she belonged. Such an approach, in his opinion, stymies advances in both scientific and religious knowledge. If religion would keep to its proper sphere—love of God and of neighbor—it would steadily grow stronger throughout the world (ibid., xii).

There are at least two ways we might understand science and Christianity to be independent of each other. The first is that they may both be investigating the same topic, but they have different methods of investigating and could arrive at different sorts of answers. These answers, however, should not be seen as competing but as different ways of describing the same thing, perhaps like a chemist and an artist might describe the same painting in very different terms without contradicting each other. An extreme version of this would be the theory of **double-truth**, which is usually attributed to Averroës, one of the most important Arabic thinkers of the Middle Ages.

Averroës (1126–1198)

Averroës, also known as ibn-Rushd, lived from 1126 to 1198. He was one of the most important Arab thinkers of the Middle Ages. He was a Muslim philosopher, physician, scientist, theologian, and scholar of the Qur'an, but his influence on subsequent Christian thought was significant and warrants inclusion here. In fact, Thomas Aquinas thought Averroës wrote the finest commentaries available on the works of Aristotle and referred to him simply as the Commentator.

Averroës's concept of double-truth was an attempt to reconcile the natural learning of humans with the supernaturally revealed truth of the Qur'an. These were viewed as two different "languages," and we should not be surprised if they say different things. Apparently, some Christians in the 13th century understood Averroës to mean that two claims could both be true even if they clearly contradict one another. Averroës's actual position was more sophisticated than this, however. For him, the doctrine of double-truth meant that a claim could have different meanings at different levels of description—a literal philosophical meaning and an allegorical or figurative theological meaning. Averroës maintained that the Qur'an was written for the masses in allegorical language. So if natural philosophers discovered that the world is different from what the Qur'an seemed to be saying, he was sure the conflict was only with the apparent meaning of scripture. We can see an application of this in Christian theology in the subsequent century.

In 1210, Aristotle's works on natural philosophy were banned at the University of Paris because they were thought to contradict the teaching of scripture. By 1255, they were back on some reading lists, but authorities still attempted to ban certain ideas contained in them. One of the most prominent of these ideas was the eternality of the world. Of course, according to Christian theology, the world was created at some point in the past. But such an idea was difficult to square with the natural philosophy of the time, which was dominated by the Aristotelian understanding. (Indeed, it was not until the 20th century that the eternality of the world was seriously challenged by scientific evidence.) Could the doctrine of double-truth be used to affirm both of these? Siger of Brabant (1240–1284) was one of the vocal defenders of the Aristotelian view at the University of Paris who tried to do just that. He wanted to affirm the eternality of the world from the scientific perspective, even though it contradicted the teachings of the Church. But the Church would have none of that. In 1270, Bishop Stephen Tempier was persuaded by the more conservative factions to condemn thirteen articles drawn from Aristotle and Averroës. The condemnation seemed to have Siger in mind specifically. If science and religion were to be kept independent, this view of double-truth would not be the way to do it. But there is another version of independence to consider.

Instead of seeing science and Christianity as independent because they have different ways of talking about the same thing, one might attempt to confine science and Christian theology to different objects of study. In the wake of Tempier's condemnations, the arts faculty at the university (which included those studying natural philosophy) attempted to circumvent conflict with the theology faculty by having each of its members swear an oath to not even consider theological questions surrounding issues like the **Trinity** or the **Incarnation**. There is a modern ring to this attempt to demarcate the boundaries of inquiry for different disciplines. In the context of the powerful Church of the Middle Ages, the conservative faction continued to push until the infamous, and even stronger, condemnations of 1277 of Bishop Tempier. The impulse to see science and theology as independent methods of inquiry was stifled, as it would be again with Galileo in the 17th century. But eventually the hegemony of the Church would be broken with respect to academic inquiry, and then the prospect for the independence would be different.

The eminent 20th-century American evolutionary biologist Stephen Jay Gould (1941–2002) defended an approach to science and religion he called **NOMA**, which is an acronym for "non-overlapping magisteria." His claim too is that religion and science are both legitimate methods of inquiry, but they should be restricted to separate spheres. The way his boundary lines were drawn in the late 20th century was that the magisterium of science is the natural world, and that of religion is values. In this view, it became illegitimate to use the Bible to correct scientists about the natural world. Gould said:

> So—and now we come to the key point—if some contradiction seems to emerge between a well-validated scientific result and a conventional reading of scripture, then we had better reconsider our exegesis, for the natural world does not lie, but words can convey many meanings, some allegorical or metaphorical ... In this crucial sense, the magisteria become separate, and science holds sway over the factual character of the natural world. (1999, 21–22)

It could be charged that his theory is hopelessly idealistic and that religion and the Bible do have something to say about the way things are in the natural world, but Gould's theory is more sophisticated than sometimes presented. He admits there is contact between these two magisteria, and even that they are absolutely inseparable, while still maintaining that they are utterly different (ibid., 65–67).

Gould cites the different attitudes of two 20th-century popes on the topic of human evolution as an example of how his approach should and shouldn't work in practice. The first is the negative model: Pope Pius XII issued an encyclical in 1950 entitled *Humani generis*. In it he admits that it may be permitted for scientists to investigate the origins of the human body along the lines suggested by evolution but that the Catholic faith obliges us to regard the human soul as an immediate creation by God (Pius XII 1950, 36). There are consequences of this position which impinge on the findings of science. Pius said:

> For the faithful cannot embrace that opinion which maintains that either after Adam there existed on this earth true men who did not take their origin through natural generation from him as from the first parent of all, or that Adam represents a certain number of first parents. Now it is in no way apparent how such an opinion can be reconciled with that which the sources of revealed truth and the documents of the Teaching Authority of the Church propose with regard to **original sin**, which proceeds from a sin actually committed by an individual Adam and which, through generation, is passed on to all and is in everyone as his own. (Pius XII 1950, 37)

It is clear that, even if Pius allows some room for scientific inquiry to proceed according to its own rules, it is the Church that gets to determine how much room science has.

The message of Pope John Paul II in 1996 seems to reverse the authority in that sphere of inquiry. He first acknowledged that since Pius's 1950 encyclical the data for evolution has become impossible to resist. Then he goes on to concede that it is science that determines the bounds of acceptable biblical interpretation:

> It is important to set proper limits to the understanding of Scripture, excluding any unseasonable [sic] interpretations which would make it mean something which it is not intended to mean. In order to mark out the limits of their own proper fields, theologians and those working on the exegesis of the Scripture need to be well informed regarding the results of the latest scientific research. (John Paul II 1996, 3)

Gould interprets John Paul's mandate of setting proper limits on biblical interpretation and theology as carving out an independent sphere for science. But for a question like the nature of human beings, it is difficult to see how these two different methods of investigation can be kept totally separate. We need a way of incorporating the insights of these two different disciplines without lapsing into the double-truth method of Averroës.

4. Two Books

Before White and Draper altered the public's perception of the relationship between science and religion by bringing the conflict metaphor to the forefront, the conversation was dominated by a different metaphor: **Two Books**. This is the idea that God has provided information or revelation to humans through two different but coordinated sources—the book of God's word (i.e., the Bible) and the book of God's world (i.e., creation). The roots of this metaphor go back to the first centuries of the Christian era to important Christian thinkers like Justin Martyr, Irenaeus of Lyons, Tertullian, and Origen. They all acknowledged God's revelation in nature in addition to revelation in scripture.

The first clear use of the metaphor might be traced to John Chrysostom (c. 347–407). He said:

> If God had given instruction by means of books, and of letters, he who knew letters would have learnt what was written, but the illiterate man would have gone away without receiving any benefit ... This however cannot be said with respect to the heavens, but the Scythian, and Barbarian, and Indian, and Egyptian, and every man that walks upon the earth, shall hear this voice; for not by means of the ears, but through the sight, it reaches our understanding ... Upon this volume the unlearned, as well as the wise man, shall be able to look, and wherever any one may chance to come, there looking upwards towards the heavens, he will receive a sufficient lesson from the view of them. (Homily IX.5, quoted in Hess 2003, 127–128)

Throughout the Middle Ages, the point was repeated by many Christian thinkers that, although book learning was available only to the privileged class of the literate who had access to the Bible, the "book of nature" was available to everyone. The Bible was difficult for the average person to understand, but everyone could "read" what God had written in nature. So just like St. Paul claimed in Romans 1, "all men are without excuse" because God can be known from creation (natural theology is explored in more depth in Chapter 7).

Two events helped to usher Western civilization into the modern era and turned this formula on its head. First, the Protestant Reformation (which itself was fueled by the printing press and increased rates of literacy) made the Bible more widely available to the masses in their languages. No longer was it the exclusive purview of the specialists in the Church to read and interpret the Bible. As we saw in the Galileo episode, the Church attempted to hold on to this privilege, but ultimately the spread of Protestantism made it possible for anyone to read the Bible, and of course not everyone would interpret its message in the same way. So today there are thousands of different Christian denominations.

Second, the widespread access to reading the book of nature was severely curtailed by the success of the **Scientific Revolution**. Science became a set of professionalized and specialized disciplines to which only a few could really contribute. The situation today is that there is a "priestly" class of scientists who disseminate to the masses the knowledge they have acquired about how nature works. Few of us today could observe the heavens and work out the heliocentric model of the solar system, let alone develop quantum mechanics or string theory. Just as the illiterate people of the Middle Ages were beholden to the specialists in the Church to read and interpret the book of scripture, today we must rely on the specialists in science to read and interpret the book of nature for us.

To be fair, if we are to take the interpretation of scripture seriously, we must rely on specialists in that discipline too. Understanding the original languages and cultural contexts is necessary for any responsible interpretation of the Bible. So the Two Books metaphor has become less straightforward. The problem here is they are not just "givens" with content that is immediately apparent. Both the world and the Bible must be interpreted. This situation gives rise to more subtle connections and lines of influence between science and Christianity rather than straightforward conflict or independence. In the next chapter, we explore some of these.

 Summary of main points:

1. The standard typology of how science and religion can be related is conflict, independence, dialogue, and integration.

2. Galileo's conflict with the Church stemmed not so much from his scientific discoveries as from his attempt as a layman to interpret the Bible.

3. Scientific and religious investigation could be independent because they use different methods and language to explain the same phenomena or because they investigate different phenomena.

4. God has given two sources of revelation: the natural world and the Bible.

Further reading

- Brooke, John Hedley. 1991. *Science and Religion: Some Historical Perspectives.* Cambridge: Cambridge University Press. A standard and significant book for understanding the history of how science and religion have interacted.
- Hallanger, Nathan J. 2012. "Ian G. Barbour." In *The Blackwell Companion to Science and Christianity*, edited by J. B. Stump and Alan G. Padgett. Malden, MA: Wiley-Blackwell. A helpful overview of Barbour's contribution to the discipline of science and religion.
- Hess, Peter M. J. 2003. "God's Two Books: Special Revelation and Natural Science in the Christian West." In *Bridging Science and Religion*, edited by Ted Peters and Gaymon Bennett. Minneapolis: Fortress Press. An article exploring the history of the Two Books metaphor for science and religion.
- Lindberg, David C., and Ronald L. Numbers, eds. 2003. *When Science and Christianity Meet.* Chicago: University of Chicago Press. A collection of articles discussing historical case studies that exemplify the complexity of the science–Christianity relationship.
- Stenmark, Mikael. 2012. "How to Relate Christian Faith and Science." In *The Blackwell Companion to Science and Christianity*, edited by J. B. Stump and Alan G. Padgett. Malden, MA: Wiley-Blackwell. An article exploring other dimensions of the science and faith relationship.

References

Barbour, Ian. 1966. *Issues in Science and Religion*. New York: Prentice-Hall.
Barbour, Ian. 1974. *Myths, Models and Paradigms*. New York: Harper & Row.
Barbour, Ian. 1990. *Religion in an Age of Science*. San Francisco: HarperSanFrancisco.
Berg, Christian. 2004. "Barbour's Way(s) of Relating Science and Theology." In *Fifty Years in Science and Religion: Ian G. Barbour and His Legacy*, edited by Robert John Russell, 61–75. Aldershot: Ashgate.
Brooke, John Hedley. 1991. *Science and Religion: Some Historical Perspectives*. Cambridge: Cambridge University Press.
Drake, Stillman, ed. 1957. *Discoveries and Opinions of Galileo*. Garden City, NY: Doubleday Anchor Books.
Draper, John William. 1896. *History of the Conflict between Religion and Science*. New York: D. Appleton and Company.
Galilei, Galileo. 1967. *Dialogue Concerning the Two Chief World Systems: Ptolemaic and Copernican*, 2nd ed. Translated by Stillman Drake. Berkeley: University of California Press.
Gould, Stephen Jay. 1999. *Rocks of Ages: Science and Religion in the Fullness of Life*. New York: Ballantine Books.
Hess, Peter M. J. 2003. "God's Two Books: Special Revelation and Natural Science in the Christian West." In *Bridging Science and Religion*, edited by Ted Peters and Gaymon Bennett. Minneapolis: Fortress Press.
John Paul II. 1996. "Message to the Pontifical Academy of Sciences on Evolution," http://www.ewtn.com/library/papaldoc/jp961022.htm, accessed 17 February 2016.
Numbers, Ronald L. 2010. "Simplifying Complexity: Patterns in the History of Science and Religion." In *Science and Religion: New Historical Perspectives*, edited by Thomas Dixon, Geoffrey Cantor, and Stephen Pumfrey. Cambridge: Cambridge University Press.
Peters, Ted. 1996. "Theology and Science: Where Are We?" *Zygon*, 31(2): 323–343.
Pius XII. 1950. *Humani generis*, http://w2.vatican.va/content/pius-xii/en/encyclicals/documents/hf_p-xii_enc_12081950_humani-generis.html, accessed 17 February 2016.
Santillana, Giorgio de. 1955. *The Crime of Galileo*. Chicago: University of Chicago Press.
Stenmark, Mikael. 2012. "How to Relate Christian Faith and Science." In *The Blackwell Companion to Science and Christianity*, edited by J. B. Stump and Alan G. Padgett. Malden, MA: Wiley-Blackwell.
White, Andrew Dickson. 1922. *A History of the Warfare of Science with Theology in Christendom*. New York: D. Appleton and Company.

CHAPTER 2

Christianity and the Origin of Modern Science

In 1633, when Galileo was forced to recant and sentenced to house arrest, a younger man in France had just prepared a scientific book for publication. René Descartes (1596–1650) was interested in the emerging science, and his manuscript *The World* assumed the heliocentric model of the universe. But Descartes was a Catholic and saw no reason to jeopardize his career by getting on the wrong side of the Church, so he decided against publishing the book.

Even so, Descartes' work over the next decade made important contributions to the Scientific Revolution. He is credited with developing algebraic solutions to geometrical problems (we still use the Cartesian coordinate system in geometry), and he developed a conception of matter which, if not ultimately correct, advanced the project of explaining physical reality by its underlying mechanical structures. But Descartes is most remembered today for what we would call his philosophical work. The distinction we make between science and philosophy was not acknowledged (or even entirely understood) in Descartes' day. Indeed, what we mean by science was still called natural philosophy in the 17th century. The important distinction for people then was between reason and revelation. Science and philosophy were systematic attempts to learn things about the world (including human beings) using our natural unaided reason, and theology was the discipline (also called a science) that drew from supernatural revelation. These correspond to the Two Books metaphor we saw in the conclusion of the previous chapter.

Descartes saw a different kind of relationship between these two disciplines than the Conflict or Independence approaches. In his most enduring philosophical

Science and Christianity: An Introduction to the Issues, First Edition. By J. B. Stump.
© 2017 John Wiley & Sons, Ltd. Published 2017 by John Wiley & Sons, Ltd.

work, *Meditations on First Philosophy*, he wrote a dedicatory letter to the theology faculty at the University of Paris describing this relationship:

> I have always thought that two issues—namely, God and the soul—are chief among those that ought to be demonstrated with the aid of philosophy rather than theology. For although it suffices for us believers to believe by faith that the human soul does not die with the body, and that God exists, certainly no unbelievers seem capable of being persuaded of any religion or even of almost any moral virtue, until these two are first proven to them by natural reason. (Descartes 1984, vol. 2, 3)

The existence of God and the immortality of the soul are two of the foundational doctrines of religion, yet, according to Descartes, unbelievers aren't going to believe them just because we appeal to revelation. But he thought that he could prove them by the use of **natural reason**. So Descartes offered his services to the Church. He wasn't claiming to have produced a new doctrine (at least he hoped the Church would see it that way), merely that he could give rational justification for what faith tells us is true. In this sense, natural reason (science and philosophy) could be called the "handmaiden of theology."

According to this metaphor, science and religion would not be in conflict with one another, nor would they be independent of each other. Instead, the two have some overlap, work together, and even influence each other. In this chapter and the next we explore a couple of the grand themes of the history of science and Christianity in which it might be most plausibly claimed that science and Christianity have significantly influenced each other. First, we consider a bit of background to the **handmaiden metaphor**.

 Questions to be addressed in this chapter:

1. What are the classical sources for the handmaiden metaphor?
2. How did 20th-century historians understand the role of Christian theology in the development of modern science?
3. What are the more recent perspectives on Christianity and the development of modern science?

---

1. The handmaiden of theology

Philo, the 1st-century Jewish thinker from Alexandria, is generally regarded as the originator of the handmaiden metaphor. He claimed that the secular disciplines should not be studied for their own sakes, but only as a means to better understand scripture and theology (Grant 2004, 105). He was influential for subsequent Christian thinkers, and Justin Martyr (c. 100–165) was perhaps the first of the Church Fathers to adopt the approach. We also see Clement of Alexandria (c. 150–215) offering an explicit defense of the handmaiden metaphor. He titled Book I, Chapter 5 of his *Stromata* (or *Miscellanies*), "Philosophy the Handmaid of Theology," claiming that the learning of the Greeks may have been a preparation for true

Christian theology. He compared secular learning to Hagar, Sarah's handmaid in the Old Testament story. When Abraham told Sarah, "Your slave is in your hands; do with her whatever you think best" (Genesis 16:6), Clement interpreted this to mean, "I embrace secular culture as youthful, and a handmaid; but thy knowledge I honour and reverence as true wife" (*Stromata* I:V; Early Christian Writings 2016).

It was Augustine (354–430) who gave the classic formulation of the handmaiden tradition to the West. He justified the approach of using non-Christian resources by allegorical appeal to another story from the Old Testament. When Pharaoh finally allowed the Hebrew slaves to leave Egypt, Moses told the people to ask their Egyptian neighbors for clothing and articles of gold and silver. "The Lord had made the Egyptians favorably disposed toward the people, and they gave them what they asked for; so they plundered the Egyptians" (Exodus 12:36). Augustine said that using secular learning to advance our understanding of theology is "plundering the Egyptians." But he thought this should be done cautiously, for there is little in secular learning that is of much importance or helpful for Christian doctrine. (See the quotation box.)

Augustine on secular learning

"Accordingly, I think that it is well to warn studious and able young men, who fear God and are seeking for happiness of life, not to venture heedlessly upon the pursuit of the branches of learning that are in vogue beyond the pale of the Church of Christ, as if these could secure for them the happiness they seek; but soberly and carefully to discriminate among them. And if they find any of those which have been instituted by men varying by reason of the varying pleasure of their founders, and unknown by reason of erroneous conjectures, especially if they involve entering into fellowship with devils by means of leagues and covenants about signs, let these be utterly rejected and held in detestation. Let the young men also withdraw their attention from such institutions of men as are unnecessary and luxurious. But for the sake of the necessities of this life we must not neglect the arrangements of men that enable us to carry on intercourse with those around us. I think, however, there is nothing useful in the other branches of learning that are found among the heathen, except information about objects, either past or present, that relate to the bodily senses, in which are included also the experiments and conclusions of the useful mechanical arts, except also the sciences of reasoning and of number. And in regard to all these we must hold by the maxim, 'Not too much of anything;' especially in the case of those which, pertaining as they do to the senses, are subject to the relations of space and time." (Christian Classics 2016a)

Almost 1000 years after Augustine, the metaphor continued to enjoy success in providing a framework for understanding the relationship of secular learning to revelation. Thomas Aquinas (1225–1274) is traditionally interpreted as seeing natural reason to be a handmaiden to theology, or what he called in Latin *ancilla theologiae*. Just how this played out for his view of the relationship between natural philosophy and revelation is a matter of some disagreement among scholars today. Aquinas argued that some truths of faith (like the claim that God is a Trinity) can only be known through revelation, but others (like the existence of God) can be shown through the use of reason. It is tempting to read back into Aquinas the modern approach of Descartes and his use of natural reason alone to prove certain truths of faith. But that would be anachronistic. The closest Aquinas came to this approach was in his *Summa Contra Gentiles* in which he claimed that his intent was to show "how the truth that we come to know by demonstration is in accord with the Christian religion" (Aquinas 1975 (I.2.4), 63). That is to say, the things we can prove with reason are consistent with revealed truths. The two cannot contradict each other. Reason complements revelation and assists in the defense of it. Aquinas did not claim that the articles of faith can be proved by reason, but rather that objections to faith can be answered with reason: "If our opponent believes nothing of divine revelation, there is no longer any means of proving the articles of faith by reasoning, but only of answering his objections—if he has any—against the faith" (*Summa Theologica* I.1.8, Christian Classics 2016b).

Others have given a different interpretation of Aquinas's thought in this regard. One of the characteristic features of his work was to carve out the proper places for reason and revelation. As such, he made theology into an independent science, distinct from other learning. Edward Grant sees this as simultaneously conferring autonomy on natural philosophy as well. "The emergence of theology as an independent science in the second half of the 13th century had an inadvertent corollary: a guarantee that natural philosophy would also be regarded as an independent science" (Grant 2004, 187). Grant's interpretation suggests that Aquinas would be more at home with the Independence thesis discussed in the previous chapter. But while there may be some legitimacy in seeing the separation of theology as an important step toward the development of **modern science**, it is difficult to maintain that Aquinas believed their proper relationship to be the sort of independence Stephen Jay Gould had in mind (as discussed in Chapter 1). It would be more accurate to say that for Aquinas natural philosophy played an important role in the demonstration and justification of theological truths. We'll see below that this role for natural philosophy was significant for the development of modern science.

> ### Roger Bacon (c. 1220–1294)
>
> A forerunner of the modern scientific method. He was a lecturer in Paris and then a Franciscan friar in England who emphasized the study of nature by empirical methods. He contributed to our understanding of optics, the reformation of the calendar, and perhaps gunpowder. (Not to be confused with Francis Bacon (1561–1626), who was also an important figure in the development of modern science.)

Aquinas's contemporary in the 13th century was Roger Bacon. In the narrative of conflict between science and Christianity, Bacon is often presented as one of the heroes for the developing science. In the previous chapter we met Andrew Dickson White who bears significant responsibility for creating and perpetuating the conflict narrative. He painted a picture of Bacon as a lone rational figure standing up against the irrational spirit of his times:

> In an age when theological subtilizing was alone thought to give the title of scholar, [Bacon] insisted on real reasoning and the aid of natural science by mathematics; in an age when experimenting was sure to cost a man his reputation, and was likely to cost him his life, he insisted on experimenting, and braved all its risks … The most conscientious men of his time thought it their duty to fight him, and they fought him steadily and bitterly. (White 1922, 387)

It is true that Bacon was censured by those in the Church who thought the new scientific reasoning would distract people from the pursuit of truth. And he was at the forefront of the movement to incorporate the study of Aristotle into Christian theology. But the scholarly consensus today is that Bacon was a thoroughly medieval thinker rather than the vanguard of modernity.

The defense of the new learning for Bacon came only on utilitarian grounds: it could serve the Church. "In none of his writings is there so much as the hint of a preference for an autonomous philosophical enterprise" (Lindberg 1987, 534). Bacon himself wrote, "the philosophy of unbelievers is essentially harmful and has no value considered by itself. For philosophy in itself leads to the blindness of hell, and therefore it must be by itself darkness and mist" (1928, 74). But he saw that the learning of the pagans could be used to advance the mission of the Church. Mathematics was the foundation of the other sciences, and so was important for understanding them. And in a manner reminiscent of Plato, Bacon also believed the study of mathematics itself was capable of elevating the mind and preparing it for higher knowledge of heavenly things. Astronomy could be used to correct the calendar for the Church. Optics—the understanding of which Bacon significantly contributed to—might be used to construct mirrors and other optical devices by which terror could be incited in unbelievers and Christian lands could be defended against invaders. Even astrology—a respected science in Bacon's day—could be used to predict the future and assist in understanding the end times. All of these were to be put to use in understanding scripture.

Bacon's goal was not to develop some independent track for secular learning but to reclaim such learning from the pagans so that it might serve the Church. As such, what we call science today was clearly the subservient handmaiden of theology in Bacon's understanding of their relationship. Christian thinkers through the Middle Ages consistently subordinated natural reason to what they believed God had revealed. In this subordinate relation, though, we find one of the most plausible instances of Christian theology influencing science. In the next section we consider how recent historians have understood the role Christianity played in the development of modern science.

2. Christianity's role in the rise of modern science: Twentieth-century views

There is no disputing the fact that modern science developed in the Christian West. The question is whether that was merely an accident of history or whether there was something inherent in and unique to Christian thought that allowed scientific thinking to flourish in that setting. Other cultures seemed to have been further along the road of scientific development in the ancient world. But their attempts at birthing science were "stillborn," to use the phrase of Stanley Jaki (whom we'll meet below). The Scientific Revolution occurred in the Christianized Europe of the 16th and 17th centuries.

Even well into the 20th century, there was the feeling that science was a uniquely Western phenomenon; the cultures of China, India, and the Middle East just didn't seem that interested. In that sense, it is no more surprising that modern science did not develop in those places than that the game of cricket did not develop in Indiana. The locals just didn't have a taste for it. The same could not be said for science in the East now.

The science faculties at major research universities today include a significant number (if not a preponderance) of names of Asian origin. And in fields of technology and applied science, like medicine and computer science, we're increasingly likely to see practitioners of the highest level from Southeast Asia or the Middle East. Even if countries in these areas have not uniformly become scientifically minded and their worldviews are remarkably syncretistic with traditional belief systems, there are significant numbers of people within their borders who have embraced a scientific mindset. There no longer seems to be a disconnect between the ethnic and cultural backgrounds of those from the East with science. If anything, it seems to be the opposite. So if these countries are capable of supporting science, we're still left with the question of why modern science did not develop in them in the past.

The history of science emerged as a professional academic discipline largely in connection to this question of the rise of modern science. The 20th century produced a considerable body of work on this topic, and there are many facets to its interpretation. We're considering here the contentious point of just how much influence Christianity had on the development of modern science.

The writings of the conflict theorists we've met—Draper and White—set the tone for much of the historical perspective of writers in the 20th century, claiming it was in spite of the influence of Christianity, rather than because of it, that science developed within a Christian context. Of course, such a claim found listening ears among the scientifically minded philosophers. Writing in 1922, Bertrand Russell claimed, "Although Chinese civilization has hitherto been deficient in science, it never contained anything hostile to science, and therefore the spread of scientific knowledge encounters no such obstacles as the Church put in its way in Europe" (Russell 2007, 193). Such sentiments suggest it would have been easier for science to develop in China where there was an older civilization, a larger population from which to draw scientific genius, and even technological innovations predating their counterparts in Europe of things like a moveable type printing press, the magnetic compass, and gunpowder. So why didn't it?

In the politically correct environment of the last part of the 20th century, it became fashionable to show respect for non-Western cultures by searching for and trumpeting their scientific achievements that had been left out of the standard history books. India, like China, had ancient civilizations with large numbers of people, and may very well lay claim to significant innovations in mathematics. Carl Sagan even saw in India's ancient Hinduism the possibility of consonance with the oscillating universe theory (which was a legitimate scientific option when he was writing):

> The Hindu religion is the only one of the world's great faiths dedicated to the idea that the Cosmos itself undergoes an immense, indeed an infinite, number of deaths and rebirths. It is the only religion in which the time scales correspond to those of modern scientific cosmology. Its cycles run from our ordinary day and a night to a day and night of Brahma, 8.64 billion years long. (Sagan 1985, 213)

But again, we've got to ask why, if the ancient Indians and Chinese were so scientifically astute, then why didn't they come to discover heliocentrism, the laws of motion, or the periodic table of elements?

Fig. 2.1 Antique Chinese spoon compass. Source: © Hans-Joachim Schneider/Alamy.

This was precisely the question Joseph Needham (1900–1995), certainly the West's greatest expert on the history of science in China, dedicated his scholarly career to answering, calling it the "Grand Question." Of course, any answer to such a question will be complex. Needham thought a large part of the answer is to be found in the different social and governmental structures in China, but he also gave a significant place to Chinese culture's different conception of God, about which he made the following two points:

> The first is that it is clear that the de-personalisation of God in ancient Chinese thought took place so early, and went so far, that the conception of a divine celestial lawgiver imposing ordinances on non-human Nature never developed. The second is that the highest spiritual being ever known and worshipped in China was not a creator in the sense meant by the Hebrews and the Greeks. It was not that there was no order in Nature for the Chinese, but rather that it was not

an order ordained by a rational personal being. Hence there was no conviction that rational personal beings would be able to spell out, in their lesser earthly languages, the divine code of laws which he had previously decreed. (Needham 1978, 305)

Even before Needham's extensive research into the culture and context of ancient China, the English philosopher Alfred North Whitehead (1861–1947) came to a similar conclusion about the more general requirements for the development of science. His 1925 book *Science and the Modern World* argued that a necessary condition for the development of modern science in the 16th and 17th centuries was faith in the order of nature. Some of this was inherited from the Greek tradition, which saw a moral order to the world in terms of fate. This idea was shaped by the Stoics into a more diffuse sense of order that came to pervade the medieval mind. While the rationality of the Middle Ages is sometimes caricatured by highlighting carefully nuanced arguments about how many angels can dance on the head of a pin, Whitehead claims that "The Middle Ages formed one long training of the intellect of Western Europe in the sense of order" (Whitehead 1925, 12).

Beyond this underlying mental commitment to order that can be traced back to the Greeks, Whitehead argued that the greatest contribution of medievalism to the development of modern science came from their belief in the Judeo-Christian God. The conceptions of God in Asia were too impersonal or arbitrary to infect thought there with the habit of thinking that every event could be correlated with antecedent events in a perfectly definite manner according to general principles or laws (ibid., 13). It was the West's intellectual commitment to the existence of a personal God who ordered creation according to rational principles that encouraged scientists to investigate creation in order to discover the secrets contained therein.

Another influential historian of science in the middle of the 20th century was Robert Merton (1910–2003). He built on the thesis of sociologist Max Weber about the importance of the Protestant work ethic and the rise of capitalism, developing his own "Merton Thesis" about Puritanism and science. He claimed that the Puritans had a practical or utilitarian orientation to their faith such that honoring God was directed toward "worldly" activities that would benefit the community, rather than expressing it in the asceticism of monastic life. As such, scientific knowledge was useful and empirical investigations were encouraged. Robert Boyle was Merton's poster child, in whom he saw the blend of **empiricism** and **rationalism** that was ideally suited for making scientific discoveries (see Merton 2002).

The Dutch historian of science Reijer Hooykaas (1906–1994) similarly saw that scientific discovery needs rationalism tempered with empirical inquiry. He thought the downfall of the ancient Greeks, who made so much progress in scientific thinking but ultimately fell short, was their unbridled rationalism. They never reined this in, so nature was not allowed to instruct them in her ways. Instead, they relied on largely a priori attempts at scientific knowledge.

Another important point in Hooykaas's analysis was the distinctive transformation in the biblical worldview that demythologizes nature. For those in the ancient Near East and other ancient cultures, the natural world was filled with personal spirits. Their whims determined the course of nature, and hence there was little motivation for studying to understand the workings of nature. But in the Hebrew tradition there was a personal God who stood outside of nature and created it. For this worldview, nature itself is impersonal, and so is capable of being described with natural laws. Thus people might profitably learn by studying nature and figuring out how nature works. And this creator who fashioned human beings in the image of God also provides the basis for rationality that Needham noted was missing from the Chinese.

Now, of course, Christians share this tradition with Jews and Muslims. Why didn't it spur them to develop modern science? Admittedly, in the Middle Ages they were further advanced and must be credited with preserving the works of the Ancient Greeks, which proved important in the European Renaissance. But, for Hooykaas, it was the **Protestant Reformation** that provides the key to understanding the importance of Christianity for science. "In the Middle Ages, then, the biblical view was only superimposed on, and did not overcome, the Aristotelian conceptions" (Hooykaas 1972, 12–13). It was the emphasis of the Reformation on the theological concept of the priesthood of all believers that allowed scientists to overcome that rationalist thinking. For this:

> implied the right, and even the duty, for those who had the talents, to study Scripture without depending on the authority of tradition and hierarchy, together with the right and the duty to study the other book written by God, the book of nature, without regard to the authority of the fathers of natural philosophy. (ibid., 109)

The key witness for Hooykaas on this point was Johannes Kepler in his unwillingness to bow to the rationalist conception of the fathers of natural philosophy that the heavenly bodies must move in perfect circles. Instead, he allowed the anomaly of eight minutes of arc in the observed orbit of Mars to convince him to abandon the dogma of circularity. "He submitted to given facts rather than maintaining an age-old prejudice; in his mind a Christian empiricism gained the victory over platonic rationalism; a lonely man submitted to facts and broke away from a tradition of two thousand years" (ibid., 36). It was the Reformation attitude of not blindly following authority that gave Kepler the permission to see the data for what it was, rather than for what it had been said to be.

A recent Roman Catholic thinker gives less credence to Hooykaas's Reformation thesis, but still finds Christian theology to be largely responsible for science. Stanley Jaki (1924–2009) was a Hungarian-born priest who earned doctorates in both theology and physics, and he made extensive study of the history of the development of modern science. His most well-known book in this area is *The Road of Science and the Ways to God* (1978). More than others, he credited the development of key concepts for the Scientific Revolution to Christian theological influences. Among these were inertial motion and the conservation of momentum, which were crucial to overcoming Aristotelian physics. Jaki claimed that they were grounded in God's creation of the universe, which gave the initial motion to the system. Furthermore, the Christian view of creation gives a dignity to human beings that was absent from other cultures. In the non-Christian cultures of the past in which science was "stillborn," there was a belief in the cyclic view of the universe or the pattern of eternal recurrence. Such a view of the universe encouraged a view of humans as nothing more than a "bubble on the inexorable sea of events whose ebb and flow followed one another with fateful regularity" (Jaki 1974, 130). Another concept was the contingent nature of the world which resulted from God's free decision to create rather than creating out of necessity. Belief in this contingency invites empirical investigation of the world, rather than the more strictly rationalist approach. Jaki even credits Christian theology with promoting the quantitative methods which were so crucial to the development of science.

 Suggested influences of Christianity on the development of modern science

- God as a personal creator who guaranteed the order and rationality of nature
- Creation as a contingent order which must be investigated
- The Hebrew tradition of depersonalizing nature
- Protestantism's valuing of utilitarian goals in understanding nature
- The Protestant Reformation's willingness to question authority

For all of his careful historical detail, there are questions about the objectivity of Jaki's analysis. Indeed, just as we are considering the influence Christian belief has had on the development of science, the charge against Jaki is that Christian belief influenced his conclusions about the relationship between Christianity and the development of modern science. Jaki's work has been cited often by Christian apologists who see an argument for the truth of Christianity by linking it to the development of science. At least in part because of this apologetic use, others have argued that Christianity's influence on the development of science was minimal and a historical accident. We consider one such view next.

3. Recent developments

In the 20th century, a school of historians of science arose which advocated that the proper way to explicate the story of science was not so much through the development of the ideas themselves as by considering the social situations in which science arose. The histories produced by this school are sometimes called "external" since they refer primarily to the institutions and social contexts which allowed or encouraged the development of science, as opposed to the "internal" histories that more directly chart the development of the ideas. Toby Huff is a recent example of an external historian. He claims that the essential ingredient for the development of modern science is the existence of "neutral spaces" in society within which discussion of ideas could take place free from political and religious censors. As such, "Science is thus the natural enemy of all vested interests—social, political, and religious—including those of the scientific establishment itself" (Huff 2003, 1). Here the conflict thesis is inflated so that any established social order which seeks to preserve itself will come into conflict with scientific inquiry. In this sense, organized religion is no different from the scientific status quo in holding back the development of science.

In Huff's view, then, modern science did not develop in the East or in Muslim cultures, because they lacked the institutional supports for the development of neutral spaces of inquiry. To be fair, Huff acknowledges that Christian theology played a role in the development of science in the West insofar as it "contained images of order, regularity, and even system-processes" and "shaped conceptions of reason and rationality as attributes of man and nature" (ibid., 4). But, for him, the development of science had to overcome the culture's Christian framework, and this was accomplished through the institution of universities. Though certainly not all at once, universities gradually led to a separation between the sacred and the secular, and legal protection was afforded to secular thinking that was not available in Chinese, Indian, or Islamic cultures. He summarizes his position as follows:

> The European medievals created autonomous self-governing institutions of higher learning; at the same time, they imported into them a methodologically powerful naturalistic cosmology that directly challenged and contradicted many aspects of the traditional Christian worldview. By institutionalizing the study of the corpus of the new Aristotle, the intellectual elite of medieval Europe established an impersonal intellectual agenda that was publicly acknowledged and available to all. Furthermore, by incorporating the Aristotelian metaphysics of naturalistic inquiry, the European intellectuals had in effect displaced the centrality of the Christian worldview as a "scientific" worldview. (ibid., 340)

There is little place in Huff's portrait of the development of science for understanding science as a handmaiden to theology. It is just such an image, though, that Stephen Gaukroger sees as the most important one for the development of science.

Gaukroger is a contemporary historian of science and philosophy, and he has embarked on a very ambitious project of writing five volumes on science and the shaping of the modern mind. The first volume (weighing in at over 500 pages) treats the emergence of science in the years 1210–1685 (Gaukroger 2006). He sees some value in the sort of external history that Huff has provided. It gives extra dimensions to the story of the development of science. But Gaukroger as a more fundamentally "internalist" historian is concerned that when those extra dimensions are portrayed as the whole story they do not stand up to closer scrutiny. For example, Gaukroger thinks that speaking of neutral spaces of inquiry in the early modern period is anachronistic. It presumes that the goal of scientific inquiry of the time is the same as we find it to be today, namely the pursuit of truth. But in the early modern period "public discussions of the value of natural philosophy tended to turn on its usefulness rather than its truth" (Gaukroger 2006, 36). This is consistent with the attitudes toward natural philosophy we saw earlier in this chapter and forces historians to answer the question "Useful for what?" about science in these cultures. We find, then, that values of specific groups must be introduced, and the idea of neutral space for inquiry becomes irrelevant (ibid., 40). Science was used in the service of other valued enterprises, not as an end in itself.

Instead of looking primarily to the kind of social factors Huff considers, Gaukroger traces the development of the ideas of natural philosophy itself. He develops the thesis in rigorous detail that Christianity played a central role in the development of natural philosophy by legitimizing it as her "handmaiden." In the 13th century, Aquinas had carved out a separate sphere for natural philosophy from theology by allowing it to provide justification and demonstration of truths of revelation. But when the Aristotelianism upon which Aquinas's natural philosophy depended was called into question, natural philosophy had to be transformed in order to maintain its position of reinforcing theology. Gaukroger summarizes:

> What emerged from this was a conception of revelation and natural philosophy as being mutually reinforcing, a reinforcement consolidated through a process of "triangulation", towards the shared truth of revelation and natural philosophy. In this way, the nature of the natural-philosophical exercise was transformed and provided with a unique vindication and legitimacy. The combination of revelation and natural philosophy—the two "books" superposed into a single volume, as it were—produced a unique kind of enterprise, quite different from that of any other scientific culture, and one that was largely responsible for the subsequent uniqueness of the development of natural philosophy in the West. This uniqueness derives in large part from the legitimatory aspirations that it takes on in the course of the seventeenth century, and I have attempted to reconstruct how these legitimatory aspirations were formed. The kind of momentum that lay behind the legitimatory consolidation of the natural-philosophical enterprise from the seventeenth century onwards, a momentum that marked it out from every other scientific culture, was generated not by the intrinsic merits of its programme in celestial mechanics or matter theory but by a natural-theological imperative. (ibid., 507)

Conclusion

It is not reasonable to deny that Christianity played an influential role in the development of modern science. Whether that role goes as far as Hooykaas and Jaki claim, whether Huff's minimalist interpretation better captures the true story, or whether Gaukroger's middle path is the best explanation remain a matter of scholarly debate. That debate is essentially about the extent to which it is reasonable to claim that Christianity has significantly influenced science. It is not a matter of debate that the science which developed in the Christian West has become much more culturally powerful than it was at its inception. Some will go further and argue that the handmaiden has usurped the queen of the sciences, and she herself has become the master. If such a picture is correct, then we have a substantial example of the opposite direction of influence to what we've considered in this chapter. It is sometimes called the **Secularization Thesis**, and we turn to it in the next chapter.

Summary of main points:

1. Augustine, Aquinas, and Roger Bacon saw secular learning (what they called natural philosophy) as useful and therefore as a handmaiden to theology.

2. Needham, Whitehead, and Merton gave Christian thinking a significant role in the development of modern science; Hooykaas and Jaki gave it the most important role.

3. Huff downplayed the importance of Christian thought, emphasizing instead the role of institutions; Gaukroger argued that Christian thinkers legitimized natural philosophy by using it to justify Christian belief.

Further reading

- Gaukroger, Stephen. 2006. *The Emergence of a Scientific Culture: Science and the Shaping of Modernity 1210–1685*. Oxford: Oxford University Press. The first of a projected five volumes on science and shaping of modernity.
- Huff, Toby E. 2003. *The Rise of Early Modern Science*. 2nd ed. Cambridge: Cambridge University Press. An examination of the religious, legal, philosophical, and institutional contexts within which science was practiced in Islam, China, and the West.
- Jaki, Stanley L. 1978. *The Road of Science and the Ways to God*. Chicago: University of Chicago Press. The Gifford Lectures from a Benedictine priest and physics professor arguing for the positive role of Christian theology in the development of modern science.

References

Aquinas, Thomas. 1975. *Summa Contra Gentiles, Book One: God*. Notre Dame, IN: University of Notre Dame Press.

Bacon, Roger. 1928. *The "Opus Majus" of Roger Bacon*. Translated by Robert Belle Burke. Vol. I. Philadelphia: University of Pennsylvania Press.

Christian Classics Ethereal Library. 2016a. "On Christian Doctrine," §58, Book II, Chapter 39, http://www.ccel.org/ccel/augustine/doctrine.toc.html, accessed 17 February 2016.

Christian Classics Ethereal Library. 2016b. "Summa Theologica." http://www.ccel.org/ccel/aquinas/summa.toc.html, accessed 17 February 2016.

Descartes, René. 1984. *The Philosophical Writings of Descartes*. Translated by John Cottingham, Robert Stoothoff, and Dugald Murdoch. Cambridge: Cambridge University Press. 3 vols. 1985–1991.

Early Christian Writings. 2016. "The Stromata, or Miscellanies," http://www.earlychristianwritings.com/text/clement-stromata-book1.html, accessed 17 February 2016.

Gaukroger, Stephen. 2006. *The Emergence of a Scientific Culture: Science and the Shaping of Modernity 1210–1685*. Oxford: Oxford University Press.

Grant, Edward. 2004. *Science and Religion, 400 BC–AD 1550*. Baltimore: The Johns Hopkins University Press.

Hooykaas, Reijer. 1972. *Religion and the Rise of Modern Science*. Grand Rapids, MI: Eerdmans Publishing Company.

Huff, Toby E. 2003. *The Rise of Early Modern Science*. 2nd ed. Cambridge: Cambridge University Press.

Jaki, Stanley L. 1974. *Science and Creation: From Eternal Cycles to an Oscillating Universe*. Edinburgh: Scottish Academic Press.

Jaki, Stanley L. 1978. *The Road of Science and the Ways to God*. Chicago: University of Chicago Press.

Lindberg, David C. 1987. "Science as Handmaiden: Roger Bacon and the Patristic Tradition." *Isis* 78: 518–536.

Merton, Robert. 2002. *Science, Technology and Society in Seventeenth-Century England*. New York: Howard Fertig.

Needham, Joseph. 1978. *The Shorter Science and Civilisation in China*. Vol 1., edited by Colin A. Ronan. Cambridge: Cambridge University Press.

Russell, Bertrand. 2007. *The Problem of China*. New York: Cosimo Classics.

Sagan, Carl. 1985. *Cosmos*. New York: Random House.

White, Andrew Dickson. 1922. *A History of the Warfare of Science with Theology in Christendom*. New York: D. Appleton and Company.

Whitehead, Alfred N. 1925. *Science and the Modern World*. New York: Macmillan.

CHAPTER 3

Secularization

Auguste Comte was a 19th-century philosopher and social thinker who was very impressed with the kind of thinking that developed out of the Scientific Revolution. He saw it as more than merely an improvement on what came before, seeing it rather as the culmination of human thinking. Famously, he articulated his **Law of Human Progress**, according to which human thinking necessarily passes through three stages: the theological, the philosophical (or metaphysical), and the scientific.

During the theological stage, humans suppose that observed phenomena are the result of the direct and unmediated action of divine beings. If an earthquake strikes or a tree bears fruit (or fails to bear fruit), there must be a god responsible for making these things happen (or not happen). In Comte's philosophical stage of human cognitive development, phenomena are explained by abstract entities like the nature or essence of an object. A tree bears fruit because that is its nature, and apples fall to the earth because they are composed of the earthy element and naturally come to rest there. In his final stage, the scientific—or what Comte liked to call the positivistic—we stop looking for causes and content ourselves with describing the laws that govern phenomena. For example, Newton's law of gravitation does not explain how or why gravity works but merely gives a mathematical description of the action of gravity. Apples fall to earth, projectiles trace out parabolas, and the moon stays in orbit according to the same general law of gravitation which could be described mathematically.

Comte himself never supposed that proper scientific language would contain only direct and immediate descriptions of phenomena without any theoretical terms. That would be the hallmark of the 20th-century school of thought known as **positivism**, which was a further development of Comte's ideas. Nor did Comte claim that everyone in a society progresses through the three stages together. Even the same individual might be simultaneously in the theological stage for one discipline, the philosophical for another, and the scientific for yet another. His claim was merely that all human theorizing—which he believed could be categorized under the six sciences of mathematics, astronomy, physics, chemistry, biology, and sociology—progresses through these stages.

Science and Christianity: An Introduction to the Issues, First Edition. By J. B. Stump.
© 2017 John Wiley & Sons, Ltd. Published 2017 by John Wiley & Sons, Ltd.

> **Comte's Law of Human Progress**
> "From the study of the development of human intelligence, in all directions, and through all times, the discovery arises of a great fundamental law, to which it is necessarily subject, and which has a solid foundation of proof, both in the facts of our organization and in our historical experience. The law is this: that each of our leading conceptions—each branch of our knowledge—passes successively through three different theoretical conditions: the Theological, or fictitious; the Metaphysical, or abstract; and the Scientific, or positive. In other words, the human mind, by its nature, employs in its progress three methods of philosophizing, the character of which is essentially different, and even radically opposed: viz., the theological method, the metaphysical, and the positive. Hence arise three philosophies, or general systems of conceptions on the aggregate of phenomena, each of which excludes the others. The first is the necessary point of departure of the human understanding; and the third is its fixed and definite state. The second is merely a state of transition." (Comte 1855, 25–26)

The question that concerns us in this chapter is whether Comte's hypothesis about the progression away from theological explanations to scientific explanations has been borne out in reality. And relatedly, if there has been such a progression away from theology, has science caused that "secularization"?

Comte would not be troubled by the conclusion of those in the previous chapter who thought that Christian thinking played an essential role in the development of modern science. He may not have agreed that it had to be Christianity in particular, but he thought that the theological thinking which posited divine agency (and especially monotheism) was a necessary first step in coming to understand natural phenomena. The claim that science always exists in that kind of dependent relationship to Christianity, however, seems to have been significantly undermined by the findings of our first two chapters.

The historical episodes described so far have demonstrated that there has not been one way that science and Christianity have been related throughout all of their existence. At times the two have been in conflict, at other times they have operated completely independently of each other, and at still other times they have influenced and engaged in dialogue with each other. It is a gross misrepresentation of history to take one of these relations and attempt to construe it as characteristic of how science and Christianity are always related to each other. In just this sense, it has become common to refer to the work of John Hedley Brooke as establishing the "complexity thesis" of the relationship between science and religion. But if Comte were correct, in spite of the diversity of individual examples, we should be able to see a general trend of science replacing religion in human thinking. The inchoate scientific thinking which was taken to be the handmaiden of theology at one stage of development inevitably becomes the master. This supposed trend is often called the secularization thesis, and it constitutes a dramatic example of how science has influenced Christianity. To judge whether the thesis is correct, however, we must first come to a clearer understanding of just what is claimed by the thesis of secularization.

Questions to be addressed in this chapter:

1. Has religious belief among scientists declined?

2. What else might we mean by "secularization"?

3. What do Taylor and Buckley see as the root cause of secularization?

1. Scientists and religious belief

Historian of science Ronald Numbers acknowledges the complexity of the relationship between science and religion as shown by Brooke, and so he thinks we are unable to provide overarching or universal descriptions of that relationship. But he does think it helpful to identify some "midscale patterns" by which to categorize and understand the history of the relationship between science and Christianity. Perhaps these patterns are not universalizable, but they might offer some help in identifying trends in the history. He offers five such midscale generalizations: naturalization, privatization, secularization, globalization, and radicalization (Numbers 2010, 264). Our concern here is with secularization.

Numbers defines secularization as "loss of faith among scientists" (ibid., 270). If human thinking tends to move from the theological to the scientific, then we would expect that individuals who have embraced the scientific way of thinking would have moved beyond their religious faith. We cannot establish this conclusion by merely recounting the personal stories of a few individual scientists. We would need longitudinal data on a larger pool of individuals. Such data is difficult to come by over the centuries since the Scientific Revolution, and even if we had such data there would be some difficulty in interpreting it regarding the supposed causal influence of science on loss of religious belief; there might be only a correlation between the two trends. (Ironically, the positivists in Comte's wake would have to concede such a point since they eschewed a search for causes in that sense.) There was one measurement done toward the beginning and the end of the 20th century, however, from which we can draw some limited conclusions.

In order to determine the religious beliefs of scientists in his day, in 1914 James Leuba sent questionnaires to a random selection of 1000 out of the 5500 scientists who appeared in *American Men of Science*. Of these 1000 questionnaires, 600 were sent to scientists of less eminent distinction and 400 to scientists of eminent distinction, as determined by the editors of *American Men of Science* (Leuba 1916, 249n). He was particularly interested in their beliefs about a personal God, which he thought were best determined by asking about their attitude toward prayer, and in their beliefs on life after death, or personal immortality (see box for the exact phrasing of the questions). About 10% of those surveyed did not reply, and about 15% returned an unmarked questionnaire. Of those who answered, 41.8% indicated belief in a personal God, 41.5% indicated disbelief, and 16.7% indicated agnosticism. When confined to the "eminent scientists," belief in a personal God dropped to 31.6%. On the second question, 50.6% of all respondents expressed belief in personal immortality, and 36.9% of those of eminent distinction expressed such belief (ibid., 250).

The Leuba Survey

1. Belief in a personal God:

- I believe in a God to whom one may pray in the expectation of receiving an answer. By "answer," I mean more than the subjective, psychological effect of prayer.
- I do not believe in a God as defined above.
- I have no definite belief regarding this question.

2. Belief in life after death:

- I believe in personal Immortality for all men or conditional Immortality, i.e., Immortality for those who have reached a certain state of development.
- I believe neither in conditional nor in unconditional Immortality of the person in another world.
- I have no definite belief regarding this question.
  (ibid., 225–226)

The conclusion Leuba drew from his findings was that disbelief in a personal God and in immortality is directly proportional to success in the sciences (ibid., 279). He reasoned from his data that the more scientific a person was, the less likely it was for that person to hold to the traditional claims of religious faith. Furthermore, he thought this trend would be reflected in the wider culture as scientific information and ways of thinking became more prevalent. In his words:

> The situation revealed by the present statistical studies demands a revision of public opinion regarding the prevalence and the future of the two cardinal beliefs of official Christianity ... The essential problem facing organized Christianity is constituted by the wide-spread rejection of its two fundamental dogmas—a rejection apparently destined to extend parallel with the diffusion of knowledge and the moral qualities that make for eminence in scholarly pursuits. (ibid. 1916, 281)

However, in 1996 and 1998, Edward Larson and Larry Witham sent the same survey questions to scientists, again drawing them randomly from *American Men and Women of Science*. In response to the question of whether they believed in a personal God (the kind to whom one might pray, expecting an answer), 40% of their respondents answered yes (Larson and Witham 1999, 90). The editors of *American Men and Women of Science* discontinued the practice of signifying "eminent" scientists, so Larson and Witham attempted to find a similar measurement by surveying members of the National Academy of Sciences (NAS)—a much more elite organization to which membership is gained only by the consent of current members. They found less than 10% of respondents indicating a belief in God as so defined. If this is approximately equivalent to Leuba's "eminent scientists," then we see a significant decline in personal theism among the most elite scientists in the country. There is disagreement over how these results are to be interpreted, with some claiming that the self-perpetuating nature of the NAS has led to a homogeneity of belief that is not truly representative (ibid., 93).

Regardless of the interpretation of the religious beliefs of elite scientists, the data on religious belief of scientists in general is remarkable for remaining consistent over eight decades. And this result clearly falsifies Leuba's prediction that religious belief among the scientifically minded would wane.

Another more recent study on the religious beliefs of scientists was done by Elaine Howard Ecklund. She surveyed nearly 1700 scientists who were employed at elite universities in the United States. Her questions were not the same as Leuba's, and her sample tended more toward the "eminent" class of scientists that Leuba surveyed. But even still, she found that 36% of her sample believed in God. This figure is markedly lower than the rate of belief of the general population in the United States, but it too indicates that the religious beliefs of US scientists has not gone away. If the thesis of secularization is that religious belief by scientists will decline, then the thesis does not seem to be supported by the evidence.

Scientists' belief in God compared to the general public's		
Which one of the following statements comes closest to expressing what you believe about God?	**Percent of Scientists***	**Percent of US Population**
I do not believe in God.	34	2
I do not know if there is a God, and there is no way to find out.	30	4
I believe in a higher power, but it is not God.	8	10
I believe in God sometimes.	5	4
I have some doubts, but I believe in God.	14	17
I have no doubts about God's existence.	9	63
Total	100	100

(Ecklund 2010, 16)
*The sample was limited to scientists working at elite American universities

There is one other point to make here about the thesis of secularism when construed as the loss of religious belief by scientists: there is an interesting difference in the religious belief of scientists when separated out by specific discipline. Leuba did some of this in his 1914 study, finding that those in the physical sciences had the highest belief in God (43.9%), followed by those in the life sciences (30.5%), and then the social sciences (24.4% for sociologists and 24.2% for psychologists). According to some studies, there seems to have been consistency over the 20th century in this discrepancy in rates of belief between practitioners of what are sometimes called the "hard sciences" of physics and chemistry and the "soft sciences" or social sciences of psychology and sociology, with biologists in between. For example, the 1969 Carnegie Commission Survey of American Academics found that professors of mathematics and the physical sciences were most likely to be religious, and professors of sociology, psychology, and anthropology were least likely (Iannaccone, Stark, and Fink 1998, 385).

Leuba thought the reason for this slide toward secularism in the social sciences was obvious: the physical scientist can accept determinism in the domain of physical entities while maintaining a belief in divine intervention among the less understood phenomena of the social sciences. But if a social scientist accepts a purely natural explanation for his domain, it wouldn't be likely for him to hold to supernatural activity in the physical sciences (Leuba 1916, 265). It should be noted, however, that in Ecklund's survey, she found little difference between social scientists and natural scientists (Ecklund 2010, 16).

2. Broadening the definition

Perhaps Numbers' definition was too narrow to show that secularization has occurred. Indeed, a significant problem presents itself when we try to pin down exactly what is meant by "secularization." Historian Peter Burke notes that the term could refer to a number of possible trends in society, some of which are mutually contradictory. Some use it to refer to the decline in wealth and status of the Church, or relatedly to the increasing autonomy of the laity and the shrinkage or dilution of the sacred; but others think secularization is best described as the replacement of spiritual values by more material ones—a usage which would ironically see the increase in wealth and status of the Church as secularization (Burke 1979, 294).

The difficulty in defining secularization is that it is dependent upon the definition of religion, which has itself been notoriously difficult to define. Our concern here is primarily with the cognitive content of religion rather than its social forms, and so the version of secularization we consider should similarly emphasize the cognitive dimension. Specifically as it relates to science, we might try to conceive of secularization as a replacement of supernatural interpretations of reality with natural explanations. This is in the neighborhood of what German social theorist Max Weber (1864–1920) famously called the "disenchantment of the world," and he believed that modern science was singularly responsible for bringing it about. But just as Brooke "complexified" any simple understandings of the general relationship between science and religion, he also argued that the process of secularization is more complex than a straightforward effect of scientific thinking on Christian belief (Brooke 2010).

First, despite the claims of disenchantment, science has not replaced theology. Even if it is conceded that science itself has been secularized in the sense that we no longer find references to divine activity in technical scientific literature—the way that even scientists of the stature of Isaac Newton and Robert Boyle referred to the divine in their scientific literature—this has not brought about the demise of theology. Just because scientists no longer rely on the divine to fill in the gaps in their scientific explanations (or otherwise conflate scientific and theological language), that does not mean theological language has been rendered obsolete in other respects. A casual survey of Christian publishing houses today shows that Christian theology is alive and well in our society. The continued use of theology in academic discussions of morality, spiritual formation, and systematic theology suggests that the secularizing effect of science was not a straightforward elimination of theology. At most we can conclude from the secularization of science that there has been a reconfiguring of the lines of demarcation between science and theology. But that hardly constitutes a secularization of society.

Percentage of population who describe themselves as "a religious person"			
Nigeria	93	Germany	51
Romania	89	Ireland	47
Brazil	85	Canada	46
India	81	France	37
Poland	81	Sweden	29
Italy	73	Turkey	23
South Africa	64	Japan	16
United States	60	China	14

Global Index of Religiosity and Atheism—2012 (WIN-Gallup International 2012, 9)

Furthermore, a survey of cultures today which share similar levels of scientific achievement shows that there is little correlation between that measure and the religious activity of those cultures. British sociologist David Martin argues that if science is the universal secularizing force that it is portrayed to be by some, then as cultures increasingly embrace a scientific outlook and way of life we should see a corresponding decline in religious influence, belief, and practice. Instead, among cultures in the United States, Russia, France, Brazil, Singapore, Uruguay, Turkey, and others we find a great diversity of religious activity despite similar levels of scientific achievement (Martin 2007, 9–11). It might be claimed that these countries themselves are not culturally uniform, and a more fine-grained analysis could show that the more scientifically astute factions of those countries are in fact less religious. In this case we are in danger of defining our terms so they will tell us what we want to hear. Martin laments that the overwhelming majority in his discipline seem to consider this question only with regard to their own academic circles and against the backdrop of a "sometimes mythic history of the relationship" between science and religion generated in the academy (ibid., 12). It would be more accurate (though less interesting) to say that, for some people and groups, exposure to science has a secularizing effect; for others, it does not.

So if it is not a simple correlation between advance of science and secularization, what is it in these cultures that might account for the differences? John Hedley Brooke argues that there are a host of differences in cultures that affect the way science has been received with respect to Christianity. One of these differences is that there has not been a constant definition of what counts as science. If that definition itself has changed over time, then it is not fair to compare how earlier cultures were affected by their science with how later cultures were affected by a different understanding of what counted as science. More subtly—but perhaps more importantly—is the way that conceptions of God's relationship to nature have changed. Samuel Clarke, the public mouthpiece for Isaac Newton, believed that natural laws are descriptions of the ways that God normally chooses to work through the natural order. For someone like that, new scientific discoveries are not going to push God out of the natural order but instead they give a better understanding of God. For others, though, natural and supernatural explanations are in competition such that if God acts in nature, then there can be no scientific account. For them, the discovery of a new scientific explanation of some natural process rules out any divine involvement in that process, and so obviously their religious beliefs will be forced to change. It appears also that political environments affect the relationship between scientific and religious elements in societies. It would be simplistic to think that science's effect on a culture would be the same in, say, the United States, where freedom and decentralization are valued, versus its reception in the former Soviet republics. Brooke summarizes, "Because different societies have experienced the tension between secular and sacred values in contrasting ways, there is no one, universal process of secularization that can be ascribed to science or to any other factor" (Brooke 2010, 114). Still, we can't escape the seemingly obvious fact that something dramatic has happened in Western cultures over the last couple of centuries, and that it is more than a coincidence that this change has been concomitant with the development of science.

3. A secular age

Canadian philosopher Charles Taylor addresses the question of secularization in his massive book *A Secular Age*, which developed out of his 1999 Gifford Lectures at Edinburgh. He surveys a couple of meanings of secularization but then settles on the specific sense he considers as "a move from a society where belief in God is unchallenged and indeed, unproblematic, to one in which it is understood to be one option among others, and frequently not the easiest to embrace" (Taylor 2007, 3). We must be careful again not to paint society with too broad a stroke, for certainly there are still communities in the Western developed world where belief in God does not seem optional. However, in most suburban and urban communities, there is little doubt that adherence to one particular religion—or to none at all—is now considered a matter of personal preference. The question for us to consider here, then, is whether this secularizing effect is somehow due to science. Taylor doesn't think so.

First, he doesn't think arguing from scientific discoveries and advances to the non-existence of God is particularly persuasive. Undoubtedly, some people have been persuaded that evolution or multiverse hypotheses definitively rule out the existence of the divine. But Taylor thinks that even when people cite scientific arguments as the reason for their abandonment of faith there are deeper reasons at work which make that abandonment a live option in society today. He describes the life of faith not just as theories or sets of belief that one subscribes to but, more importantly for our question, as the context or framework (what Taylor calls the background) within which beliefs are held. This framework is part of the lived experience that is faith. So, faith in God today might be different from faith in God 500 years ago because of the different context within which that belief is held. Taylor says, "It is this shift in background, in the whole context in which we experience and search for fullness, that I am calling the coming of a secular age" (ibid., 14). The real story, then, is the rise of the background Taylor calls **exclusive humanism** which makes possible a range of religious beliefs or none at all.

According to exclusive humanism, there is no transcendent order and no ultimate goals beyond that of human flourishing. All previous societies in the Western world understood humans not to be the pinnacle of existence. There were beings above us on the **Great Chain of Being**, for instance, and those beings provided the chief end of life—to glorify God, regardless of any human's flourishing. This picture of things broke down coincident with the development of modern science, but Taylor argues that the real causal factor was the change in morality which stemmed primarily from **deism**. In deism, God may oversee an impersonal natural order, but has nothing more to do; so God is practically irrelevant to life. As such, humans have no meaningful engagement with anything transcending themselves. The objector to Taylor might reply, "But wasn't it science that brought about deism by replacing the supernatural explanations with natural ones? So science is still implicated in the process of secularization."

No one would deny that science has played a contributing factor, but the claim by many who are proponents of the Conflict thesis is that science has single-handedly defeated religion (or at least has been primarily responsible for its demise). Interestingly, though, Taylor argues that deism did not come from scientists to begin with. One element of deism stems from a suspicion of miracle claims. Today, it is natural for us to think that the demise of belief in miracles was due to the success of scientific explanations that replaced supernatural explanations. But the original issue with miracles was not that they compromised the natural order but rather that they were poorly established historically. Even as late as David Hume's influential treatment of miracles in 1748—well into the Scientific Revolution—the primary argument was that miraculous events contradict our experience, and as such it is more reasonable for us to believe that the testimonies to the miraculous were mistaken. Furthermore, all the religious traditions had their own miracle stories, which were disbelieved by others, and this leads to a mutual cancelling-out of all the testimonies.

If the origin of deism is not primarily found in science, where should we look? Taylor's answer is in league with Michael Buckley's analysis in his own massive work, *At the Origins of Modern Atheism*. Buckley's thesis is that the theologians of the 16th and 17th centuries treated atheism as if it were a philosophical problem rather than a religious one, and in so doing denied the relevance of the person and teachings of Jesus Christ in answering skeptics and atheists of the time. Instead, they tried to defend a philosophical idea—the "god of the philosophers" as it has come to be known—rather than the Christian Trinity. That is what led to deism and then ultimately to the atheism that characterized much of the French intelligentsia of the 18th and 19th centuries and continues to dominate academia today. Buckley summarizes:

> The remarkable thing is not that d'Holbach and Diderot found theologians and philosophers with whom to battle, but that the theologians themselves had become philosophers in order to enter the match. The extraordinary note about this emergence of the denial of the Christian god which Nietzsche celebrated is that Christianity as such, more specifically the person and teaching of Jesus or the experience and history of the Christian Church, did not enter the discussion. The absence of any consideration of Christology is so pervasive throughout serious discussion that it becomes taken for granted, yet it is so stunningly curious that it raises a fundamental issue of the modes of thought: How did the issue of Christianity vs. atheism become purely philosophical? To paraphrase Tertullian: How was it that the only arms to defend the temple were to be found in the Stoa? (Buckley 1987, 33)

So, on this reading—which is amply supported by historical detail—any decline in Christian belief throughout the Scientific Revolution seems ultimately traceable to the methods adopted by Christians to defend Christianity itself. They contented themselves with arguing for theism in general and thereby denuded the cognitive content of their religion of the rich moral and experiential resources of the Christian tradition. The bare theism with which they were left was unable to support the wider context of the life of faith.

Conclusion

Has science influenced Christianity? Undoubtedly so. It is no longer part of mainstream, orthodox theology that the earth is motionless in the center of the universe. Has Western society become more secularized? If we mean by the term that religious institutions have come to play a less significant role in society, then of course this is true too. And even if we mean, as Taylor does, that religious belief has become optional, then again there is little controversy that this is so for many in the Western world. But the data doesn't show that scientists in general have become less religious. For the versions of secularization that have occurred, it is difficult to maintain that there is a straightforward causal relationship between the advance of science and secularization.

This supposed relationship between science and secularization seems to belong to the same category as the Conflict thesis: generally assumed to be true but incapable of being confirmed by the facts in anything but isolated instances. Those isolated instances receive most of the attention and are incautiously made to stand for the whole relationship. We've seen, however, that both are more complex than such one-dimensional analyses can portray.

For a history as rich and complex as the one between science and Christianity, a one-size-fits-all approach will not do. We have to use different tools to understand different parts of the history of how science and Christianity have been related to each other. Perhaps we might make the case that the Independence view is the default tool to be used. Most of what goes on in scientific laboratories has very little direct relevance for how we understand Christianity, and we ought to respect their disciplinary boundaries. But there are some topics—and these can seem more prominent than they really are because they receive the preponderance of attention—for which Independence does not do justice to the relationship. There are points of conflict. And there are points of dialogue. At such points, we must use a different tool to understand the relationship. Perhaps an analogy from science helps to make this point. For most applications, engineers do just fine using Newtonian mechanics to solve problems. When building a backyard patio, a sophisticated automobile, or a suspension bridge across a gorge, we don't have to account for Einstein's relativistic phenomena. But there are some applications—GPS satellite programs, for example—that require a different tool (general relativity in this case) to address the situation accurately.

More prosaically, we might even say the different disciplines of science are different tools, or different methodologies. We must select the appropriate tool depending on the subject matter being studied. If we want to know about the effects of certain chemicals on an ecosystem, we don't call a physicist or a geologist. In the same way that science has specialized to address natural phenomena ever more carefully and accurately, we might insist that the discipline looking at the relationship between science and Christianity needs to do the same. Lots of Independence theorists will be needed to look at the vast swaths where science and Christianity appear not to be overlapping at all. But sometimes we'll need a Conflict theorist to sort out what has happened in episodes where science and Christianity do legitimately give competing answers to the same question. And at other times we'll want to see someone specializing in dialogue to help us understand how science and Christianity have influenced each other. Recognizing disciplinary distinctions can be a tricky business at the boundaries, but that does not mean there are no meaningful distinctions. Or to switch metaphors, no longer can we paint the history of science and Christianity with one color; the colors run together at places, but often can be clearly recognized.

These first three chapters have surveyed some history in order to illustrate the complexity that attends the relationship between science and Christianity. In the next chapter, we turn to more recent history that gets a lot of attention from Christians, and almost no attention from scientists.

 Summary of main points:

1. The data about religious belief among scientists shows consistency throughout the 20th century.
2. Secularization is a complex concept, capable of being defined in several ways.
3. Taylor and Buckley think the secularization of society was ultimately the result of Christian thinkers abandoning specifically Christian theology and opting for a more generic philosophical theism.

Further reading

- Brooke, John Hedley. 2010. "Science and Secularization." In *The Cambridge Companion to Science and Religion*, edited by Peter Harrison. Cambridge: Cambridge University Press. A succinct treatment of secularization by one of the world's leading historians of science.
- Ecklund, Elaine Howard. 2010. *Science vs. Religion: What Scientists Really Think*. Oxford: Oxford University Press. The results of a systematic study of scientists' religious beliefs.
- Taylor, Charles. 2007. *A Secular Age*. Cambridge, MA: The Belknap Press of Harvard University Press. The magnum opus of one of the most significant philosophers of our time.

References

Brooke, John Hedley. 2010. "Science and Secularization." In *The Cambridge Companion to Science and Religion*, edited by Peter Harrison. Cambridge: Cambridge University Press.

Buckley, Michael J. 1987. *At the Origins of Modern Atheism*. New Haven: Yale University Press.

Burke, Peter. 1979. *The New Cambridge Modern History*. Vol. XIII. Cambridge: Cambridge University Press.

Comte, Auguste. 1855. *The Positive Philosophy of Auguste Comte*. Translated by Harriet Martineau. New York: Calvin Blanchard.

Ecklund, Elaine Howard. 2010. *Science vs. Religion: What Scientists Really Think*. Oxford: Oxford University Press.

Iannaccone, Laurence, Rodney Stark, and Roger Finke. 1998. "Rationality and the 'Religious Mind'." *Economic Inquiry*, 36(3): 373–389.

Larson, Edward J., and Larry Witham. 1999. "Scientists and Religion in America." *Scientific American*, 281: 88–93.

Leuba, James H. 1916. *The Belief in God and Immortality: A Psychological, Anthropological and Statistical Study*. Boston: Sherman, French, and Company.

Martin, David. 2007. "Does the Advance of Science Mean Secularisaton?" *Science and Christian Belief*, 19: 3–14.

Numbers, Ronald L. 2010. "Simplifying Complexity: Patterns in the History of Science and Religion." In *Science and Religion: New Historical Perspectives*, edited by Thomas Dixon, Geoffrey Cantor, and Stephen Pumfrey. Cambridge: Cambridge University Press.

Taylor, Charles. 2007. *A Secular Age*. Cambridge, MA: The Belknap Press of Harvard University Press.

WIN-Gallup International. 2012. "Global Index of Religiosity and Atheism," http://www.wingia.com/web/files/news/14/file/14.pdf, accessed 17 February 2016.

CHAPTER 4

Young Earth Creationism and Intelligent Design

In the hot summer of 1925 in Dayton, Tennessee, one of the most famous trials in American history took place. Legally, it was the prosecution of a high school science teacher, John Scopes, for teaching evolution in violation of a law that had been passed recently. Really, though, the trial was just the stage for a high-profile debate between two of America's most prominent citizens.

Clarence Darrow was known as the greatest defense lawyer in the country. He came to Dayton to defend John Scopes, knowing that his client had clearly broken the law and would be convicted. Darrow's hope was that the trial would bring the law into public view and expose the supporters of the law as hopelessly unscientifically minded, thereby getting the law overturned.

The prosecution had an equally large personality in William Jennings Bryan, who had run for the presidency of the United States three times (unsuccessfully). He had taken to campaigning in favor of anti-evolution laws in several states. The climax of the trial occurred when Bryan agreed to take the stand to be questioned by Darrow. Of course, such a stunt had little to do with the trial, but made for fantastic theatre. The event didn't even happen inside the courtroom, as the judge feared the crowds would collapse the floor, so the proceedings were moved outside onto the lawn.

Bryan himself understood the situation, and even convinced the judge to let it proceed, stating from the makeshift stand that Darrow's defense team "did not come here to try this case, they came to try revealed religion. I am here to defend it" (Larson 1997, 5). Darrow's version was, "We have the purpose of preventing bigots and ignoramuses from controlling the education of the United States, and that is all" (ibid., 6). So the questioning proceeded, not directly about evolution but about Bryan's beliefs concerning the Bible. Just as we saw in the episode

Science and Christianity: An Introduction to the Issues, First Edition. By J. B. Stump.

between Galileo and the Church, the real source of conflict was not so much the scientific theories themselves as it was the authority of—and the authority to interpret—Scripture.

The **Scopes trial** was a watershed moment for science and Christianity in America. For many, the question became whether scientific explanations for natural phenomena would be allowed to alter—or even trump—the traditional explanations that had been taken from the Bible. Subsequent chapters in this book examine biblical interpretation and **methodological naturalism**—doctrines key to understanding the controversies about science among Christians today. In this chapter, we conclude Part 1 with some historical perspective on two contemporary schools of thought which have been enormously influential among Christians in America. We first address **Young Earth Creationism,** and then end up back in the courtroom to see the influence and particular approach to science and religion characterized by the movement known as **Intelligent Design**.

 Questions to be addressed in this chapter:

1. What led to the development of Young Earth Creationism?
2. What is the status of Young Earth Creationism today?
3. Where did Intelligent Design come from?
4. What is the strategy of Intelligent Design?

1. Setting the stage for Young Earth Creationism

In one sense, all Christians are creationists—Christians believe that God is the creator of all things. But of course there are different senses in which one could hold to God creating things, and the significant distinction in this chapter will be how the relationship is understood between scientific accounts or explanations and the theological attribution of "God created." For example, we might say that God created the Hawaiian Islands; but since we can still see the lava pouring out into the ocean, adding to the Big Island today, it is pretty clear that God did not say, "Let there be the Hawaiian Islands" and they materialized instantaneously *ex nihilo* or *de novo*. There are natural processes at work that can be understood scientifically. Some Christians claim that these natural processes describe the "how" of creation without detracting at all from the "who" of creation. Creationists, on the other hand, as the term is generally understood in the science and religion discussions, believe that God has created in ways that defy scientific explanation, and they typically reserve the word "created" for God's "special" or *de novo* acts of creation. This relationship between scientific and theological explanations is subtler and deserves careful analysis. It is the subject of Chapter 7. Our attention in this section is on the development of the Young Earth Creationist position that God created the earth and the species of life on it through acts of special creation in the relatively recent past—six to ten thousand years ago.

> **Creation *ex nihilo*** [ex nee-hill-o]
> Literally, creation out of nothing. This phrase is used to signify the claim that God created the universe out of nothing, rather than creating from existing materials or from out of himself.
>
> **Creation *de novo*** [day noh-voh]
> Literally, creation from new. This phrase is used to signify the claim that some things were created quickly and completely, not through a long process using intermediate forms.
>
> **Special creation**
> This phrase is used to signify the claim that God contravened natural processes to bring about some things miraculously.

Before the 19th century, there was little extra-biblical reason to question the chronology of Scripture as presenting facts of history (as we understand history today). The science of the day (or more accurately for the period, natural philosophy) could support neither an older nor a younger special creation because, as we saw briefly in Chapter 2, it was far more common to understand science as most supportive of an eternal natural world. In that case, God's creation of the natural world could no more be justified scientifically as occurring billions of years ago as it could be justified as occurring thousands of years ago. So at that time, science wasn't the relevant method of inquiry if one was trying to determine the age of the world.

Based on biblical interpretation, then, we can find people who argued for a literal reading and hence a young earth and others who argued for a figurative or metaphorical reading which allowed for longer stretches of time in earth's history. The most famous of the former category was James Ussher, an Anglican archbishop and the Primate of All Ireland in the 17th century. By piecing together the genealogies in Scripture, he determined that the moment of creation occurred in 4004 BCE on October 22 at 6pm! Saint Augustine and Aquinas are paradigmatic examples of the latter category, urging caution in reading the Genesis account too literally. Augustine is often quoted for his wise words about this matter (and biblical interpretation in general):

> In matters that are obscure and far beyond our vision, even in such as we may find treated in Holy Scripture, different interpretations are sometimes possible without prejudice to the faith we have received. In such a case, we should not rush in headlong and so firmly take our stand on one side that, if further progress in the search of truth justly undermines this position, we too fall with it. That would be to battle not for the teaching of Holy Scripture but for our own, wishing its teaching to conform to ours, whereas we ought to wish ours to conform to that of Sacred Scripture. (Augustine 1982, 41).

In the 19th century, developments on two fronts forced Christians to consider the relationship between science and the Bible with more nuance. One was the science that was bringing to light a seemingly ancient history of the earth. Fossils and geological layers were discovered and most naturally interpreted as evidences of a very old earth. The other development was the discovery of other texts from the ancient Near East in the genre of Genesis 1–11, suggesting that the Bible should be read in a literary way in keeping with that genre rather than in a simplistic literal way.

During the early 20th century, the most popular way of reconciling the scientific findings of an old earth with the Bible was what is known as the gap theory. This held to as literal a reading of Genesis 1 as possible, but allowed for there being a long gap of time between the first verse, "God created the heavens and the earth" and the six days of creation. With this view, fossils and the geologic layers could be accounted for as having developed during that gap before the special creation of the species we see today.

By the middle of the 20th century, Professor Bernard Ramm urged Christians to abandon the gap view as hopelessly unable to account for the geologic evidence. He urged a more moderate concordism according to which the Bible and geology tell generally the same story, but claimed there is no need to correlate the specific days with geologic events. He even interpreted the flood of Noah as a local event to Mesopotamia, rather than being worldwide (in our sense of the term today). Such a move away from a literal interpretation of Genesis was welcomed by some Christians, but not by all.

2. Today's Young Earth Creationism

John Whitcomb was a Bible professor who was much angered at the liberalizing tendency of Ramm's work. In 1957, he wrote a lengthy manuscript on the Genesis Flood as a response to Ramm. The conservative Christian publisher Moody Press was interested in the work, but thought that the scientific aspects of Whitcomb's argument would be more effective if written by a scientist. He struggled to find someone with the necessary scientific credentials who agreed with his literal interpretation of the flood. Then he met Henry Morris, a civil engineer with a PhD in hydraulics, who was a staunch proponent of a worldwide flood and a young earth. Whitcomb and Morris teamed up to write the seminal book of today's Young Earth Creationist movement, *The Genesis Flood*. After reviewing the manuscript, Moody Press declined to publish the book for fear that it would offend its constituency (showing how far the view was outside of American evangelicalism at the time). Instead, the book was published by the Presbyterian and Reformed Publishing Company in 1961.

There is no doubt that *The Genesis Flood* has had an enormous impact in orienting the thought of Christians in the latter half of the 20th century. Whitcomb and Morris's insistence on a literal reading of Genesis 1–11 fell on ears eager to counteract liberalizing tendencies of American society. This phenomenon seems influenced by the tendency of many Christians to buy into the dualism created by the culture wars that pits the sacred against the secular. Almost invariably, Young Earth Creationists today are first convinced that the Bible gives a very different explanation for natural history than "secular" science does. Then some ersatz science is rounded up to confirm their beliefs. Some of this "Creation

Science" can sound like it makes plausible points. But scientific theories are supple enough that some degree of support can be found for most positions. There are always anomalies to reigning scientific theories, so if you highlight them and take them out of context for what they explain successfully, then you can make a case for something that goes contrary to the established positions.

Ellen White (1827–1915)

One of the founders of the Seventh-day Adventist Church. She was known for her visions, which were regarded as authoritative by her followers. One of these is recognized as the origin of the modern Young Earth Creationist movement, when she claims to have been carried back to the time of creation and shown that it occurred in a week just like every other week.

George McCready Price (1870–1963)

An Adventist follower of White who helped to bring her ideas into the mainstream. He was a self-taught amateur geologist who pioneered Flood geology in an attempt to give Young Earth Creationism a scientific basis.

This approach is reflected in *The Genesis Flood*, which begins with an endorsement of the verbal inspiration and **inerrancy** of Scripture (these are discussed further in the next chapter). Then Whitcomb gives the biblical case for why the teaching of the Bible is for a universal flood, and this leads Morris to present a starkly defined choice: if the Bible clearly teaches a worldwide flood, then you have two options: reject the inspired word of God, or reject the testimony of the many thousands of trained geologists (Whitcomb and Morris 1961, 117–118). There is no question of allowing science to inform the interpretation of the Bible or to otherwise work toward reconciling the messages of science and the Bible. Morris claimed to be a proponent of the "Two Books" approach (discussed in Chapter 1) but couldn't countenance the possibility that God's world would reveal anything contrary to his understanding of God's word. And since he was absolutely sure of what the Bible said, he had to develop an alternative science that would support those views.

The Young Earth Creationist position dramatically increased in popularity among conservative Christians in the latter part of the 20th century. Today, Young Earth Creationism is committed to these core tenets:

- The universe and the earth are relatively recent creations—six to ten thousand years ago.
- Adam and Eve were created *de novo* on the sixth day of Creation. They are the first human beings and the ancestors of all human beings.
- Adam and Eve sinned, causing the Fall—before which no death had occurred even among animal life—and transmitting original sin to all subsequent human beings.

- There was a worldwide flood at the time of Noah, completely covering the earth and accounting for the geological features of the earth today.

Jason Rosenhouse is a mathematics professor who began following the Young Earth Creationist movement because of the battles over science education in Kansas. He has written a book about his attendance at their conferences and personal interactions with its proponents. He says that the stage and the pulpit are the natural venues for the discussion and dissemination of creationism. "So long as the audience is generally sympathetic and there is no opportunity for counterpoint, its confident fanaticism is infectious." But when placed in the medium of calm deliberation and rigorous evidential standards it becomes much less impressive. "Shorn of its emotionalism, nothing remains beyond its gross scientific errors" (Rosenhouse 2012, 5). This description may be accurate with respect to 99% of Young Earth Creationists. Fowler and Kuebler (2007, 195) quote Kurt Wise, an influential Young Earth Creationist with a PhD in geology from Harvard, estimating that 95% of Young Earth Creationists are concerned consumers. They comprise the overwhelming majority of audience members at Young Earth Creationist conferences and events who soak up the sermons and rhetoric without question. According to Wise, another 4% are the "crusaders" who are the primary public figures of the movement and have been largely responsible for the successes of spreading the doctrine and for creating a bad name within the scientific community. Then there remains the 1% who, Wise says, are the serious scientists who are building explanatory systems to try to support their beliefs. These systems sometimes stray rather far from the mainstream of science, but Young Earth Creationist scientists are driven to them because of their prior commitment to a particular reading of Scripture. In the next chapter we look at the various ways that Christians might read Scripture; before that, though, we need to consider another contemporary movement that has been influential in the science and Christianity discussions.

 Creationist organizations

Answers in Genesis

Founded in 1994, the most visible and influential of the Young Earth organizations. Its president, Ken Ham, and its Creation Museum are icons of the Young Earth movement.

The Creation Research Society

Founded by Henry Morris in 1963 to sponsor scientific research and publications from the creationist perspective. It publishes the *Creation Research Society Quarterly*.

The Institute for Creation Research

Founded in 1972 in California by Henry Morris and Duane Gish as an apologetics organization for Young Earth Creationism. After Morris died in 2006, the organization relocated to Dallas, Texas.

3. Intelligent Design

Another approach that sometimes gets lumped together with creationism is what is known as Intelligent Design. The most prominent organization defending Intelligent Design is the Discovery Institute in Seattle. It is a think tank concerned to counter a materialistic worldview and its effects in science, economics, politics, and religion. Specifically with regard to science, the Discovery Institute says that it seeks "to counter the materialistic interpretation of science by demonstrating that life and the universe are the products of intelligent design and by challenging the materialistic conception of a self-existent, self-organizing universe and the Darwinian view that life developed through a blind and purposeless process" (Discovery Institute 2016).

It can be misleading to label Intelligent Design as "creationist," since most Intelligent Design proponents accept the old age of the universe, and many accept the theory of common ancestry. What they do not accept—and have in common with creationists—is that there is an adequate scientific theory for explaining the development of life. Or perhaps it is more accurate to say that they do not think scientific explanations which do not include an explicit appeal to "mind" or an "intelligent cause" are adequate. Whether such appeals are proper to scientific explanations is the crux of the disagreement between Intelligent Design theorists and mainstream scientists. That is why their opponents charge that they aren't really doing science (and that they are just creationists in disguise), since they appeal to supernatural entities. We take up this debate about methodological naturalism in Chapter 6.

It is somewhat curious that the Intelligent Design movement has figured so prominently in recent discussions of science and religion since it is not essential to identify the intelligent designer with God. It is a matter of fact that the overwhelming majority of Intelligent Design advocates are Christians, but this is downplayed by the Discovery Institute. Two reasons might be given for suppressing an overt connection with religion: first, Phillip Johnson, one of the founders of the Intelligent Design movement, advocates using what he calls the "wedge strategy" against the "materialistic prejudice" of Darwinism. They are unwilling to consider theistic arguments directly, so Johnson thinks it is better to begin by exposing the weaknesses of their scientific theories first, and that will open the way for theism later. He says:

> To put things on a more rational basis, the first thing that has to be done is to get the Bible out of the discussion. Too many people, including journalists, have seen the movie *Inherit the Wind* and have become convinced that everyone who questions Darwinism must want to remove the microscopes and textbooks from the biology classrooms and just read the book of Genesis to the students. It is vital not to give any encouragement to this prejudice, and to keep the discussion strictly on the scientific evidence and the philosophical assumptions. This is not to say that the biblical issues are unimportant; the point is rather that the time to address them will be after we have separated materialist prejudice from scientific fact. (Johnson 1999, 22)

Another reason for downplaying religious connections is the desire of the Intelligent Design community to see their theory taught in American public schools. If their theory really is just science, then it should not be barred from public education. But history has not been kind to them in this regard, and here is where their link with creationism is more difficult to deny.

The 1925 Tennessee law at the heart of the Scopes trial forbade the teaching of "any theory that denies the Story of the Divine Creation of man as taught in the Bible." But in 1947, the United States Supreme Court ruled that states had to abide by the restrictions of the US Constitution from the so-called establishment clause. And, in 1968, the Court struck down an Arkansas law that was similar to the Tennessee law. Since they could no longer outlaw the teaching of evolution, creationists instead turned to the scientific development of their theories, and started using the phrase "creation science" or "scientific creationism." They did not hide the fact that they were Christians, but claimed that their theories could be justified on purely scientific grounds. Most scientists disagreed, and judges ruled against scientific creationism again and again. By the turn of the century, supporters of Intelligent Design had become more sophisticated in their scientific defenses and cagier about their religious commitments. The strategy came to a head in 2004 when the school board in Dover, Pennsylvania voted to require science teachers to read a statement to their classes that evolution is just a theory, and Intelligent Design is an alternative scientific theory. Students were referred to a pro-Intelligent Design textbook called *Of Pandas and People*. A group of parents and teachers filed a lawsuit against the school, and Intelligent Design got its day in court.

High-profile witnesses were called for both sides. The essential argument was whether Intelligent Design could legitimately be called science. The prosecution set out to establish that Intelligent Design was just an outgrowth of creationism, and their case was particularly compelling. The textbook in question, *Of Pandas and People*, was shown to have originated as a work of scientific creationism, and then in later drafts "creationists" was replaced with "design proponents" throughout the text. In one particularly damning passage the text reads, "cdesign proponentsists accept the latter view"—an obvious error in the find and replace procedure (Matzke 2009, 383).

Judge John E. Jones III, himself a conservative Republican appointed by President G. W. Bush, wrote a 139-page decision finding the mandate of the Dover school board unconstitutional (the conclusion of this decision is quoted in the box). He was convinced by the testimony that Intelligent Design does not qualify as science because it appeals to supernatural causation. To understand this charge better, we should look at some of the specific arguments Intelligent Design uses.

Judge Jones' conclusion

"The proper application of both the endorsement and *Lemon* tests to the facts of this case makes it abundantly clear that the Board's Intelligent Design Policy violates the Establishment Clause. In making this determination, we have addressed the seminal question of whether Intelligent Design is science. We have concluded that it is not, and moreover that Intelligent Design cannot uncouple itself from its creationist, and thus religious, antecedents.

"Both Defendants and many of the leading proponents of Intelligent Design make a bedrock assumption which is utterly false. Their presupposition is that evolutionary theory is antithetical to a belief in the existence of a supreme being and to religion in general. Repeatedly in this trial, Plaintiffs' scientific experts testified that the theory of evolution represents good science, is overwhelmingly accepted by the scientific community, and that it in no way conflicts with, nor does it deny, the existence of a divine creator.

"To be sure, Darwin's theory of evolution is imperfect. However, the fact that a scientific theory cannot yet render an explanation on every point should not be used as a pretext to thrust an untestable alternative hypothesis grounded in religion into the science classroom or to misrepresent well-established scientific propositions.

"The citizens of the Dover area were poorly served by the members of the Board who voted for the Intelligent Design Policy. It is ironic that several of these individuals, who so staunchly and proudly touted their religious convictions in public, would time and again lie to cover their tracks and disguise the real purpose behind the Intelligent Design Policy.

"With that said, we do not question that many of the leading advocates of Intelligent Design have *bona fide* and deeply held beliefs which drive their scholarly endeavors. Nor do we controvert that Intelligent Design should continue to be studied, debated, and discussed. As stated, our conclusion today is that it is unconstitutional to teach Intelligent Design as an alternative to evolution in a public school science classroom.

"Those who disagree with our holding will likely mark it as the product of an activist judge. If so, they will have erred as this is manifestly not an activist Court. Rather, this case came to us as the result of the activism of an ill-informed faction on a school board, aided by a national public interest law firm eager to find a constitutional test case on Intelligent Design, who in combination drove the Board to adopt an imprudent and ultimately unconstitutional policy. The breathtaking inanity of the Board's decision is evident when considered against the factual backdrop which has now been fully revealed through this trial. The students, parents, and teachers of the Dover Area School District deserved better than to be dragged into this legal maelstrom, with its resulting utter waste of monetary and personal resources.

"To preserve the separation of church and state mandated by the Establishment Clause of the First Amendment to the United States Constitution, and Art. I, § 3 of the Pennsylvania Constitution, we will enter an order permanently enjoining Defendants from maintaining the Intelligent Design Policy in any school within the Dover Area School District, from requiring teachers to denigrate or disparage the scientific theory of evolution, and from requiring teachers to refer to a religious, alternative theory known as Intelligent Design." (Jones 2005, 136–138)

4. Irreducible complexity and information

One of the main arguments used by the Intelligent Design movement is for what they call **irreducible complexity**. The biochemist Michael Behe wrote one of the seminal books for Intelligent Design in 1996 entitled *Darwin's Black Box*. In it he argues that evolution cannot explain how certain structures developed over time through slow, successive modifications. Irreducibly complex structures have many parts working together, such that the absence of one of them renders the entire structure nonfunctional. Behe uses the analogy of a mousetrap to explain the concept: a mousetrap needs a base, spring, hammer, catch, and holding bar; without any one of these, it is not as though the mousetrap would be marginally less effective—it wouldn't work at all to catch mice. So, claims Behe, are structures like the flagella of bacteria, or the blood clotting system. Certain bacteria have flagella which require some 40 different proteins to work properly. It is too outrageously coincidental to think that all 40 developed through random mutations at once to make the structure work; and without any one of the 40 proteins it wouldn't work at all. So Behe claims that the best explanation is that there is an intelligent designer behind this development, rather than merely chance mutations and natural selection.

Of course, most evolutionary biologists are not convinced by this argument. In the years after the publication of *Darwin's Black Box*, many scientists brought forth examples of how supposedly irreducibly complex structures could have developed piecemeal through natural processes, often by the co-option of existing structures for other purposes. Although some of these explanations seem convincing, it must be admitted that there are many things about the evolution of specific structures we still don't understand (and perhaps never will). So long as that gap in our knowledge persists, proponents of Intelligent Design can continue to claim that their explanation is viable.

> "By irreducibly complex I mean a single system composed of several well-matched, interacting parts that contribute to the basic function, wherein the removal of any one of the parts causes the system to effectively cease functioning. An irreducibly complex system cannot be produced directly (that is, by continuously improving the initial function, which continues to work by the same mechanism) by slight, successive modifications of a precursor system, because any precursor to an irreducibly complex system that is missing a part is by definition nonfunctional." (Behe 1996, 39)

There is another argument used by Intelligent Design theorists for their position. Underlying the complexity of cells, their component parts, and the proteins that these are built out of is the information in the genetic code of all living things. If new structures suddenly appear without precursors, then massive amounts of information have to suddenly appear in the DNA. But even if supposedly irreducibly complex structures can be explained in other ways, another prominent Intelligent Design author, Stephen Meyer, thinks that there is still an information problem that can't be explained by random genetic mutations and natural selection.

DNA functions as a set of instructions for cells to build the specific proteins needed to sustain our biological functions. The human genome is over three billion base pairs long, and the DNA of even the simplest organisms still has hundreds of thousands of base pairs (the smallest known to date is the 112,000 base pair genome of *Nasuia deltocephalinicola*—a microbe living inside a plant-eating insect).

The question Meyer asks is how huge amounts of functionally specified information could have arisen in DNA in the first place. There are four different nucleotide bases (adenine, thymine, guanine, and cytosine) out of which the DNA strand is built. Every three base pairs code for one of 20 naturally occurring amino acids; and then a chain of hundreds or thousands of amino acids makes up a protein, and the sequence of these amino acids determines the structure and function of the protein. There is no debate that DNA is information—vitally important information for life.

In his 2009 book, *Signature in the Cell,* Meyer considers the candidates for scientific explanation of the origin of this information. These include chance, self-organization, and the **RNA World Hypothesis,** Meyer's strategy is similar to Behe's: survey the best candidates scientists have put forward as "natural" explanations, and argue that they are all inadequate to the task; then remind the readers that we know that conscious minds can create large amounts of information; so conclude that the best explanation available for the origin of DNA is that there is an intelligent consciousness that is ultimately responsible. Meyer published another book in 2013, *Darwin's Doubt,* in which he applies the same strategy to the massive explosion of life forms throughout the Cambrian period.

There are some standard responses to Intelligent Design's conclusion that the natural world can only be explained by asserting there is an intelligent consciousness behind it. One is that there is also considerable evidence of poor design in natural systems. For example, as human brain size increased in comparison to other primates, our jaws had to shrink so the head could still fit through the birth canal (and it is only recently that we've resorted to Cesarean Section births to avert the previously all-too common deaths in childbirth of mother and infant). Our smaller jaws don't have enough room for all our teeth, so wisdom teeth have to be removed and others are crowded. There are other instances of "design" that seem to count

Fig. 4.1 Wasp larvae eating their way out of a caterpillar. Source: Courtesy of Kevin Collins.

against a wise and beneficent engineer who set things up this way. Darwin's infamous example was of the Ichneumonidae wasp, which lays an egg inside a caterpillar, and when it hatches, the young wasp eats its way out, keeping the caterpillar alive as long as possible to feed on. These and other examples of "natural evils" are countered by Young Earth Creationists as being a result of sin and the Fall. Prior to Adam and Eve's sin, they contend, there were no such problems in nature (not even predation). But most Intelligent Design proponents have accepted enough science to know that these "problems" were part of nature long before human beings came onto the scene (the problem of natural evil is considered further in Chapter 12).

Another response to the Intelligent Design conclusion is that it just isn't science anymore if we have to posit a supernatural cause in the midst of an otherwise natural explanation. Some Christians seem to find succor in these supernatural interventions, believing them to keep God involved in the affairs of the world. In reality, though, putting God into the gaps in the natural explanations is already a concession to the deism they are trying to avoid. For the implication is that if there is a natural explanation, then God must not be required. Holding onto these gaps seems to be the only way in their minds to keep God engaged. But as scientific explanations have gotten better and better, the God of the Gaps has less and less to do. There is not much difference between the deistic god who started things off and then sits back and watches and the Intelligent Design god who sits back and watches for a while then inserts himself into the process for a bit to make something work to then go back to sitting and watching. The Discovery Institute resists the claim that they rely on a God of the Gaps strategy. They are adamant that they have not resorted to intelligence only because there are no other explanations but because it is the best explanation, all things considered. At the root of their disagreement with other scientists, though, is whether it still counts as scientific when one element of that explanation is "an intelligent designer made it that way." We consider this issue in more detail in Chapter 6. First, we need to spend some more time on how the Bible is used by Christians in discussions of science.

 Summary of main points:

1. Young Earth Creationism was a reaction to the "liberalizing" tendencies of some Christians in the wake of the development of modern theories of science.

2. Young Earth Creationists today are convinced that their literal reading of Scripture is correct, and therefore try to develop alternative scientific theories to support that reading.

3. Intelligent Design has suppressed its religious motivations and accepts most mainstream science, but is still not viewed as properly scientific by mainstream scientists and the courts.

4. Intelligent Design attempts to show that natural explanations of certain phenomena are inadequate and that the best explanation appeals to an intelligent designer.

Further reading

- Davis, Edward B. 2012. "Science Falsely So Called: Fundamentalism and Science." In *The Blackwell Companion to Science and Christianity*, edited by J. B. Stump and Alan G. Padgett. Malden, MA: Wiley-Blackwell. An account of fundamentalism in America and its relationship with science.
- Meyer, Stephen. 2012. "Signature in the Cell: Intelligent Design and the DNA Enigma." In *The Blackwell Companion to Science and Christianity*, edited by J. B. Stump and Alan G. Padgett. Malden, MA: Wiley-Blackwell. A summary of his large book arguing that information in DNA is best explained by positing an intelligent designer.
- Moran, Jeffrey P. 2012. *American Genesis: The Evolution Controversies from Scopes to Creation Science*. Oxford: Oxford University Press. An exploration of the social forces contributing to the rise of Young Earth Creationism and Intelligent Design.
- Numbers, Ronald L. 1992. *The Creationists: The Evolution of Scientific Creationism*. New York: Alfred A. Knopf. The definitive account of the intellectual history of scientific creationism as it developed in the 20th century.
- Rosenhouse, Jason. 2012. *Among the Creationists: Dispatches from the Anti-Evolutionist Front Line*. Oxford: Oxford University Press. An atheist gives an illuminating and sympathetic account of his attendance at Young Earth Creationist conferences.

References

Augustine. 1982. *The Literal Meaning of Genesis*. Vol. 1. Mahwah, NJ: Paulist Press.

Behe, Michael J. 1996. *Darwin's Black Box: The Biochemical Challenge to Evolution*. New York: The Free Press.

Discovery Institute. 2016. "About Discovery," http://www.discovery.org/about. php, accessed 17 February 2016.

Fowler Thomas B., and Daniel Kuebler. 2007. *The Evolution Controversy: A Survey of the Competing Theories*. Grand Rapids, MI: Baker Academic.

Johnson, Phillip E. "The Wedge: Breaking the Modernist Monopoly on Science." *Touchstone: A Journal of Mere Christianity* 12, no. 4 (July/August 1999).

Jones, John E., III 2005. "Kitzmiller v. Dover, Memorandum Opinion," http://web.archive.org/web/20051221144316/http://www.pamd.uscourts. gov/kitzmiller/kitzmiller_342.pdf, accessed 17 February 2016.

Larson, Edward J. 1997. *Summer for the Gods: The Scopes Trial and America's Continuing Debate over Science and Religion*. New York: Basic Books.

Matzke, Nick. 2009. "But Isn't It Creationism? The Beginnings of 'Intelligent Design' in the Midst of the *Arkansas* and *Louisiana* Litigation." In *But Is It Science: The Philosophical Question in the Creation/Evolution Controversy*, edited by R. T. Pennock and M. Ruse. Amherst, MA: Prometheus Books.

Rosenhouse, Jason. 2012. *Among the Creationists: Dispatches from the Anti-Evolutionist Front Line*. Oxford: Oxford University Press.

Whitcomb, John C., and Henry M. Morris. 1961. *The Genesis Flood: The Biblical Record and Its Scientific Implications*. Philadelphia: The Presbyterian and Reformed Publishing Company.

CHAPTER 5

The Bible

Christians are people of a book. The Bible plays a foundational and for-
mational role for Christians in all areas of life—including their take on
science. But of course not all Christians use or view the Bible in the same
way. One of the chief differences exists between Protestants and Catholics.

Not long after the Protestant Reformation in the 16th century, there was growing consensus among leaders in the Catholic Church to take steps toward its own
institutional and administrative reform. Protestants had brought up significant
theological issues, and Catholics felt the need to respond to these. Chief among
them was an issue with the doctrine of justification, which Protestants proclaimed
to be *sola fide, sola gratia* (faith alone, grace alone), but there were also differences
about Scripture. Protestants had endorsed the **sola scriptura** principle too, claiming that the final authority of doctrine and practice is the Bible, not the Church. In
Martin Luther's famous speech before Holy Roman Emperor Charles V, he said he
would not change his opinions "unless convicted by Scripture and plain reason—I
do not accept the authority of popes and councils, for they have contradicted each
other—my conscience is captive to the Word of God" (Bainton 1978, 144).

Catholics responded on April 8, 1546 at the Fourth Session of the Council of
Trent with this decree about Scripture:

> Furthermore, to check unbridled spirits, it decrees that no one relying on his
> own judgment shall, in matters of faith and morals pertaining to the edification
> of Christian doctrine, distorting the Holy Scriptures in accordance with his own
> conceptions, presume to interpret them contrary to that sense which holy mother
> Church, to whom it belongs to judge of their true sense and interpretation, has
> held and holds, or even contrary to the unanimous teaching of the Fathers, even
> though such interpretations should never at any time be published. (Leith 1982,
> 403–404)

This statement lays the groundwork for the Church's conflict with Galileo. As
described in Chapter 1, Galileo ran into trouble not so much for his scientific
discoveries as for his presumption to interpret Scripture contrary to the Catholic Church. The Church believed Scripture to be authoritative, and it believed
itself to be the authoritative interpreter of Scripture. By claiming *sola scriptura*, the

Science and Christianity: An Introduction to the Issues, First Edition. By J. B. Stump.
© 2017 John Wiley & Sons, Ltd. Published 2017 by John Wiley & Sons, Ltd.

Reformers denied that the Church had such authority. For them, Scripture alone had ultimate authority.

But it is not always straightforward to know what Scripture claims. And especially when we try to use it in dialogue with science, there is the difficulty of sorting out the culture-bound claims and assumptions from the timeless message. This is why the Catholic Church retains for itself the authority to interpret the Bible and say what it means. For Protestants who hold to the *sola scriptura* principle, there is also an interesting comparison with the "Two Books" concept discussed in Chapter 1. We'll address these two issues first before turning to the nature of Scripture itself and what this implies for its discussion with science.

Questions to be addressed in this chapter:

1. How does *sola scriptura* fit with the Two Books model?

2. What is the challenge of interpreting Scripture in the *sola scriptura* model?

3. What does the text itself seem to indicate about how God inspired the Bible?

4. How does this view of inspiration affect discussions with science?

1. Two Books vs. *sola scriptura*

As we saw in Chapter 1, there is a long tradition of seeing the created order as another source of God's revelation to us—the book of God's works. But how are the two books to be correlated with each other? And what does this do to the Reformation principle of *sola scriptura*?

The doctrine of *sola scriptura* began as a means of uniting Protestants against the Catholic Church. At its heart, the Protestant Reformation was about who had the authority to determine the content and practice of Christianity—individuals or the institution of the Church. In the view of the Reformers, the Church had become corrupt and self-serving. It could no longer be trusted to regulate itself, and it was necessary to look to an authority outside of the Church hierarchy. So Martin Luther took his stand against the Catholic Church with his Bible in hand. In the Bible he found no teaching about popes and purgatory, or indulgences and the role of works in salvation, so he rejected these. His original intention was not to found a new denomination, but there could be no reconciliation with the institution once he had pulled the rug out from under it by asserting the right of the individual to determine orthodoxy through his or her own reading of Scripture. But then this doctrine which began as a unifying cry against the institution very quickly became the grounds for endless divisions. Luther's reading of Scripture was questioned by Zwingli and Calvin; theirs was questioned by the Anabaptists. And so on. At last count, the number of distinct Christian denominations worldwide exceeds 33,000 (Barrett, Kurian, and Johnson 2001, 18).

Given this state of affairs in Protestant Christianity today, it is obvious that there is more to the doctrine of *sola scriptura* than the popular and pious-sounding slogan, "The Bible says it; that settles it." The Reformers themselves—despite some quotations that could be produced—would not have advocated such an approach to the Bible. They were not advocating the arch-individualism to Bible reading that has arisen in the American context. The Reformers understood that our reading of Scripture must be informed and guided by church tradition and the creeds. It was just that they did not think such tradition carried the same weight as the Bible itself. Even John Wesley, the 18th-century theologian and founder of **Methodism**, acknowledged roles for tradition, reason, and experience in shaping the way we understand the Bible, though all the while maintaining that Scripture is the single highest authority.

But in America in the 18th century, the spirit of democracy permeated most of life, and the approach to science and to the Bible was no exception. Instead of being regulated by an authoritarian process, both science and the Bible were approached democratically. This was held to be the safest protection against the tendencies of tradition to corrupt (Noll 2009, 6). But how would you know if your interpretation was correct? It must be plain to see. There was an underlying assumption to this approach, namely, that the message of Scripture is clear if one would but pay attention to it.

From the time of the Church Fathers in the Christian tradition, there had been a multifaceted approach to the interpretation of Scripture. Besides the literal meaning of the words, the "professional" interpreters would also discern the spiritual sense of the text, which could include an allegorical sense, a tropological or moral sense, and an anagogical or future sense. Understandably, these spiritual senses of the text were much more ambiguous, so if a clear message was desired, there would have to be an increased emphasis on the literal meaning of Scripture.

Cassian and Augustine on the four-fold sense of Scripture

Augustine wrote in his *The Literal Meaning of Genesis*: "In all the sacred books, we should consider eternal truths that are taught [the allegorical], the facts that are narrated [the literal or historical], the future events that are predicted [the anagogical], and the precepts or counsels that are given [the tropological or moral]." (§1.1.1, Augustine 1982, 19)

John Cassian (c. 360–435) gave an illustration of this: "The one Jerusalem can be understood in four different ways, in the historical sense as the city of the Jews, in allegory as the Church of Christ, in anagoge as the heavenly city of God 'which is the mother of us all' (Gal 4:26), in the tropological sense as the human soul." (Cassian 1985, 160)

One of the effects of the emphasis on the literal meaning was to diminish the distinctiveness of Scripture from other books: if there was no legitimate spiritual sense to the words, then it was not much different from other texts which told of historical events and could be read in a similar way (Harrison 1998, 124). Perhaps individuals could draw different morals from the story of Jonah or Noah or Adam, but those were applications of the text. The Bible itself was thought to be clear in its message: these were historical figures and their stories happened just as described—otherwise we wouldn't be able to trust the message of Scripture.

The emphasis on the literal sense of Scripture also stimulated more careful examination of nature (Noll 2009, 2). One way we see this is in the labors of the Renaissance scholars who gave careful scrutiny to ancient texts (including the Bible) in order to understand the words being used. For example, in translating texts from the ancient world, words for the names of plants and animals could simply be transliterated, as the Arab translators had done throughout the Middle Ages, without concern for correlating them with contemporary species. Or an attempt could be made to identify species based on the description of them in the texts. This forced the Renaissance translator to leave the academy and go into the field and make careful observations (Harrison 1998, 78).

With increased attention on the natural world, the Two Books metaphor came to resonate more with those who were involved in science and religion. But then the issue of the relation between the information of these Two Books inevitably came into play. Without much serious reflection, it was assumed by many that there should be a straightforward correlation between what information the Bible gives and what we discover from nature. One popular book on science and Christianity today endorses this principle explicitly: "If Scripture has anything to say about the natural world, then what is revealed in Scripture should not contradict what is revealed by studying the natural world itself" (Haarsma and Haarsma 2011, 73). But Mark Noll sees this need to harmonize nature and the Bible as one of the assumptions that creates the conflict between science and religion (Noll 2009, 2). For example, when Jesus is quoted in Matthew saying the mustard seed is the smallest of all the seeds (13:31–32) and then careful observers of nature discover that there are in fact many smaller seeds, what are we to do?

Those committed to the Two Books model cannot just discount such statements in Scripture which on a plain, literal reading contradict what we learn from nature. Of course, sometimes what we "learn" from nature turns out to be wrong (i.e., we learn something else that turns out to be a better explanation). But it is not likely that the heliocentric solar system will be overturned; nor will scientists find that there was a flood covering the whole earth sometime in the last several thousand years; nor will the common ancestry of life be replaced. And yet there are statements in the Bible that seem to contradict all of these. If we are committed to the claim that "what is revealed in Scripture should not contradict what is revealed by studying the natural world itself," we need a more sophisticated method of interpreting Scripture—which is what Haarsma and Haarsma push for, and what we turn to next.

2. Interpretation

There is a way of looking at science and the Bible so as to see a parallel—though not an exact match—between how Christians use Scripture and how scientists use empirical data. With this view, it can be claimed that there is no conflict between the natural world and the Bible, but there might be conflict between our interpretation of the Bible and our interpretation of the natural world. These interpretations are human attempts at understanding and explaining, whereas nature and the Bible are the God-given revelations—the Two Books—which cannot contradict each other. So, any perceived conflicts are the result of our misinterpretations of one or other (or both) of these sources. To assess this approach, we need to spend some time understanding the surprisingly complex process of interpretation, or what is sometimes called **hermeneutics**.

The first point to make is that the data almost always underdetermines the theories that explain it. That is to say, the data doesn't absolutely compel us to believe a specific theory; or another way to say that is that more than one theory can be consistent with the data. To illustrate this a bit abstractly, and with some fancy Latin terminology, let's say the dots in the following diagram are the *explananda* (the things we want to explain):

●
●   ●
●

These *explananda* are individual data points, like the measurements from an experiment, or individual claims made in Scripture. What we aim to do with scientific or theological theories is to provide an explanation—called the *explanans*—that accounts for these data points. In this illustration, let's say that the *explanans* is the shape implied by the dots. So if we have these four dots, the interpretive question to consider is, "What shape do they seem to be making?" And the underdetermination problem is that more than one shape is consistent with these dots. In fact, mathematically speaking, there are an infinite number of shapes that could incorporate these four dots. So we, perhaps unconsciously, assume that simplicity is a virtue of potential explanations, and that narrows the field considerably, but still we find several viable candidates: a diamond, a circle, or a cross would all fit these points very well.

What good explanations should do, then, is predict or be able to incorporate further data points that may be found, and presumably these future data points will help to clarify just what shape is the best. So, for example, the "circle theorists"

would say that future data points in these positions would be confirming evidence for their explanation:

But the "diamond theorist" might claim that the new data points have too much experimental error, or even that the basic diamond explanation still holds, with some appropriate "circular" embellishments:

In the same way, Christian theologians look to the Bible as a source of revelation about God. And they take individual statements made as part of the "data" to be explained. For example, in a very simplistic version of this, we see that Scripture claims that God is the creator (Genesis 1:1) and that God created everything in six days (Exodus 20:11). That seems to show that Young Earth Creationism has the best explanation of the data. But then someone else might produce another data point from the Bible, "with the Lord a day is like a thousand years" (2 Peter 3:8 and Psalm 90:4); this person might conclude that the claim of six days is capable of being explained in a nonliteral sense. Another person might produce the verse from Romans (5:14) in which the Apostle Paul seemingly appeals to Adam as a historical figure; he might claim that this provides the interpretive key for deciding whether the correct theological explanation demands that all human beings were descended from one pair of humans who resided in the Garden of Eden. Others go to great lengths to explain away or reinterpret that data point so that it fits their explanation better.

Unfortunately, this is the level at which much of the biblical engagement takes place by those who endeavor to take Scripture seriously as an authoritative source of revelation. There is an underlying assumption that each direct statement taken from Scripture must be incorporated into the *explanans*, and the resulting "shape" is claimed to be the true biblical position. Within conservative Christian denominations, this has led to affirmations of **biblical inerrancy**—the claim that the Bible (at least in its original manuscripts) contains no errors in its factual claims. The most well-known articulation of this position comes from the "Chicago Statement on Inerrancy," developed by a host of evangelical leaders in 1978 at a meeting in Chicago.

> Excerpt from "Chicago Statement on Inerrancy"
> "Being wholly and verbally God-given, Scripture is without error or fault in all its teaching, no less in what it states about God's acts in creation, about the events of world history, and about its own literary origins under God, than in its witness to God's saving grace in individual lives." (Center for Reformed Theology and Apologetics 1978)

So how do inerrantists handle the clear statements in Scripture that do contradict what we've discovered in nature? Of course, there are some who deny that we have discovered common ancestry (we discuss evolution in Chapter 9) or clear evidence that there was not a global flood in recent history. They usually do not, however, deny heliocentrism or that there are smaller seeds than the mustard seed. Instead, they must employ a range of interpretive strategies—embellishing the "shape" of their *explanans*. Perhaps Jesus was exaggerating for effect in calling the mustard seed the smallest; or perhaps he was referring only to the kinds of seeds with which his audience was familiar. Perhaps when Joshua commanded the sun to stand still (Joshua 10), God was accommodating his language to his original audience (how would they have responded if Joshua had commanded the earth to stop rotating?!).

Suggesting just these instances should give us pause about the implicit assumption of *sola scriptura* that the message of the Bible is clear and perspicuous. If these seemingly straightforward readings turned out not to be the correct way to read Scripture, what else might we be getting wrong on such a reading? It appears that interpretation is an inescapable component of saying what Scripture means. But once this admission is made, the doctrine of inerrancy carries much less force. Very few people would claim that their interpretations are inerrant, so as soon as they try to say what passages of Scripture mean, their interpretations can be challenged by others who claim to have a better interpretation. Sociologist Christian Smith surveyed the way the Bible functions in conservative American Protestant contexts in which a version of *sola scriptura* (**biblicism**) is adhered to, and he describes the problem as follows:

> The very same Bible—which biblicists insist is perspicuous and harmonious—gives rise to divergent understandings among intelligent, sincere, committed readers about what it says about most topics of interest. Knowledge of "biblical" teachings, in short, is characterized by pervasive interpretive pluralism. What that means in consequence is this: in a crucial sense it simply does not matter whether the Bible is everything that biblicists claim theoretically concerning its authority, infallibility, inner consistency, perspicuity, and so on, since in actual functioning the Bible produces a pluralism of interpretations. (Smith 2011, 17)

> "Biblicism" Christian Smith (ibid., 4–5) defines biblicism with 10 assumptions or beliefs about the Bible's nature, purpose and function. Some of these are:
>
> • Divine Writing: The Bible, down to the details of its words, consists of and is identical with God's very own words written inerrantly in human language.

- Democratic Perspicuity: Any reasonably intelligent person can read the Bible in his or her own language and correctly understand the plain meaning of the text.
- Commonsense Hermeneutics: The best way to understand biblical texts is by reading them in their explicit, plain, most obvious, literal sense, as the author intended them at face value, which may or may not involve taking into account their literary, cultural, and historical contexts.
- Solo Scriptura: The significance of any given biblical text can be understood without reliance on creeds, confessions, historical church traditions, or other forms of larger theological hermeneutical frameworks, such that theological formulations can be built up directly out of the Bible from scratch.
- Inductive Method: All matters of Christian belief and practice can be learned by sitting down with the Bible and piecing together through careful study the clear "biblical" truths that it teaches.

"Pervasive interpretive pluralism" is the result of what we earlier called the "underdetermination problem." Using the analogy of the dots again, there are just too many different shapes that can be made to fit a configuration of dots. In a sense, this might be thought to be beneficial for the Bible's interaction with science: the meaning of Scripture can be manipulated enough to fit anything science throws at it. But this resolves potential conflict at the expense of rendering the Bible almost meaningless. This is close to Gould's non-overlapping magisteria approach (discussed in Chapter 1) according to which religion is cordoned off from empirical matters and confined to the realm of values.

In the next section, we consider a different approach to the Bible which acknowledges more of the complexity of the interpretive process.

3. What kind of inspiration?

Deciding the proper method of interpreting the Bible depends on recognition of what kind of book it is. What is too often overlooked is that it is actually a collection of books, and this is a fact that accounts for some of the interpretive difficulties. When the Psalmist says that the earth is set on pillars (Psalm 75), are we to interpret that as a claim about cosmology? When the Apostle Paul says that women should be silent in the churches (1 Corinthians 14:34), is he speaking to everyone in all cultures, or does that command apply only to the original audience? Should we read the historical narratives in Genesis the same way we read the historical narrative in the book of Acts? Answers to such questions depend on knowing something about the origin and purpose of the texts. The traditional Christian position is that God inspired the writing of Scripture. But what does that mean?

The Book of Common Prayer includes a prayer for the second Sunday of Advent which begins with, "Blessed Lord, who hast caused all holy Scriptures to be written for our learning." Claiming that the Lord caused Scripture to be written no more answers the question about inspiration than does the Apostles' Creed line, "God the Father, Almighty, maker of heaven and earth," provide an explanation for how God brought the natural world into existence and to the way we find it today. The affirmation that God is the creator is consistent with all manner of scientific theories about the development of the natural world. Therefore, if we want to know how God created, we must look to the natural world and investigate what we find there.

In the same way, the affirmation that God caused Scripture to be written is consistent with a range of theories about what it means for the Bible to be inspired. God could have caused Scripture to come into being by supernaturally dropping fully formed Bibles out of heaven into church pews. Or God could have caused Scripture to be written by dictating to people who wrote down the exact words being whispered in their ears. Or God might have more subtly influenced the minds of the human authors without eliminating the human element of their writing (their language, culture, and worldview). If we want to know which method of inspiration God used, we will have to actually look at the text and see what kind of writings we find there.

Of course, there are more options than these for how God might have inspired Scripture; we'll consider just two broad categories. The first conforms generally to the first assumption of the biblicist picture described by Christian Smith: divine writing (the Bible, down to the details of its words, consists of and is identical with God's very own words written inerrantly in human language). The dictation method is one way this might have happened; or perhaps God inaudibly "dictated" in the sense that the human author was not aware of the fact that God was using him, but God nonetheless caused each word to be written exactly as God desired.

The other broad category is what I'll call "bearing witness." On this model, there was an act of special revelation to which the writings bear witness. For the Gospels, that revelation was the person of Jesus Christ who became human and dwelt among some people in 1st-century Palestine. For Saul/Paul, that revelation was the risen Jesus who appeared to him on the Damascus Road. We could even say that for the Old Testament Prophets and John in the New Testament, God revealed himself to authors in visions (though, of course, authorship is more complex than this for almost all of the biblical books in the form we have them in today). But this differs from the divine writing model in the fact that God did not predetermine the words that would be written in response to that revelation. We might say that God guided (i.e., inspired) their thoughts, but it was the human beings with their language and their understanding of the world at the time it was written who wrote the words. So according to this view, we cannot assume that the words of Scripture are God's very words. They are the words of people and communities to whom God revealed himself.

So, what kind of text would we expect there to be in each of these scenarios? One question we might ask would be whether we'd expect the message of the Bible to be clear and consistent (on at least the most important topics) if God was primarily responsible for the words. It seems that the answer to this would be affirmative. Even if God accommodated the words to the languages and cultures of the time, God should be seen as coordinating the overall message. If, however,

God gave a revelation and the human authors responded (even if God was influencing their thoughts to a degree), it would seem more likely that there could be significant differences in how those humans respond. In this way, these two models of how God might have inspired Scripture make predictions of what we should expect to find in Scripture. It remains, then, to do the empirical work of checking whether the message of the Bible is in fact clear and consistent. If it is, then, that would provide some confirming evidence for the divine writing model; if not, then the evidence points toward the bearing witness model.

When I have asked this question to groups of Christians, they usually have the first response of affirming that the message of Scripture is clear and consistent on the central issues with which it is concerned. But it doesn't take very long to show that it just is not the way we find the texts to be, even about the most important topics. Consider the accounts of the resurrection of Jesus in the four gospels:

- Matthew: Mary Magdalen and the other Mary went to the tomb; when they got there, an angel appeared and rolled back the stone and sat on it. They left the tomb and met Jesus, who told them to tell his brothers to go to Galilee, where they would see him.
- Mark: Mary Magdalene, Mary the mother of James, and Salome went to the tomb; the stone had already been rolled away by the time they got there. They went into the tomb and there saw an angel, who told them to tell the disciples to go to Galilee, where they would see Jesus.
- Luke: Mary Magdalene, Joanna, Mary the mother of James, and the other women went to the tomb; the stone was already rolled away and they entered the tomb. There two men stood beside them; they went and told the disciples, and Peter ran to the tomb to inspect it.
- John: Mary Magdalene went to the tomb alone and found that the stone had been removed; she went back to tell Peter and John, who ran to the tomb. After they left, Mary saw two angels in the tomb, and Jesus appeared to her. Then Mary went and told the disciples.

These accounts conform to what we would expect from human eyewitness accounts. If a car accident happened at an intersection and was witnessed by people standing on the four corners, we'd probably get slightly different accounts of what happened, concerning whether the traffic light turned, which car was at fault, and so on. The witnesses certainly attest adequately to the fact that there was an accident, just as the gospel writers clearly attest to the fact that the tomb was empty. But it seems strange that God would dictate different versions of the details to each writer.

Or consider the message of salvation and what we must do to be saved. The Apostle Paul in his letters emphasizes that salvation comes by grace through faith—not by works (e.g., Ephesians 2:8–9); and this is usually taken as the orthodox position. But in the book of James we're told that a person is justified by works and not by faith alone (James 2:24); and in the parable of the sheep and the goats (Matthew 25:31–46), Jesus himself is portrayed as attributing the final judgment and rewards of people to the actions that they performed. We could provide similar examples from the doctrines of **eschatology** (the study of the end times),

predestination, **atonement**, and almost any other doctrine. It may be that individuals or certain traditions develop clear and consistent theologies of these, but the claim here is that they do so at the expense of ignoring or explaining away recalcitrant passages of Scripture that do not fit with their theory (just like the analogy of shapes and dots earlier in this chapter). The text itself is messier than that. This evidence suggests that the Bible is a record in which human authors—with all their limitations—bore witness to the divine disclosures among them. What might this mean for its relationship to science today?

4. Science and the Bible

If Scripture itself is not always clear and consistent, it is the goal of the theologian to develop explanations (i.e., theology) that are clear and consistent. These explanations, then, provide interpretive "lenses" through which we view other parts of Scripture and the world itself. Such interpretations, though, must be in constant conversation with the rest of our experience. Here is the point most relevant for the Bible's interaction with science. Instead of attempting to mine Scripture for scientific insights, we ought to allow for an ongoing conversation between what we learn about the created order and what we find in Scripture. Some Christians get nervous when we talk of allowing science to influence our interpretation of Scripture, but there is no denying that it has done so. The obvious allusions in the Bible to the movement of the sun were once interpreted literally, but no longer are, because of science.

Some Christians will affirm that such a conversation even allows science to correct (not just influence) our interpretation of Scripture. In a sense, this might be a positive approach for the relation between science and the Bible. It acknowledges that there is a culture-bound aspect to Scripture and that this ought not to be taken as the inspired message of Scripture. New scientific discoveries about the world (e.g., heliocentrism, ancient age, common descent) can help to correct our reading of Scripture when we've taken the cultural-bound language as absolute. However, even this approach implies that there is one correct interpretation of Scripture, and implicitly it seems still to hold to the view that the Bible is simply a collection of true statements (even if their meaning is difficult to discern at times).

Another way we might understand the conversation between science and the Bible is that our changing understanding of the natural world calls for fresh interpretations of Scripture which are relevant to the context in which we find ourselves. In this regard, Christians might learn something from the ancient Jewish tradition of Pharisees who studied Torah, not to discover some single authoritative meaning of Scripture but to encounter the divine presence in the fresh meanings they discovered from interacting with the text and applying them to the burning issues of their day (Armstrong 2007, 81–82). There are Christians, as well, who use similar language. New Testament scholar N. T. Wright says:

> The Bible seems designed to challenge and provoke each generation to do its own fresh business, to struggle and wrestle with the text … Each generation must do its own fresh historically grounded reading, because each generation needs to *grow* up, not simply to *look* up the right answers and remain in an infantile condition. (Wright 2014, 29–30)

Of course, Wright is not advocating that any interpretation of Scripture is just as good as any other. The conversation between Scripture and our experience is guided by church tradition (both generally and within specific denominational traditions) and reason. Rather, this is a commitment to the fecundity of Scripture to speak across cultures and generations.

These kinds of insights about the interpretation of the Bible bring us back to considering the spiritual meanings of the text instead of just the literal meaning. The 3rd-century church father Origen saw too that the design of the Bible does not lend itself to flat, superficial readings. He thought it was impossible to consistently follow the literal or historical meaning of Scripture, even claiming that if people attempted to do so they could not revere the Bible as a holy book because of the inconsistencies at that level (Armstrong 2007, 109). This was not a liability of the text according to Origen but that which drives us to consider deeper, spiritual meanings.

In conclusion, Christians use the Bible variously with regard to science. It seems, though, that the approach that is most consistent with the kind of text(s) we find in the Bible is to allow for conversation between the original witnesses of God's revelation and the situation we find ourselves in today. This approach takes the Bible seriously as inspired by God, but also creates space for scientific inquiry. In the next chapter, we consider one of the purported hallmarks of scientific inquiry—methodological naturalism—and how well it fits with a commitment to Christian faith.

 Summary of main points:

1. *Sola scriptura* forced an emphasis on the literal meaning of Scripture, and this brought some passages of Scripture into conflict with what was learned from the "book" of nature.

2. Scripture underdetermines the doctrines drawn from it, and so *sola scriptura* gives rise to pervasive interpretive pluralism.

3. Scripture itself is not always clear and consistent, suggesting that God did not dictate the words of scripture but allowed humans to bear witness to God's revelation.

4. A conversation between Scripture and experience (including science) enables us to find fresh meanings of Scripture in light of what we know about the world.

Further reading

- Harris, Mark. 2013. *The Nature of Creation: Examining the Bible and Science.* Durham: Acumen. A sustained examination of the creation texts of the Bible in the light of contemporary science.

- Harrison, Peter. 1998. *The Bible, Protestantism, and the Rise of Natural Science.* Cambridge: Cambridge University Press. Explores the role played by the Bible in the development of natural science.
- Noll, Mark. 2009. "Evangelicals, Creation, and Scripture: An Overview," http:// biologos.org/uploads/projects/Noll_scholarly_essay.pdf, accessed 17 February 2016. A concise treatment of the changing understanding and use of Scripture by evangelicals in America.
- Smith, Christian. 2011. *The Bible Made Impossible: Why Biblicism Is Not a Truly Evangelical Reading of Scripture.* Grand Rapids, MI: Brazos Press. A prominent Christian sociologist shows how conservative Christians use the Bible to defend significantly different views.

References

Armstrong, Karen. 2007. *The Bible: A Biography.* New York: Grove Press.

Augustine. 1982. *The Literal Meaning of Genesis.* Vol. 1. Mahwah, NJ: Paulist Press.

Bainton, Roland H. 1978. *Here I Stand: A Life of Martin Luther.* Nashville, TN: Abingdon Press.

Barrett, David B., George T. Kurian, and Todd M. Johnson, eds. 2001. *World Christian Encyclopedia.* Oxford: Oxford University Press.

Cassian, John. 1985. *Conferences.* Translated by Colm Luibheid. New York: Paulist Press.

Center for Reformed Theology and Apologetics. 1978. "Chicago Statement on Biblical Inerrancy," http://www.churchcouncil.org/ICCP_org/Documents_ICCP/English/01_Biblical_Inerrancy_A&D.pdf, accessed 17 February 2016.

Haarsma, Deborah B., and Loren D. Haarsma. 2011. *Origins: Christian Perspectives on Creation, Evolution, and Intelligent Design.* Grand Rapids, MI: Faith Alive Christian Resources.

Harrison, Peter. 1998. *The Bible, Protestantism, and the Rise of Natural Science.* Cambridge: Cambridge University Press.

Leith, John H., ed. 1982. *Creeds of the Churches,* 3rd ed. Louisville, KY: Westminster John Knox Press.

Noll, Mark. 2009. "Evangelicals, Creation, and Scripture: An Overview." http:// biologos.org/uploads/projects/Noll_scholarly_essay.pdf, accessed 17 February 2016.

Smith, Christian. 2011. *The Bible Made Impossible: Why Biblicism Is Not a Truly Evangelical Reading of Scripture.* Grand Rapids, MI: Brazos Press.

Wright, N. T. 2014. "Do We Need a Historical Adam?" In *Surprised by Scripture: Engaging the Contemporary Issues,* 26–40. San Francisco: HarperOne.

CHAPTER 6

Methodological Naturalism

The 19th-century British mathematician and philosopher Augustus De Morgan included this now famous story in his *A Budget of Paradoxes*:

> Laplace once went in form to present some edition of his "Systeme du Monde" to the First Consul, or Emperor, Napoleon, whom some wags had told that this book contained no mention of the name of God, and who was fond of putting embarrassing questions, received it with—"M. Laplace, they tell me you have written this large book on the system of the universe, and have never even mentioned its Creator." Laplace, who, though the most supple of politicians, was as stiff as a martyr on every point of his philosophy or religion, … drew himself up, and answered bluntly, "Je n'avais pas besoin de cette hypothèse-là" [I have no need of that hypothesis]. (De Morgan 1872, 249–250)

De Morgan's account might not be accurate in its detail, but there is probably some truth to this supposed encounter between Napoleon and Laplace. The astronomer William Herschel preserved a record of a visit by Napoleon to Malmaison (Josephine's estate) on August 8, 1802 where Hershel and Laplace were visiting. After a discussion with Herschel, Napoleon also addressed himself to Laplace and had a considerable disagreement with him. Hershel said of it:

> The difference was occasioned by an exclamation of the First Consul's [Napoleon], who asked in a tone of exclamation or admiration (when we were speaking of the extent of the sidereal heavens), "and who is the author of all this?" M. de LaPlace wished to shew that a chain of natural causes would account for the construction and preservation of the wonderful system; this the First Consul rather opposed. (Lubbock 1933, 310)

Laplace was advocating what philosophers and scientists today call methodological naturalism. Laplace's theological beliefs are debated, but even if he had said "I have no need of that hypothesis" that wouldn't be support for attributing atheism to him. He meant that his scientific explanation didn't need to appeal to supernatural causation.

Science and Christianity: An Introduction to the Issues, First Edition. By J. B. Stump.
© 2017 John Wiley & Sons, Ltd. Published 2017 by John Wiley & Sons, Ltd.

It is fairly easy to give examples at the ends of the spectrum of what counts as natural and what counts as supernatural: a scientific theory that appeals to angels or spirits as the explanation for the elliptical orbits of planets around the sun would not qualify as a scientific theory for those who hold to methodological naturalism; and the theory that claims the diversity of life today can be explained by random mutations of the genetic code and natural selection would qualify. But if methodological naturalism is supposed to be the criterion of demarcation for separating true science from false, there are some gray areas where it is not so clear—both throughout history and in scientific practice today. And even if we could determine just what is meant by methodological naturalism, not everyone agrees whether it is the only or the proper way to do science. It is the aim of this chapter to explore the concept of methodological naturalism and assess the claim that it is the appropriate (or only) way to do science.

 Questions to be addressed in this chapter:

1. What is the trouble with understanding methodological naturalism?
2. Is Duhemian science possible?
3. Does methodological naturalism provide a criterion of demarcation for science?
4. What is one reason for affirming methodological naturalism?

---

1. Defining methodological naturalism

To begin, we need to get clearer on what we mean by methodological naturalism. The first word of the phrase is relatively easy to deal with. It is customary to contrast *methodological* naturalism with *metaphysical* naturalism. **Metaphysical naturalism** (sometimes called **ontological naturalism**) is the view that all that exists are natural entities. That is to say, there are no supernatural beings, like gods or demons, and there are no supernatural events, like miracles. By contrast, methodological naturalism makes no claims about whether there are supernatural beings or events but merely claims that science should not appeal to them in scientific explanations. So the proper "methods" for scientific inquiry ought to remain within the natural realm.

All metaphysical naturalists will be methodological naturalists, but it does not work the other way. Christians will typically reject metaphysical naturalism (though there are some who call themselves theistic naturalists) because they believe that God is a supernatural being and that God may interact with the world in supernatural ways. The question for Christians, then, is whether it is appropriate in the discipline of science to pursue only natural explanations. Sometimes that is explained as bracketing off the supernatural while doing science, or acting "as if" naturalism were true in the metaphysical sense while one works in the laboratory, even if one accepts the supernatural outside the laboratory.

For the Christian, there is no assumption that the tools of science give an exhaustive description of reality. Rather, if they hold to methodological naturalism, they are committed to the claim that science is necessarily limited in what it can discover about reality, because it does not deal with the supernatural. To get a better idea of what those limits are, we need to know something further about the second word of the phrase—what the "natural" of methodological naturalism refers to. This turns out to be surprisingly difficult to define.

It appears as though the term "methodological naturalism" was coined by philosophy professor Paul de Vries in 1983 in a conference paper which was subsequently published as "Naturalism in the Natural Sciences." His claim was that Christians should accept methodological naturalism, by which he meant that the natural sciences ought to "establish explanations of contingent natural phenomena strictly in terms of other contingent natural things—laws, fields, probabilities" (Vries 1986, 388). Since this explanation of the term contains two instances of "natural," it doesn't work as a definition unless we already know what phenomena and things are to be counted as natural. With this approach, we can't determine what phenomena are natural by whether or not there are natural explanations for them, or we are in danger of begging the question, of becoming embroiled in a circular argument?

A definition that is not so obviously circular says that methodological naturalism "is an approach to scientific investigation that seeks to take phenomena on their own terms to understand them as they actually are" (Bishop 2013, 10). But digging just a little deeper, we have the same problem. How do we know what they actually are? Through investigation. But then aren't our methods of inquiry going to set the parameters for the kinds of things we find? To use a rough example, if we trawl the sea with a net with two-inch holes, you can bet we won't find things less than two inches in diameter. But it would be rash to conclude that there are no smaller things in the sea. Likewise, if we restrict our scientific investigations to empirical methods, are we sure our results have completely described the objects we studied? Only if we know beforehand that there are no non-empirical aspects to the objects.

The philosopher Paul Draper says that methodological naturalism is the doctrine that "scientists should not appeal to supernatural entities when they explain natural phenomena" (Draper 2005, 279). Of course, it wouldn't break us out of the definitional circle to use "supernatural" without further explanation, but Draper does attempt to provide further definitions. He says natural entities are those which are physical entities, or causally reducible to physical entities. And physical entities are "the entities currently studied by physicists and chemists" (ibid., 277). So, at least for the case of physicists and chemists, this means that when they are explaining the objects of their inquiry they should only appeal to the same kind of objects that they are studying. The problem here is that there is no set and abiding list of the things scientists study. That has changed over time. For example, astrology was once considered properly scientific, but the study of the mind was not. Most scientists today think that situation is reversed.

The trouble with adopting methodological naturalism is that it seems we have to predetermine what counts as natural. And that will inescapably involve metaphysical notions and values that are not properly scientific by the standards of methodological naturalism. In that case, our metaphysics is going to affect our science, so long as we're committed to science as explanatory. That raises the concern that methodological naturalism seems to lead to metaphysical naturalism. Treating objects "as if" they are wholly natural while doing science implicitly commits one to the view that there is nothing relevant about them that is non-natural. One way to avoid this implication is to deny that science is about providing explanations—whether natural or not—at all. We consider this view of science and its response in the next section.

2. Duhem and the aims of science

Pierre Duhem was a French physicist in the late 19th and early 20th century who argued that science was properly restricted to the observation and classification of experience. He thought that saying science aims to explain why our experience is what it is would necessarily subordinate science to metaphysics, and then science would be bogged down in metaphysical disputes that were unproductive to the advancement of science. He himself was a devout Catholic believer, and hence had strong and particular metaphysical views, but he thought these should have no effect on his science. He summarized his position on this as:

> There you have, then, a theoretical physics which is neither the theory of a believer nor that of a nonbeliever, but merely and simply a theory of a physicist; admirably suited to classify the laws studied by the experimenter, it is incapable of opposing any assertion whatever of metaphysics or of religious dogma, and is equally incapable of lending effective support to any such assertion. (Duhem 1954, 291)

In his view, science has nothing to say about the underlying causes of phenomena. All the scientist can do is report on and try to classify the purely empirical findings of experimentation, for example: "object x rose in temperature 3 degrees when we performed experiment y" or "the position or mass of our object did thus and such when we did this." These descriptions would satisfy Duhem as being scientific, because none of them includes any attempt at explanation. To go further and ask, "Why did x rise in temperature 3 degrees?" cannot be answered by the Duhemian scientist. To say something like, "because there is a fluid substance called 'caloric' which flows from 'hotter' bodies where the fluid is present more densely to 'cooler' areas" should have no part of his science. That is a claim of the philosopher.

C. S. Lewis on science
"Science works by experiments. It watches how things behave. Every scientific statement in the long run, however complicated it looks, really means something like, 'I pointed the telescope to such and such a part of the sky at 2:20 a.m. on January 15th and saw so-and-so,' or, 'I put some of this stuff in a pot

and heated it to such-and-such a temperature and it did so-and-so.' Do not think I am saying anything against science: I am only saying what its job is. And the more scientific a man is, the more (I believe) he would agree with me that this is the job of science—and a very useful and necessary job it is too. But why anything comes to be there at all, and whether there is anything behind the things science observes—something of a different kind—this is not a scientific question. If there is 'Something Behind,' then either it will have to remain altogether unknown to men or else make itself known in some different way. The statement that there is any such thing, and the statement that there is no such thing, are neither of them statements that science can make. And real scientists do not usually make them. It is usually the journalists and popular novelists who have picked up a few odds and ends of half-baked science from textbooks who go in for them. After all, it is really a matter of common sense. Supposing science ever became complete so that it knew every single thing in the whole universe. Is it not plain that the questions, 'Why is there a universe?' 'Why does it go on as it does?' 'Has it any meaning?' would remain just as they were?" (Lewis 2001, 22–23)

If science can be separated from philosophy like this, then perhaps methodological naturalism can consistently be upheld as the proper way of doing science. But Duhem's view is actually more subtle than this. He says the goal of scientific theories is merely the classification of what we observe. But even he thought that if this is done well it will be able to make predictions of what our future experience will be like, and correct predictions will "prove that it is the reflection of a real order" (ibid., 29). Duhem calls this "natural classification," and it must certainly qualify as some sort of an explanation.

Our goal here is not to give a comprehensive interpretation of Duhem, but merely to take one who has been touted as the spokesperson for the separation of science and philosophy, and show that even he can't get away from explanations. And, ironically, his work itself provided the basis for the 20th-century philosophy of science which convincingly undermined the stark separation of science from philosophical considerations. Duhem had said, "the physicist can never subject an isolated hypothesis to experimental test, but only a whole group of hypotheses" (ibid., 187). This principle was extended by the philosopher Willard Van Orman Quine in the middle of the 20th century (in what is sometimes called the **Duhem-Quine Thesis**) by claiming that all knowledge claims have an interdependency with background beliefs, and thus form a "web of beliefs" which confronts experience only on the periphery. Deep down in the web—almost immune to experience—are the background beliefs. Then philosopher Thomas Kuhn, in his groundbreaking book *The Structure of Scientific Revolutions*, called these webs of beliefs "paradigms" and argued that competing paradigms (those with different background beliefs) may be "incommensurable." That is to say, they can't be objectively compared and assessed, because even the standards of assessment are parts of the paradigms. Observation is theory-laden, and facts and values are inescapably intertwined. This is exactly Duhem's concern: once you involve philosophical commitments in your scientific theories, science will no longer have universal reach.

Willard Van Orman Quine (1908–2000)

One of the foremost analytic philosophers of the 20th century. He attempted to adopt the methods of science to understand science itself, which has come to be called "naturalized epistemology." Part of this project was the realization that no hypothesis is tested in isolation, but assumes background beliefs. This creates the web of beliefs which confronts experience as a whole.

Fig. 6.1 Willard Van Orman Quine (1908–2000). One of the most important philosophers of the 20th century. Source: © President and Fellows of Harvard College.

Thomas S. Kuhn (1922–1996)

The most important figure in the philosophy of science in the 20th century. His book *The Structure of Scientific Revolutions*, first published in 1962, drew the philosophy of science out of the rationalistic and ahistorical views, and highlighted the social and institutional aspects of science. His account of theory change or "paradigm shift" has become influential outside of science and philosophy.

Let's apply this trajectory of thought to our question of methodological naturalism. We've already shown that commitment to methodological naturalism is not a scientific claim according to its own definition of how science should operate. Instead, we might call it an epistemic value that is operative in the production of scientific knowledge. This is to say, methodological naturalism is a commitment to a certain kind of phenomenon as the proper domain of scientific explanation; and it is a commitment to what theories must be like in order to constitute scientific knowledge; and it is a commitment to certain kinds of reasoning, evidence, and proof as how scientific theories must be established. Gerald Doppelt (2007) gives a careful analysis to show that such epistemic values are not merely the product of scientific knowledge—counteracting the notion that we could use the methods of science to show that the epistemic values we use in our theories are in fact the most reliable. Critics might try to show that, for example, the kinds of phenomena we look at, the kinds of theories we use to explain the phenomena, and the methods we use for arriving at those theories are in fact the most reliable in attaining true theories about the world. But this only pushes the problem back another level: what count as true theories about the world? Predictive success or explanatory power? The simplest theory or the one that unifies the most disparate phenomena? And so on. These kinds of questions are as value-laden as the bodies of scientific knowledge they hope to evaluate (ibid., 206).

The upshot of this is that the aims, problems, and methods of science change from time to time, varying with local evaluations of what counts as a legitimate scientific theory. It is this recognition that gives Christian philosopher Alvin Plantinga the license to utilize epistemic values and metaphysical systems that are most consistent with his Christian theism when doing science. He wrote a series of articles in the 1990s arguing for what he called **Augustinian science** over the perceived methodological naturalism of "Duhemian science." Augustine was invoked as having spoken of the struggle between the City of God and the City of the World, and that Christians ought to be consciously adopting the stance of the City of God, even in science: "I shall argue that a Christian academic and scientific community ought to pursue science in its own way, starting from and taking for granted what we know as Christians" (Plantinga 1997, 340).

At this point it might be objected that even if science cannot operate without extra-scientific concepts and commitments, it is still possible to employ only naturalistic metaphysics (things like natural laws and material substances), but not supernatural things like gods and miracles. Thus it is maintained that science properly conducted still contains no reference to the supernatural. As such, methodological naturalism can be seen as what defines science, or demarcates it from non-science. We consider this proposal in the next section.

3. Methodological naturalism and the problem of demarcation

In Chapter 4 we saw the trial concerning Intelligent Design in Dover, Pennsylvania. One of the fundamental claims of the prosecution was that it is the intention of the Intelligent Design community to change what is accepted as science to include the supernatural. Judge Jones claimed, "ID violates the centuries-old ground rules of science by invoking and permitting supernatural causation" and concluded, "It is therefore readily apparent to the Court that ID fails to meet the essential ground rules that limit science to testable, natural explanations" (Jones 2005, 64, 70).

Ernan McMullin, a committed Catholic philosopher (and Plantinga's long-time colleague at the University of Notre Dame), accepts that science is limited. He gives no support for metaphysical naturalism. But he seems to go along with Judge Jones and his characterization of what properly counts as science. McMullin says, "Methodological naturalism does *not* restrict our study of nature; it just lays down which sort of study qualifies as *scientific*. If someone wants to pursue another approach to nature—and there are *many* others—the methodological naturalist has no reason to object. Scientists *have* to proceed in this way" (McMullin 1991, 168). For McMullin, other approaches might contribute to our overall knowledge of reality; he just doesn't want to call them science if they don't adhere to methodological naturalism.

There is something to be said for recognizing disciplinary boundaries. Michael Ruse (2005, 46) compares methodological naturalism to going to a doctor and expecting not to be given any political advice. The doctor may have very strong political views, but it would be inappropriate for him or her to disseminate them in that context. So, too, the scientist ought not to disseminate religious views, as they are not relevant to the task at hand. But Plantinga counters that in assessing grand scientific theories we will necessarily cross disciplinary lines in order to use all that we know that is relevant to the question. For the Christian, he thinks this properly allows the use of biblical revelation in assessing whether something like the theory of common ancestry is a correct explanation. And he believes that can be called Augustinian, or theistic, science.

Furthermore, we've already shown that methodological naturalism is a normative commitment. It is therefore hubris on the part of its proponents to declare that they have discovered the heretofore elusive criterion of demarcation that separates all legitimate science from the illegitimate. The universality of methodological naturalism just doesn't hold historically—science changes, and not just the conclusions of science but also the methods and aims of science. Philosopher Jeffrey Koperski sums up the situation:

> The bottom line is this: The future use or suspension of [methodological naturalism] depends on what is discovered. If the best explanation for some new phenomenon is design, even supernatural design, it would still count as a scientific explanation. It borders on academic incompetence to pretend that science has strict boundaries and then gerrymander those boundaries to keep out the riffraff. Philosophers of science in particular should know better. (Koperski 2008, 440)

Even Quine (one of the leading naturalist philosophers of the 20th century) concurs, saying: "If I saw indirect explanatory benefit in positing sensibilia, possibilia, spirits, a Creator, I would joyfully accord them scientific status too, on a par with such avowedly scientific posits as quarks and black holes." (Quine 1995, 252).

So the question comes down to a definition of terms: who gets to decide what counts as science and what doesn't? That can't be decided non-arbitrarily by science or by philosophical analysis. The meanings of terms are a function of communities and how the terms are actually used. History attests to changing norms and values in this regard, and it would be naïve to think that these won't continue to change. It is a fact that the mainstream of science operates right now according to methodological naturalism. The proponents of Augustinian Science, or Intelligent Design, or any other alternative conception of science are perfectly free to adopt local values different from the mainstream regarding what counts as legitimate scientific explanation. It is even possible that they could ultimately win the day and persuade the mainstream that their view of science is "better." The most we can say now is that methodological naturalism is a contingent value that is accepted by most scientists today. We cannot say that it is a necessary condition of any legitimate science. But perhaps there are pragmatic reasons for abiding by it. We consider these next.

4. Reasons for abiding by methodological naturalism

From the philosophical point of view, there don't seem to be any necessary or compelling reasons for acknowledging methodological naturalism as the *sine qua non* of scientific inquiry. But there may be pragmatic reasons for abiding by the general principle of what Alan Padgett calls the "nature-bias" of the natural sciences. In his view, even approaching scientific work "as if" naturalism were true carries too high a risk of the methodology turning into an ontology. But acknowledging a nature-bias has nothing to do with a full-blown ontology or a philosophical worldview. It is just a contingent tradition and rational bias, and "unless and until a very significant and powerful combination of evidence and reason forces a major change," the natural sciences should stick with their nature bias (Padgett 2012, 91). Against the proponents of Intelligent Design and others who claim to be doing science when they appeal to intelligent agency, Padgett claims that is social science, not natural science according to the accepted definitions. Appeal to intelligent agency is at the center of the traditions of inquiry like economics and linguistics. In the natural sciences, though, there is a long tradition of successful explanations in terms of non-intelligent causes. And unless we are compelled to abandon this because such theories are unable to provide the kinds of explanations we want, then it makes sense to stick with them.

Inserting supernatural agency or events into explanations has a fairly poor track record historically. Science has been remarkably successful at figuring out the causes of phenomena that once were explained by supernatural agents—from thunder and solar eclipses, to disease and epilepsy. Of course that doesn't mean that science will be able to figure out everything in the future. But it should give us pause before thinking we've found some phenomenon for which there will never be any scientific explanation. To do otherwise would be to inhibit scientific investigation. Take the example of how the first living cell came about. Scientists don't have very promising models right now for how that could have happened through natural means. Plantinga thinks this should allow us to conclude that God must have intervened in a special way. He says:

> If, after considerable study, we can't see how it could possibly have happened by way of those regularities—if, as is in fact the case, after many decades of study the enormous complexity and functional connectedness and integrity of even the simplest forms of life make it look increasingly unlikely that they could have orig- inated in that way—the natural thing to think, from the perspective of Christian theism, is that probably God did something different and special here ... And why couldn't one draw this conclusion precisely as a scientist? Where is it written that such a conclusion can't be part of science? (Plantinga 1996, 380)

Of course, the difficulty is knowing how much "considerable study" is enough. Plantinga's approach seems to give license to giving up the search. He says that he does not mean that inquiry should halt but that our conclusions should always be provisional. It should just be the best explanation we have at present and further inquiry might change that. But should we call it the best scientific explanation we have at present if we say, "and then a miracle happened" and there was life? It seems more in keeping with our present usage to say, "At present we have no scientific explanation for that phenomenon."

Furthermore, the push to limit scientific explanations to natural phenomena is an effect of the shift that allowed science to become so successful. Previously, inquiry into the natural world was known as natural philosophy, and natural philosophers sought to understand objects in the Aristotelian sense of knowing their essences. For them the real world was an amalgam of qualities and mean- ings that defied mathematization. In the scientific revolution in physics, scientists limited themselves to those properties which could be mathematized—sometimes called the "primary qualities." Those same objects that were studied scientifically might have additional perspectives from which they might profitably be viewed. Allowing for specialization can be an important impetus to discovery. Science is one such specialized way of looking at reality.

This brings us to the final point. **Scientism** is often the label given to the view that the natural sciences are the only source of genuine knowledge about the world. From what is discussed in this chapter, it should be seen that scientific descriptions are not complete descriptions of reality, and thus scientism is false. This gives us another pragmatic reason for holding (however weakly and tenta- tively) to methodological naturalism. If we are to give the term "science" to the broader, more inclusive quest for knowledge that includes supernatural sources for Christians, then we would agree with scientism on the comprehensive role of science. Of course, they wouldn't agree with scientism on just what counts as science, but there is an implicit acceptance of the scope of science. It seems to me that the wiser approach is to agree with scientism that science limits itself to nat- ural explanations but to disagree that science can explain everything.

The correct implication to draw from the commitment to methodological nat- uralism is not that reality itself is completely describable by science. Rather, it is to assert that science provides only a limited view of reality. Science is one "epistemological portal" or one "window" on reality (Michael Peterson quoted in Applegate 2013, 42–43), and methodological naturalism does not imply that it is the only one. Still, it has proved to be an enormously fruitful window on reality, and ought to be pursued on the basis of methodological naturalism until such a time as there has proven to be a more fruitful way to understand nature.

In the next chapter, we consider whether scientific examination of the world can yield any knowledge of God—natural theology.

 Summary of main points:

1. There doesn't seem to be a non-circular way of determining what counts as natural.

2. Duhemian science—the claim that scientific inquiry can proceed independent of philosophical commitments—does not seem possible.

3. Methodological naturalism is a contingent value accepted by most scientists today, but not a criterion of demarcation for all science.

4. It seems that it is wise to restrict science to natural explanations.

Further reading

- Numbers, Ronald. 2003. "Science without God: Natural Laws and Christian Beliefs." In *When Science & Christianity Meet,* edited by David C. Lindberg and Ronald L. Numbers. Chicago: University of Chicago Press. Gives a history of methodological naturalism.
- Padgett, Alan. 2012. "Practical Objectivity: Keeping Natural Science Natural." In *The Blackwell Companion to Science and Christianity,* edited by J. B. Stump and Alan G. Padgett. Malden, MA: Wiley-Blackwell. Argues for the nature-bias of the natural sciences.
- Pennock, Robert T., ed. 2001. *Intelligent Design Creationism and Its Critics.* Cambridge, MA: MIT Press. Contains several of the papers by Plantinga and McMullin (and others) on methodological naturalism.

References

Applegate, Kathryn. 2013. "A Defense of Methodological Naturalism." *Perspectives on Science and Christian Faith,* 65: 37–45.

Bishop, Robert. 2013. "God and Methodological Naturalism in the Scientific Revolution and Beyond." *Perspectives on Science and Christian Faith,* 65: 10–23.

De Morgan, Augustus. 1872. *A Budget of Paradoxes.* London: Longmans, Green, and Company.

Doppelt, Gerald. 2007. "The Value Ladenness of Scientific Knowledge." In *Value-Free Science? Ideals and Illusions,* edited by Harold Kincaid, John Dupré, and Alison Wylie. Oxford: Oxford University Press.

Draper, Paul. 2005. "God, Science, and Naturalism." In *The Oxford Handbook of Philosophy of Religion*, edited by William J. Wainwright. Oxford: Oxford University Press.

Duhem, Pierre. 1954. "Physics of a Believer." In *Aim and Structure of Physical Theory*, 2nd ed., 273–311. Princeton: Princeton University Press.

Jones, John E. III. 2005. United States District Court for the Middle District of Pennsylvania. Case no. 04cv2688. Memorandum Opinion.

Koperski, Jeffrey. 2008. "Two Bad Ways to Attack Intelligent Design and Two Good Ones." *Zygon*, 43(2): 433–449.

Lewis, C. S. 2001. *Mere Christianity*. San Francisco: HarperSanFrancisco.

Lubbock, Constance Ann. 1933. *The Herschel Chronicle: The Life-story of William Herschel and his Sister, Caroline Herschel*. New York: The Macmillan Company.

McMullin, Ernan. 1991. "Plantinga's Defense of Special Creation." *Christian Scholar's Review, 21: 55–79*. Citations taken from the reprint in *Intelligent Design Creationism and its Critics*, 2001, edited by Robert T. Pennock. Cambridge, MA: MIT Press.

Padgett, Alan. 2012. "Practical Objectivity: Keeping Natural Science Natural." In *The Blackwell Companion to Science and Christianity*, edited by J. B. Stump and Alan G. Padgett. Malden, MA: Wiley-Blackwell.

Plantinga, Alvin. 1996. "Science: Augustinian or Duhemian?" *Faith and Philosophy*, 13: 368–394.

Plantinga, Alvin. 1997. "Methodological Naturalism?" *Perspectives on Science and Christian Faith 49*. Citations taken from the version in *Intelligent Design Creationism and its Critics*, 2001, edited by Robert T. Pennock. Cambridge, MA: MIT Press.

Quine, W. V. O. 1995. "Naturalism; Or, Living within One's Means." *Dialectica*, 49: 251–261.

Ruse, Michael. 2005. "Methodological Naturalism under Attack." *South African Journal of Philosophy*, 24(1): 44–60.

Vries, Paul de. 1986. "Naturalism in the Natural Sciences." *Christian Scholar's Review*, 15: 388–396.

CHAPTER 7

Natural Theology

A s discussed in Chapter 5, Christianity is a religion that is founded on purported episodes of divine revelation. Christians believe that God spoke to
and through the Hebrew patriarchs, the prophets, and Jesus Christ. The
Bible is thought to be a collection of this revelation (though variously interpreted
by different Christian communities), and it forms an important part of the Christian religion. As such, Christians (along with Jews and Muslims) are sometimes
called "people of a book."

To explain and defend their beliefs within some cultures or communities, it is
sufficient for Christians to point to the relevant passages of the Bible, because these
are acknowledged as a source of truth. But what about cultures and audiences
which do not accept, or are at least suspicious of, the Bible as revealed truth? In
such cases, Christians have to appeal to some other ground of justification—some
other body of data or evidence—which has more widely accepted provenance.
The practice of arguing to theological conclusions from generally accepted premises drawn from reason or experience of the natural world is traditionally called
natural theology.

Christians will often (somewhat paradoxically?) appeal to the Bible itself in
support of natural theology. Two passages in particular are cited, the first from the
Old Testament:

> The heavens declare the glory of God;
> the skies proclaim the work of his hands.
> Day after day they pour forth speech;
> night after night they reveal knowledge.
> They have no speech, they use no words;
> no sound is heard from them.
> Yet their voice goes out into all the earth,
> their words to the ends of the world. (Psalm 19:1–4, NIV)

And from the New Testament letter to the Romans:

> The wrath of God is being revealed from heaven against all the godlessness and
> wickedness of people, who suppress the truth by their wickedness, since what
> may be known about God is plain to them, because God has made it plain to

Science and Christianity: An Introduction to the Issues, First Edition. By J. B. Stump.
© 2017 John Wiley & Sons, Ltd. Published 2017 by John Wiley & Sons, Ltd.

them. For since the creation of the world God's invisible qualities—his eternal power and divine nature—have been clearly seen, being understood from what has been made, so that people are without excuse. (Romans 1:18–20, NIV)

Both of these passages seem to suggest that all people can know at least some things about God just by paying attention to the world around them. As those observations become more systematic and rigorous, it is the practice of science that provides data for natural theologians. But just what can be known in this "natural" way?

 Questions to be addressed in this chapter:

1. What are some of the specific arguments used by natural theologians?
2. What objections are there against the general practice of natural theology?
3. How does a theology of nature differ from natural theology?

---

1. Classic arguments of natural theology

Many texts that have a section devoted to natural theology parade a series of arguments for the existence of God. These are purportedly consistent with the observations of the biblical texts cited above in that they draw from natural data provided by our senses and reason. In more technical language, these arguments draw theistic conclusions from natural and neutral premises. That is to say, the premises of the arguments do not presuppose any supernatural revelation or ideological commitment. They are drawn from common experience of the natural world, and indeed there is a common sense appeal to them on the surface.

For example, what is called the **Argument from Design** (or sometimes the Teleological Argument) appeals to our intuition that there is a noticeable difference between naturally occurring objects and those that couldn't have come to be as they are without the intervention of a designer. The argument has had many different versions over the centuries, and we'll encounter some current versions of it later in this book. But the classic formulation comes from the early-19th-century work of William Paley (see the excerpt in the box). He claimed that just as we can see that an intricate mechanism like a watch couldn't have self-assembled, so too we can "see" that features of nature are similarly intricate and dependent on a designer or master craftsman. Paley specifically discussed the human heart and eyeballs as "mechanisms" that show clear signs of purpose and therefore require an explanation and a designer.

"In crossing a heath, suppose I pitched my foot against a *stone*, and were asked how the stone came to be there. I might possibly answer that, for anything I knew to the contrary, it had lain there forever; nor would it perhaps be very easy to show the absurdity of this answer. But suppose I had found a *watch* upon the ground, and it should be inquired how the watch happened to be in that place; I should hardly think of the answer which I had before given, that, for anything I knew, the watch might have always been there. Yet why should not this answer serve for the watch as well as for the stone? Why is it not as admissible in the second case as in the first? For this reason, and for no other, viz. that when we come to inspect the watch, we perceive (what we could not discover in the stone) that its several parts are framed and put together for a purpose ... This mechanism being observed (it requires indeed an examination of the instrument, and perhaps some previous knowledge of the subject, to perceive and understand it; but being once, as we have said, observed and understood,) the inference, we think, is inevitable; that the watch must have had a maker; that there must have existed, at sometime, and at some place or other, an artificer or artificers, who formed it for the purpose which we find it actually to answer; who comprehended its construction, and designed its use." (Paley 1837, 5–6)

Again, there is a common sense appeal to this reasoning. But as we dig deeper into it, we see that there are significant problems with arguing for the existence of God by analogy with human designers. The watch was not designed and created by one person in an instant, but was the result of a long process of trial and error by many craftsmen who only gradually perfected their design. The skeptical Scottish philosopher David Hume put forward such an objection to the Teleological Argument in a dialogue, through the character of Philo. Philo said that when we reason through analogy things will always break down without proving the case. For example, he wondered, what can we infer about the workman who built a ship? That he was ingenious? But what if we found out that he was just a "stupid mechanic," who imitated the art of others, which "through a long succession of ages, after multiplied trials, mistakes, corrections, deliberations, and controversies, had been gradually improving?" (Hume 1998, 36). Do we then have to say of the creator of the universe that he might have botched and bungled many universes through the ages and arrived at this one only through trial and error?

And can we infer anything about the moral status or even the current existence of the designer of a watch or ship by examining it today? Then why do we think the designer of the universe is morally perfect? These are troubling questions for those who want Paley's version of the Design Argument to yield a theistic conclusion.

Still, it might be contended that the argument does open the door for the supernatural, even if it doesn't give much information about the kind of supernatural being required to explain these purportedly designed objects. For this reason the argument had a tremendous popular appeal and significantly influenced the understanding of natural theology in the early 19th century. But the common sense appeal to the argument was drastically undermined in the second half of the century when Darwin suggested a purely natural mechanism by which the appearance of design could be explained without appeal to a supernatural designer. Of course, this debate continues today, and it is examined more extensively in Chapter 9.

The **Cosmological Argument** is another of the classic arguments of natural theology. There are many versions of this argument, but essentially they rely on the common sense insight that everything we see in nature had to come from somewhere and could not have been self-caused. The 13th-century theologian Thomas Aquinas gave expression to this in his Second Way (see the box on this) of arguing for the existence of God. He claimed that within the natural order of things we find that one event or object is caused to be the way it is because of an earlier event or object. For example, people do not just come to exist without being caused to come into existence by their parents. Their parents too were caused to come into existence, and so on. This chain of causes applies equally to trees and mountains and waterfalls; these things are caused to exist by something else. But, said Aquinas, the chain cannot go on forever within the natural order. So there must be a first cause—something that doesn't need a cause to explain its existence. And that first cause is God (Christian Classics 2016).

 The Five Ways of Thomas Aquinas

Thomas Aquinas was a Dominican monk from Italy who lived from 1225 to 1274. He was a prolific writer, and continues to be one of Roman Catholicism's most influential theologians. In his best-known work, the *Summa Theologica* (or summary of theology), he claims that the existence of God can be proved in five ways. These have become known as the Five Ways. In summary, they are:

1. Because things change, there must be something which is the ultimate cause of all change.
2. Because things are caused, there must be a first cause.
3. Because the world is contingent (did not have to exist), something had to bring it into being.
4. Because we recognize degrees of perfection, there must be a maximally perfect thing.
5. Because we recognize purpose in the world, it must have been designed.

Objectors to the Cosmological Argument insist that positing God as the uncaused cause does no more explanatory work than positing nature itself as self-caused or eternally existing. For can't we also ask where God came from, or what caused God? Supporters, though, will claim that the relevant distinction is that, while natural objects do need causes to explain their existence because they are not eternally existing, something that is beyond the natural order of things may not need to be caused. It is just such a supernatural entity that is required to get the causal chain started in the first place.

The 20th-century articulation of Big Bang cosmology seemed to support the notion that there was a beginning to the universe, and the common sense intuition is that it could not have come into existence without a cause. Many natural theologians see this as a confirmation of Aquinas's argument. But recent developments in cosmology are pushing beyond the Big Bang in purely natural terms. We explore the implications of this further in Chapter 8.

Even if successful, the Cosmological Argument can still be objected to by saying that a first cause does not really resemble the God of Christian theism. At most we can infer an eternally existing being that could start a chain reaction of causes. To supplement this, some natural theologians defend another of the classic arguments for the existence of God: the **Ontological Argument**. This argument does not proceed from scientific theories or observations, but it fits within natural theology in a broader sense because it is an argument based purely on a logical analysis of the concept of God. Anselm of Canterbury first developed the argument in the 11th century. Basically, he argued that we can all form an idea or concept of the greatest imaginable being. He then purported to show from that concept that such a being must exist in reality, not just in the imagination (Anselm 2001, 7). This argument has the feeling of smoke and mirrors to many who have pondered it. They feel that something must be wrong with the argument, but it is difficult to pin down just exactly what the problem is. To motivate the method of discovering something by conceptual analysis, consider the following example.

I have an Aunt Pat. Even those who know nothing at all through experience of my Aunt Pat should be able to deduce some information about this person from the concept "aunt." Of course, Aunt Pat will be female; otherwise, she wouldn't be an aunt. Then by persevering further in the analysis of the concept, it can be deduced that Aunt Pat must have a sibling who has children (or, in the looser sense of aunt, she could be married to someone whose sibling has children). When we come to fully understand what is meant by "aunt," we recognize that these are necessary characteristics or properties of all aunts. By contrast, conceptual analysis won't reveal that Aunt Pat has red hair or that she lives in Tennessee, for those are not necessary properties of aunts.

In the same way, Anselm claimed to be able to deduce "exists" as one of the necessary properties of God. His argument rests on two key premises:

1. God is the greatest imaginable being.

2. It is greater to exist than not to exist.

If both of these premises are true, then God must exist, just like Aunt Pat must be female. To see why this is so, imagine one God-like being that is all-powerful, all-knowing, etc. but which doesn't really exist; and imagine another God-like being that is all-powerful, all-knowing, etc. and really does exist. Which one is greater? The existing one, according to Anselm. So the greatest imaginable being must exist.

It is claimed, then, that this greatest imaginable being has all the perfections traditionally associated with the God of Christian theism: God is not just all-powerful and all-knowing but also perfectly good and just. It's not so clear, according to the objectors, that the concept of God really does include all of these properties, or even that existence is a property that things have (like being blue or six foot tall or all-knowing). The Ontological Argument hinges on a very subtle analysis of language and logic. It has continued to be taken seriously by some philosophers today, but the discussion has become very technical and less accessible to non-specialists.

These are just a sampling of some of the common traditional arguments from natural theology. Our concern in this chapter is not to give a detailed exposition of these but to show the general way natural theologians have argued. The fact that not everyone finds such arguments persuasive seems to be a strike against them. These are supposed to be arguments drawn from experience and data that is available to everyone. Why, then, doesn't everyone accept the conclusions?

Some think that if the arguments are developed ever more carefully they can be made rationally compelling. Others, though, suggest that the enterprise of natural theology is wrong-headed to begin with. We now turn to consider their objections.

2. Objections to natural theology

There is an objection to the overall project of natural theology, based on the theological doctrine of the Fall and original sin. Articulated and defended by John Calvin and Karl Barth, this objection is that our natural reason has been marred by sin and is not trustworthy. Therefore, whatever supposed knowledge we have gained through natural means is itself suspect. Christians disagree on the effects of sin upon our reasoning faculties. The extreme position defended by Calvin and his followers seems to render not only natural theology but also any kind of rational work—including science and theology—impossible. The obvious success of reason in many arenas—even by the "unregenerate" non-believers—makes this objection a non-starter for those interested in a serious dialogue between science and Christianity.

John Calvin (1509–1564) and Karl Barth (1886–1968) are two of the most important Reformed theologians of Protestant Christianity. Calvin was born in France and spent most of his adult life in Switzerland, where he was the head of the Reformed Church in Geneva. His most famous and enduring work is *The Institutes of the Christian Religion*. Barth was a Swiss theologian and proponent of the **Neo-Orthodoxy Movement** of the 20th century. His greatest work is the *Church Dogmatics*.

Another objection (or a different version of the same objection), also associated with Barth, needs to be taken more seriously. He saw natural theology as an attempt at autonomy from God. That is to say, in developing arguments for the existence and nature of God based on natural reason, people attempt to know God apart from what God has revealed to them. But, Barth argued, there is no more secure or certain ground for our knowledge of God than God's word, and any attempt to find such a ground takes us further from God. In 1934, the

Swiss theologian Emil Brunner wrote that Barth's rejection of natural theology had gone too far. He claimed, among other things, that natural theology could be the foundation for belief and an important point of contact with non-Christians. Barth's famous German response to Brunner was "Nein!" He vehemently held that any attempt to ground belief in reason is to divorce faith from the good news of Jesus Christ as revealed by God to us. We believe, because God has spoken, Barth claimed (see Brunner and Barth 2002 for the exchange).

Epistemology
The branch of philosophy concerned with the theory of knowledge. Epistemologists attempt to answer such questions as, "What is knowledge?", "How do we obtain knowledge?", and "What is the difference between knowledge and opinion?"

To many people today, Barth's dogmatic pronouncement sounds like **fideism**— belief without rational grounds. Barth might respond by claiming that the charge of fideism makes sense only against the epistemology that developed in the 17th century beginning with Descartes, that is the epistemology Barth was rejecting. To follow this line of reasoning we need a brief historical excursus.

In Chapter 1, we briefly met the Muslim scholar Averroës (1126–1198, also known as ibn-Rushd) who was concerned with the apparent discrepancies between the revealed truth of the Qur'an and the dictates of reason. For example, the Qur'an clearly teaches that God created the universe, but Averroës was convinced philosophically that the universe is eternal. So he developed a theory of double-truth according to which seemingly contradictory claims can be reconciled at different levels. He maintained that the Qur'an was written for the masses who were not intellectually equipped to handle deep philosophical truths, so its message was presented allegorically to capture the imagination and emotions of these uneducated people. When understood as such, we realize that there is no real contradiction with the true understanding of things that the philosopher seeks.

This method of double-truth has been an influential one in the history of science and religion, for it seemingly creates a way to eliminate any conflict between reason and revelation. But it does so at the expense of eliminating truth claims about the world from religious language, and in the next century Thomas Aquinas would have none of that. As we've already seen, Aquinas produced proofs for the existence of God, believing that some of what has been revealed supernaturally could also be shown with natural reason. He acknowledged that many of these proofs were difficult and, in agreement with Averroës, admitted that the masses would not understand them. But, contrary to Averroës, Aquinas would not accept that there are two versions of the truth. There is only one truth, and it cannot contradict other truth.

Aquinas defended the notion that we can "know" things by faith, but this is a different species of knowledge than what we can "know" by reason, and he was concerned not to confuse the two. Aquinas said that we "believe" those things to be true which are known by faith, and we "see" those things to be true which are known by reason. He held that there are some things that we can only believe by faith, for example that God is a Trinity. This is revealed to us, and nothing in reason will contradict it, but neither can it be shown by reason to be true. There are other points of revelation, he thought, that can also be demonstrated by reason—God's existence and God's role as creator, for example. Some Christians will never work through the rational proofs for these and will only ever accept them as articles of revealed faith. But for the one who does see them by reason, they cannot also be articles of faith.

Sometimes the solution of Aquinas is called the **Thomistic synthesis**, but this is misleading in a way, because what he has done is not to synthesize theology and philosophy/science into one discipline but to clearly carve out separate domains for them. They will not contradict each other when done properly, but they are separate ways to the truth. Aquinas held together these two separate ways to produce one coherent system of knowledge (hence the appropriateness of the term "synthesis"), but later Christian thinkers would not be so concerned to do so. Hence, the two ways of knowing began to produce very different results which, even if not strictly contradictory, were yielding very different portraits of God. Some hold that the God of revelation in the stories of the Bible is a pre-rational, or even mythological, figure; reason produces a very different concept, the "God of the Philosophers." Jesus as the Incarnate Son of God is absent from the latter, and as a historical figure he becomes nothing more than a good moral teacher. Christology is given no relevance in the natural theology of the period, and we are left with a generic theism.

Here we see the relevance of Barth's criticism of natural theology. From his perspective, natural theologians have bought into the separation of faith and reason, and the distinctiveness of Christianity is left out of the equation. Modern philosophers sought certainty for their beliefs, and the path to certainty came not through stories that had been passed down but by the application of reason. René Descartes (1596–1650) thought he was providing a valuable service to theology by giving belief in God and the immortality of the soul a certain foundation in philosophical reason. Others see that move as reducing Aquinas's Christian theism to philosophical theism, which would become deism and then atheism. In this objection, natural theology divorced from revelation is inherently unstable and incapable of justifying Christian faith.

There is a further development of this objection. When reason becomes the only acceptable foundation for belief, religious experience is no longer deemed adequate for grounding faith. But some claim that there is something fundamentally wrong with eliminating this subjective element. Contemporary philosopher of religion Paul Moser claims that natural theology treats God as an object, similar to the objects that natural science investigates. In so doing, the arguments of natural theology fail to detect the personal being who is the God revealed to Abraham, Paul, and (most significantly) Jesus. Instead, the appropriate cognitive basis for the Christian faith is found in the relationship one can have with God through God's intervening personal Spirit. According to Moser, the goal of the Christian God for us is not merely intellectual or cognitive information but rather our moral transformation. Arguments from natural theology offer evidence of a God who is static and reveals himself independently of humans' volitional attitudes toward him. But this is not the God Christians should be looking for, claims Moser. The Christian God conceals himself in response to human volitional resistance, because God is non-coercive and desires that we learn to love unselfishly as God does. The true God is not revealed in the "spectator evidence" of natural theology, but is made known to us only as we enter into relationship with God. And God enters into relationship with us only if we are willing to undergo the moral transformation God desires for us—namely to become perfectly loving toward all people, even one's enemies, because that is the nature of God (Moser 2012, 156–157).

Moser's is a powerful argument from a subjective Christian perspective, but critics will object that he does not leave enough room for the role of objective evidence. Could it be that the traditional arguments do have some value in making it seem plausible that there could be such a thing as God? Then, perhaps, once someone accepts the possibility of there being something supernatural, he or she is more willing to seek relationship with the kind of God Moser describes. In this way, objective evidence could open the door to belief in God that moves beyond the spectator evidence.

But we must consider one more objection to natural theology, namely that it is not even possible in the first place. If natural theology is supposed to be argumentation from objective or neutral premises that anyone should accept, then the philosophy of the last half of the 20th century seriously calls into question whether there is such a thing. This is because many would claim that there are no neutral premises. Just as natural theologians of the Modern period thought that the separation of faith and reason allowed them to demonstrate theological claims from reason alone, so too they believed a sharp distinction between facts and value would serve their interests. Facts were thought to be objective, publicly accessible, and treated by science; values, on the other hand, were deemed to be subjectively chosen matters of conscience. Natural theologians purportedly drew from these objective facts to derive their conclusions.

But while many people today still blindly assume the legitimacy of the fact–value distinction, the story of its falling on hard times is well known in philosophy of science circles (e.g., Putnam 2002). In brief, it was David Hume who classically articulated the fact–value distinction by claiming that you can't derive an "ought" from an "is." To sustain this distinction he needed a clear notion of a "matter of fact," which he delineated from "relations of ideas." His definition of a fact as something that can give us a sense impression became deeply problematic with the continuing development of the physical sciences in which unobservables like electrons came to play significant roles. The logical empiricists of the first half of the 20th century tried various solutions to keep the realm of fact pure and untainted. But ultimately W. V. O. Quine (1980) showed to the satisfaction of most philosophers that a stark separation between matters of fact (what he called **synthetic propositions**) and relations of ideas (**analytic propositions**) is untenable. Instead, we experience the world through complex webs of beliefs, and the result is that beliefs cannot be neatly sorted into purely factual beliefs and value commitments. Instead, we find that there is a deep entanglement of facts and values. And more specifically to the realm of science, Thomas Kuhn (1970) famously contended that scientific theories are more like paradigms through which we view the world. Even the observation of "facts" is influenced by and laden with our complex systems of belief, and values form an ineliminable part of science.

3. Natural theology for the 21st century

So, what is left for natural theology? Certainly there are arguments offered which purportedly start from nature and argue for the existence of God. These have convinced some people and even contributed to their conversions to Christianity. That much is not in dispute. The relevant question here, though, is whether this is really natural theology in the sense of beginning with neutral objective premises and arguing to theological conclusions. And if it is not, then what is to become of natural theology?

Increasingly, there is a push to transform the classic practice of natural theology into what might more properly be called a theology of nature. Nature had been understood to be the value-neutral realm of facts from which natural theologians drew premises for their arguments. But consistent with the dissolution of the fact–value distinction, it turns out that nature itself is not a completely objective concept. The concept of nature is a social construction, and it has been constructed in significantly different ways throughout the centuries (McGrath 2009, 6).

The ancient Greek philosopher Aristotle divided up reality into nature, art, and chance. Art (*techne*) was understood to be the result of human intervention in the world, such as buildings and football games, and philosophy conferences. Nature (*physis*) was designated as those regularly occurring things that needed no human involvement, like mountains, seasons, and the tides. And there was also the category of chance (*tyche*), which he invoked for seemingly random and unpredictable occurrences that did not depend on human agency, like the appearance of an unknown comet or the weather on any given day. Clearly, nature was taken to be regular and in need of no intervention by agents of some sort. Regularity that was imposed from the outside (i.e., not naturally occurring) was excluded from the concept of nature.

Throughout the scientific revolution of the 17th and 18th centuries the concept of nature was transformed. It came to be thought that the defining characteristic of nature was that it consisted of extended bodies that could be treated mathematically. Scientists were increasingly successful at deciphering the mathematics in nature, and in turn became increasingly adept at imposing mathematical regularities on their artifacts. By the time of Paley at the beginning of the 19th century, Aristotle's categories had blurred. "Nature" was seen to be a giant clock-like machine by natural theologians. Machines were not part of nature for Aristotle; they were products of the artisans. But in the Modern period, natural theologians could look at nature and see the work of an artisan: human hearts and eyes couldn't exist as they do on their own; they show the clear marks of design, so there must be a Grand Designer.

> "A Christian natural theology gives a robust theoretical foundation to this process of beholding, understanding, and appreciating nature, by providing an intellectual framework that affirms and legitimates a heightened attentiveness to the world around us." (McGrath 2008)

The development of quantum mechanics in the 20th century helped to undermine the mechanistic view of nature. Today there are many competing concepts of nature from which to choose, none of which comes without bias or preconceived notions: environmentalists, outdoor sports enthusiasts, Hindu pantheists, and others see nature differently. In all of these instances, the preferred image of nature corresponds to the prejudices of a particular community which are read onto their subject. Nature is not an uninterpreted concept.

So even scientists work from a concept of nature that is not merely "the given." We see things "as" something according to theoretical presuppositions—especially as we move away from individual observances of a tree or an elephant or a waterfall and talk about a giant collective entity we call nature. But rather than despairing of this situation or pretending it isn't so, contemporary scientist-turned-theologian Alister McGrath (2009) sees it as an opportunity to reclaim the Christian notion of nature as creation. Nature is not uninterpreted, but that doesn't mean in some postmodern sense that every interpretation is just as good as the others. Seeing nature as God's creation may be an interpretation, but if Christians are right, it is the *correct* interpretation of what nature is.

In this sense, Christian natural theologians will see the natural order as imbued with purpose, and the more scientists reveal the ordered and lawful behavior of the natural order, the more natural theologians will revel in God's provision for creation. Scientists discover "facts" about the natural order that are surprising and incredible (in the literal sense of not easily believed)—perhaps the physical constants that seem to have been selected to allow for life; perhaps the evolutionary convergences that seem to be conspiring to bring about life forms like us. From McGrath's perspective, these are not so incredible when viewed through the lens of Christian theism. He claims that they are just what Christians would expect from the God revealed in the Christian tradition.

Because the data is capable of being interpreted in different ways, there is plenty of room for disagreement about the significance of specific issues we find at the intersection of science, philosophy, and Christianity. Disagreement does not mean there can be no dialogue, however. Generous and thoughtful minds will find much profit in considering these issues and engaging with others who see them differently. It is to the specific issues that we now turn.

Summary of main points:

1. The Teleological, Cosmological, and Ontological arguments are some of the traditional arguments of natural theologians.
2. Some argue that natural theology supplants revelation and others that it treats God as an object rather than a personal being worthy of worship.
3. A theology of nature argues that nature exhibits the qualities we would expect to find in God's creation.

Further reading

*   Buckley, Michael. 1987. *At the Origins of Modern Atheism*. New Haven: Yale University Press. Argues that theologians should not have ignored Christology in their defense of the faith.
*   Craig, William Lane, and J. P. Moreland, eds. 2009. *The Blackwell Companion to Natural Theology*. Oxford: Blackwell Publishers. A collection of detailed articles on the typical arguments offered by natural theologians for the existence of God.
*   McGrath, Alister E. 2008. *The Open Secret: A New Vision for Natural Theology*. Oxford: Blackwell Publishers. Argues that natural theology is fundamentally about seeing nature in a certain way—for Christian natural theologians, through the lenses of Christian theology.
*   Moser, Paul. 2010. *The Evidence for God: Religious Knowledge Reexamined*. Cambridge: Cambridge University Press. Makes the case that natural theology is not capable of revealing the relational Christian God.
*   Pruss, Alexander, and Richard Gale. 2012. "Problems for Christian Natural Theology." In *The Blackwell Companion to Science and Christianity*, edited by J. B. Stump and Alan G. Padgett. Malden, MA: Wiley-Blackwell. Details the problems some scholars find with the classic arguments of natural theology.
*   Stump, J. B. 2012. "Natural Theology after Modernism." In *The Blackwell Companion to Science and Christianity*, edited by J. B. Stump and Alan G. Padgett. Malden, MA: Wiley-Blackwell. Considers the possibility of natural theology after the fact–value distinction is dissolved.

References

Anselm. 2001. *Proslogion*. Translated by Thomas Williams. Indianapolis: Hackett Publishing Company.

Brunner, Emil, and Karl Barth. 2002. *Natural Theology: Comprising "Nature and Grace" by Professor Dr. Emil Brunner and the reply "no!" by Dr. Karl Barth*. Translated by Peter Fraenkel. Eugene, OR: Wipf and Stock Publishers.

Christian Classics. 2016. "Whether God Exists?" http://www.ccel.org/ccel/aquinas/summa.FP_Q2_A3.html, accessed 17 February 2016.

Hume, David. 1998. *Dialogues Concerning Natural Religion*, 2nd ed., edited by Richard H. Popkin. Indianapolis: Hackett Publishing Company.

Kuhn, Thomas. 1970. *The Structure of Scientific Revolutions*, 2nd ed. Chicago: University of Chicago Press.

McGrath, Alister E. 2008. *The Open Secret: A New Vision for Natural Theology*. Oxford: Blackwell Publishers.

McGrath, Alister E. 2009. *A Fine-tuned Universe: The Quest for God in Science and Theology*. Louisville, KY: Westminster John Knox Press.

Moser, Paul. 2012. "Religious Epistemology Personified: God without Natural Theology." In *The Blackwell Companion to Science and Christianity*, edited by J. B. Stump and Alan G. Padgett. Malden, MA: Wiley-Blackwell.

Paley, William. 1837. *Natural Theology*. Boston: Gould, Kendall and Lincoln.

Putnam, Hilary. 2002. *The Collapse of the Fact/Value Dichotomy*. Cambridge, MA: Harvard University Press.

Quine, W. V. O. 1980. "Two Dogmas of Empiricism." In *From a Logical Point of View*, 2nd ed. Cambridge, MA: Harvard University Press.

CHAPTER 8

Cosmology

The study of **cosmology** has long been fodder for dialogue and argument between science and religion. As far back as Plato's *Timaeus* in the 4th century BCE we find tension between what we today call a natural explanation of the existence of the cosmos and a supernatural explanation. We might expect that as science advances and develops more accurate theories, theological explanations would recede—the way they have for explanations of weather-related phenomena. But this expectation does not hold in cosmology. The fantastic discoveries of 20th-century cosmology—general relativity, the Big Bang, stellar nucleosynthesis, black holes, and so on—have not chased away those who see the hand of God at work in the universe. And in the case of fine tuning, a better understanding of the science of the cosmos has reinforced or even resurrected a theological impulse among some thinkers. In this chapter, we attempt to understand the connection between cosmology and theology by looking at some of their central points of contact today: the **Big Bang, fine tuning**, and the **multiverse hypothesis**.

> **(?) Questions to be addressed in this chapter:**
>
> 1. What is the Big Bang?
> 2. How should we respond to the apparent fine tuning we observe in the universe?
> 3. What can we conclude about multiverses?

1. Big Bang cosmology

What does it mean?
The term "Big Bang" refers to a couple of different scientific concepts, and it is important to keep them straight. Sometimes the term "Big Bang" is used as a label for the model of our current understanding of the development of the cosmos. As such, it refers to the entire history of the expansion of the universe. Alternatively,

Science and Christianity: An Introduction to the Issues, First Edition. By J. B. Stump.
© 2017 John Wiley & Sons, Ltd. Published 2017 by John Wiley & Sons, Ltd.

if we talk about the "Big Bang" as a singular event, things get more confusing because we don't really know what that refers to. Cosmologist Sean Carroll calls this sense of "Big Bang" merely a placeholder for our lack of complete understanding regarding the genesis of our universe (Carroll 2012, 186). By about one second after the Big Bang event, we have very precise theories and impressive empirical evidence. These form the basis of the Big Bang model which is firmly established as the reigning cosmological explanation. Before that first second, though, things are significantly sketchy.

It's not quite so bad from about 10^{-43} seconds after the beginning to one second. During that period cosmologists believe that our current understanding of physics (quantum mechanics and general relativity) is capable of describing the development of the universe. The problem is we don't know how these two highly confirmed theories fit together, so we are left with one way of describing the world on large scales (general relativity) and another at small scales (quantum mechanics). Before 10^{-43} seconds—the era known as Planck time in honor of physicist Max Planck, a pioneer of quantum theory—these two scales have to be integrated for us to make sense of things, so our inability to do so precludes anything more than speculation.

The theory itself originates from the scientific work of a Belgian priest named Georges Lemaître. In 1931, he wrote a brief letter to the journal *Nature* suggesting the beginning of the universe was like an atom that decayed and initiated cosmic expansion (Lemaître 1931, 706). The term "Big Bang" was coined by cosmologist Fred Hoyle as a term of derision for the theory being put forward by George Gamow and others that the universe is expanding. In a BBC radio address in 1949, Hoyle used the term "Big Bang" three times to refer to Gamow's theory (Kragh 2013, 15). Hoyle continued to defend a model of the universe known as the "steady state" theory into the 1950s and 1960s. But the evidence for the Big Bang model became increasingly persuasive, and in something of a rarity in the scientific community, Hoyle publicly admitted his steady state theory was wrong in *Nature* (see the quotation box). Just what is the evidence for the Big Bang?

"Opinion has generally moved toward the view that the equations of physics contain a singularity. I have always had a rooted objection to this conclusion. It seems as objectionable to me as if phenomena should be discovered in the laboratory which not only defied present physical laws but which also defied all possible physical laws. On the other hand, I see no objection to supposing that present laws are incomplete, for they are almost surely incomplete. The issue therefore presents itself as to how the physical laws must be modified in order to prevent a universal singularity, in other words, how to prevent a collapse of physics.

"It was with this background to the problem that several of us suggested, some twenty years ago, that matter might be created continuously. The idea was to keep the universe in a steady-state with creation of matter compensating the effects of expansion. In such a theory the density in the universe would not be higher in the past than it is at present. From the data I have presented here it seems likely that the idea will now have to be discarded, at any rate in the form it has become widely known—the steady-state universe." (Hoyle 1965, 113)

What is the evidence?

Like most of our current theories about the cosmos, the Big Bang theory traces its origin to Albert Einstein. In 1915, Einstein formulated his equations for the theory of general relativity. These explained gravity not as some mysterious force which reaches out from the sun to hold the earth in orbit, or from the earth to hold us to its surface, but as the nature of matter/energy to warp space itself. Just as the line of a golf ball is affected on the green by a depression which causes the putt to break downhill, so too bodies moving through space are drawn "downhill" toward the depressions in space caused by massive objects.

Einstein's equations describe with mathematical precision the state of matter/energy at each point in the universe and at each time. But he was alarmed by the implication of the mathematics that the density of matter/energy cannot remain the same throughout time. Because of the gravitational "depressions" throughout space and the universal gravitation between all objects, that density would always have to be increasing or decreasing. And since the amount of matter/energy remains constant, the only way to affect the overall density is to change the volume of its container. That is to say, space itself must always be expanding or contracting. This contradicted the accepted view of a static universe so starkly that Einstein was compelled to introduce an additional factor in his equations—called the **cosmological constant**. This constant supposedly described a pervasive force that would eliminate the unwanted implication of the mathematics. Later in life Einstein called that ad hoc move his greatest blunder, for it was not long until empirical data would provide confirming evidence that space is in fact expanding.

In 1929, Edwin Hubble observed through what was then the largest telescope on earth that the light from more distant galaxies was redder than the light of stars in our own galaxy. That meant that the wavelength of that light was longer than that emitted by closer stars. Assuming that the composition of the stars is essentially the same, the difference in wavelength could most plausibly be explained by supposing that the distant galaxies are moving away from us. This is an application to light waves of the well-known Doppler effect in sound waves. Think of standing by the side of the road during a motorcycle race. As a speeding (and very noisy) motorcycle approaches you, the sound is perceived at a higher pitch. As it passes and fades into the distance, the pitch we hear drops noticeably. The motorcycle itself makes a constant sound, but from the perspective of the listener the sound waves are bunched closer together when the motorcycle is moving toward the listener, and they are spread out further as the motorcycle moves away. These correspond to the higher and lower pitches we hear. The same works for light waves moving through space. Instead of hearing a lower pitch, light waves that are normally in the orange or yellow range are perceived by us as being more in the red range. Thus the effect of retreating galaxies is known as the red shift.

Sometimes we speak loosely as though stars and galaxies are moving away from us through space. According to Einstein's theory, though, it is space itself that is stretching and expanding. So the light waves in that space between us and distant stars are being stretched into longer wavelengths as the space expands.

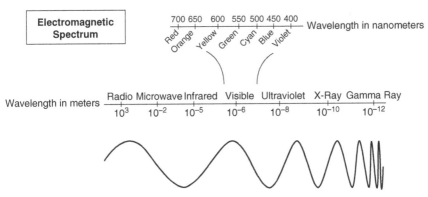

Fig. 8.1 Wavelengths of the electromagnetic spectrum.

Now, of course, if space is expanding as we move through time, we should be able to run the clock backward (theoretically speaking) and calculate when all of space was compressed into a singular point. That would be the "beginning" of the universe or the Big Bang event. Early measurements of the expansion rate were not very precise, and Hubble's first calculation of the age of the universe was 1.8 billion years. This was problematic, since geologists claimed that the earth itself was older than that. Such errors in the early data prevented the community of cosmologists from reaching consensus. But another empirical discovery came in the 1960s that settled the issue.

In the late 1940s, George Gamow conjectured that if the universe began with a big bang the immense number of photons given off should still be pervading space today. But space is a lot bigger now, and just like an aerosol can cools when the contents are released, the photons in an expanding universe will "cool" (of course, in the can, the volume of the can remains constant while the contents are reduced, but it is the same principle as keeping the contents constant while increasing the volume of the container). When photons cool, their frequency decreases and they pass out of the visible realm into the infrared and then the microwave range. Some of Gamow's associates calculated that this photon radiation today should be about five degrees above absolute zero, putting their frequency in the microwave band of electromagnetic radiation. But these calculations were ignored by the physics community, and no one would devote the resources to testing this empirical prediction.

It wasn't until the mid-1960s that the idea of **cosmic microwave background radiation** was revived by a couple of physicists at Princeton. Coincidentally, while they were mulling over the theory, two physicists from Bell Laboratories called to ask if they might have any ideas for why their new radio communications antenna was constantly hissing, no matter which direction they pointed it. To make a long story short, they had accidentally detected the radiation predicted by Gamow. And the observed value was remarkably close to the original prediction. Today the temperature of the radiation has been precisely measured by the orbiting spacecraft known as WMAP (Wilkinson Microwave Anisotropy Probe) to be 2.725 degrees above absolute zero.

What is the significance for Christianity?

At first blush, the Big Bang model of the universe with its very specific dating of the age of the universe seems to stand in tension with traditional Christian beliefs. Some Christians have read the Bible as providing specific dating for the age of the universe, and the age obtained by this method is radically different. The most infamous of these was put forth by James Ussher, an Anglican archbishop and the Primate of All Ireland, in the 17th century. By piecing together the genealogies in Scripture, he determined that the moment of creation occurred in 4004 BCE on October 23! But even conservative biblical scholars today admit that such genealogies are not meant to reveal the dating of the universe, and most have reconciled their faith to an old earth (see Chapter 4 for some discussion of the recalcitrant Young Earth Creationists).

Once the dating was accommodated with Christians' beliefs, some saw an opportunity for consonance here with the doctrine of *creatio ex nihilo*. The Cosmological Argument has been around for a long time and can be found in many different varieties. One version that has been particularly amenable to the scientific discoveries of the 20th century is the *kalām* Cosmological Argument. It was developed by Muslim theologians in the Middle Ages, most notably Al-Ghazâlî (c. 1055–1111). The foremost defender of the argument in recent times has been the Christian apologist William Lane Craig (b. 1949). He presents the argument most simply as follows:

Premise 1:   Whatever begins to exist has a cause.
Premise 2:   The universe began to exist.
Conclusion: Therefore the universe has a cause.

The argument has always had defenders on philosophical grounds, but because the available scientific evidence in previous centuries fit most easily with a picture of the universe as static and eternally existing, it was not until recently that the argument garnered much scientific attention. It is, of course, the second premise that is relevant for the Big Bang. Craig is convinced that the scientific evidence for the premise now makes the argument work. And he thinks the cause of the universe indicated by the conclusion is most plausibly taken to be an uncaused, beginningless, spaceless, and immaterial cause—which fits well with the traditional conception of the Christian God. Furthermore, Craig argues that a case can even be made that this cause is personal. He claims not only that there is currently no scientific explanation of a first state of the universe but also that there never can be. Instead, it is personal explanation (see discussion of this in Chapter 10) that has to be appealed to for such an event (Craig and Sinclair 2009). Of course, not everyone accepts this line of reasoning.

An earlier objection to the premise that the universe began to exist was that the evidence is equally supportive of an oscillating universe. That is to say, perhaps the universe expands until its gravity slows, stops, and reverses the expansion, culminating in a big "crunch" which bounces and starts everything over again. Now, however, this speculation seems to have been soundly defeated. The 2011 Nobel Prize winners in physics (Perlmutter, Schmidt, and Riess) have shown that not only is the expansion of the universe not slowing it is accelerating—thus rendering implausible the claim that we are part of an eternally oscillating universe.

In his popular book *The Grand Design*, Stephen Hawking gives another objection to the Cosmological Argument. He draws a parallel with eliminating the edge of the world when we realized that the earth is round. Now we realize that time can behave as another dimension of space in extreme events of warpage like the early conditions of the universe. Thus the "beginning" becomes a smooth boundaryless moment that has no moments prior to it—just like the South Pole has no points further south. If we were to walk south, there is a point at which we begin heading back north even though we continued in a straight line (albeit on the surface of a sphere); Hawking claims that if we were to travel back in time to the beginning, we would find that time folds back on itself and further travel in the same direction would begin taking us forward in time again (Hawking and Mlodinow 2010, 133–136).

It should be noted that Hawking's objection shifts the focus off the second premise of the *kalām* argument to the first. There is a beginning to the universe in his model; it is just that there is no time boundary to that event, and as such it becomes meaningless to speak of a cause that precedes the beginning. If Hawking is right, the beginning of our universe could be described as an uncaused quantum event. But because the Plank era of the Big Bang model is still shrouded in mystery, owing to our lack of a successful theory of quantum gravity, any explanation of the "beginning" is speculative right now and lacks direct empirical support. One of the candidates receiving significant attention these days postulates that our universe began as a phase of a more encompassing multiverse. The multiverse theory could offer the religious skeptic a way to avoid the theological implications of the Cosmological Argument, and it also presents an objection to the other major topic at the intersection of Christianity and cosmology: fine tuning. Before examining the merit of the multiverse idea, we first turn to fine tuning.

2. Fine tuning

What does it mean?
Fine tuning has come to be the term used for a contemporary version of the Design or Teleological Argument (*telos* is Greek for "goal" or "purpose"), other versions of which have been around for centuries. Thomas Aquinas included a design argument in his famous Five Ways for demonstrating the existence of God. He claimed that it is obvious that natural bodies exist for certain purposes and that these purposes must have come from a being external to themselves, whom we call God (Christian Classics 2016). Another particularly influential version of the Design Argument arose in the 19th century as biological inquiry uncovered the intricacy of living systems (this is discussed in Chapter 7, on natural theology). The fine tuning version of the Design Argument draws from the empirical discoveries of physics and cosmology in the 20th and 21st centuries. Essentially, the argument claims that the existence of the universe as we find it is too improbable to have happened by chance. Therefore, the argument concludes, the existence of a designer who determined—or fine-tuned—many of the features of the universe is the best explanation for the evidence.

What is the evidence?

The kind of evidence needed for an argument like this one must satisfy two conditions: (1) that evidence must be statistically improbable; and (2) it must conform to some pattern external to the event itself. For example, suppose the license plate for an automobile consisted of seven numbers and that these were randomly assigned when the automobile was registered. In these conditions, receiving any particular number is statistically improbable (1 out of 10 million). But that only satisfies the first condition, and on that basis alone we would not be surprised to receive an "improbable" license number. But suppose I receive a license number that corresponded exactly to my telephone number. Even though that number is no more statistically improbable than any of the others, a normal response would be some skepticism that the assignment of numbers really was random. It would be a reasonable response to think that someone must have fiddled with the assignment process to make the outcome conform to my personal circumstances—perhaps my wife ordered a personalized plate for me or the license branch has started routinely using the phone numbers they have on file.

> Don't confuse cosmic *inflation* with mere *expansion*. The traditional Big Bang model of the cosmos posited that space is expanding; the theory of inflation adds to this model by suggesting there was a period of extremely rapid expansion in the early universe.

The situation with the evidence for fine tuning in the cosmos is similar to this story—with one notable alteration. Of the possible values for some physical constants, laws of nature, or initial conditions, we don't think that they have an equal probability of being realized. Given what we do know of the laws of physics, these values should have fallen within a specific range. And yet the observed values do not come close to adhering to these expectations. It's as though the randomly distributed license plates are all numbers, and yet when my license plate shows up, it is all letters ... spelling out my last name—all the more reason to suspect the outcome was not really random.

For example, based on the current very successful theories of cosmological inflation, there is a kind of energy that pervades all of space called "vacuum energy." It is that energy that accounts for the rapid inflation of the universe very early in its history, and the observed value of the vacuum energy is less than 10^{-8} ergs per cubic centimeter. But based on calculations of very well-established quantum field theory, we should expect that value to be about 10^{112} ergs per cubic centimeter—a huge difference of 120 orders of magnitude, called "the worst theoretical prediction in the history of physics" (Hobson, Efstathiou, and Lasenby 2006, 187). Yet if there had been much more vacuum energy than the observed value, space would be expanding so rapidly that stars and galaxies could not have formed—presumably a necessary condition for life to develop. So if things had gone the way we expect them to go on their own, it doesn't seem that the universe would have been hospitable for life. But here we are. So, when we come to understand the value of vacuum energy and the physical laws that give rise to it, it is something like receiving a supposedly randomly assigned license plate that spells out your name.

There are other examples of fine tuning among the physical constants (see Rees 2000 and Collins 2009). We know of no reason that the force of gravity has the (relatively weak) value that it does. It is the force countering the expanding force of dark energy, so a slight difference here would have catastrophic effects similar to changing the expanding force: if gravity had been stronger or weaker by only one part in 10^{60}, then the exploding universe would have blown apart too quickly or collapsed back on itself without allowing life to form. Similarly, the initial distribution and density of mass/energy in the early universe needed to be incredibly "tuned" for our universe to develop (sometimes called the **flat-ness problem**). According to Roger Penrose, one of the leading theoretical physicists of our day, the precision necessary for a habitable universe was one part in 10 to the power of 10^{124} (Penrose 2011, 127). This incomprehensible number is approximately equal to the fraction of space that one proton occupies out of the entire visible universe! Besides these, we could talk about the strength of the strong nuclear force, the **Pauli Exclusion Principle**, and the mass of protons. These too are examples of fine tuning that make it seem like the universe has been "designed" with life like ours in mind.

It might be expected that the kind of evidence just cited would be highly controversial. But that is not the case here. Almost all physicists agree that there is an appearance of design in this data. The question is how we might explain that appearance.

> "Our everyday world, plainly moulded by subatomic forces, also owes its existence to our universe's well tuned expansion rate, the processes of galaxy formation, the forging of carbon and oxygen in ancient stars, and so forth. A few basic physical laws set the 'rules'; our emergence from a simple Big Bang was sensitive to six 'cosmic numbers'. Had these numbers not been 'well tuned', the gradual unfolding of layer upon layer of complexity would have been quenched." (Rees 2000)

What is the significance for Christianity?
What does the evidence for fine tuning mean for Christianity or theism in general? It depends on how you weigh the relative plausibility of the following options for explaining the evidence:

1. We just got lucky. You could just say we beat the incredible odds and things turned out in our favor. The more we learn about those odds, though, the less plausible this answer seems to be.

2. Life could have been different. All of these parameters end by saying something like, "Life as we know it could not have existed." Is it possible that life could thrive under significantly different conditions? Perhaps we shouldn't rule this out, but we have no way of imagining how life could exist without stars and relatively stable atomic structures.

3. The science is wrong. It might be claimed that the scientific theories that form the framework against which the evidence is understood are drastically wrong. After all, there have been scientific revolutions in the past that have radically altered theories. True, but even a revolution as radical as Einstein's does not throw out Newtonian physics; it incorporates it into a more general theory. Whatever theories that might be developed in the future will have to do the same with quantum physics and general relativity. They are just too well confirmed to be thrown out.

These first three options are possible in the broadest sense of the term, but few people take them as very plausible. Instead, the debate today is focused on two other options:

4. God did it. Christians see the evidence as just the sort of evidence we would expect to see if there is a creator and designer of the universe who is interested in the existence of life like ours. This does not amount to a deductive proof of the existence of God, but it is claimed that it is the best explanation for the evidence.

5. The odds are improved in a multiverse. It has been increasingly popular among cosmologists to suppose our universe is only one among a huge number of universes, each having a different set of laws and constants. Then it is not surprising ours has the features it does, because it is the only one where we could find ourselves.

Of course, it is possible for Christians also to accept the multiverse hypothesis as the means by which God brought our universe into being. But the relevant option for us to consider here is whether a multiverse theory can explain the fine tuning evidence on a purely naturalistic basis. So it is to the multiverse we must turn.

3. The multiverse

What does it mean?
The term "multiverse" obviously comes from combining the prefix "multi-" with "universe," but as such it sounds like an oxymoron. The UNI-verse is supposed to denote the one all-encompassing reality of everything that exists. How could there be more than one of these? It turns out there could be several different ways. Cosmologist Brian Greene discusses nine different kinds of multiverses in his book *The Hidden Reality* (2011). There is the **many worlds theory** originating in quantum physics according to which it is hypothesized that, of the many possible outcomes of quantum events, they are all realized in parallel universes that split off from each other. Then there are several varieties of multiverses that stem from different considerations of string theory. And there are a couple that use the possible realities of computer simulations to generate a multiverse. The kind of multiverse that especially concerns us here, though, comes from the inflationary theory of cosmology.

Open, closed, or flat?
Because gravity warps or curves space itself according to Einstein's theory of **general relativity**, we can ask about the overall curvature of space. This will be related to the average density of matter/energy in space, which affects the ultimate fate of the universe. If there is more than the critical density, space will close back on itself like the three-dimensional equivalent of the surface of a sphere; and if there are no other factors affecting the process (like a cosmological constant), space will ultimately stop expanding and contract back to a singularity. If there is less than the critical density, space will be open like the surface of a saddle and expand forever. If there is exactly the critical density, space will be flat like a sheet of paper, and the expansion rate will slow to zero at infinity (again, unless there are other factors).

As far back as the late 1970s, cosmologist Alan Guth was developing the theory of inflation as the solution to two problems that vexed cosmologists. One of those problems is known as the **horizon problem**. This arises because of the observed uniformity of the cosmic microwave background radiation discussed above. At the moment of the Big Bang explosion, there would have been regions of space with very different temperatures. In order for equalization of these to occur, the warmer and cooler regions must be in contact with each other. But on the previously accepted model, these regions of space became separated from each other before the equalization could take place. So Guth's inflationary hypothesis suggests that the expansion of the universe at its very early stage was slower than the earlier model predicts. In that way, warmer and cooler regions would be in contact with each other long enough to equalize. And then in order to get the spatial separation we observe today, there was a period of extremely rapid inflation.

The second issue that inflation resolved for Guth is the flatness problem mentioned above. The initial density of matter/energy appears to have been precisely tuned to allow for a flat universe. Guth's inflationary hypothesis, however, shows that if the universe underwent extremely rapid inflation, no matter how dense the initial universe was, the density would settle on the critical value allowing for a "flat" universe.

Of course, we can't go back and observe whether or not inflation really occurred. But the empirical evidence is mounting as the predictions of inflationary theory are confirmed. Inflation is important for the multiverse theory because we know of no scientific reason why inflationary bubbles couldn't occur in more than one area of a much larger universe. The empirical data we have now is just as consistent with there being many different regions of space-time that have inflated as it is with there being only our one inflated "universe." If there are many, they would be separated from each other beyond the capability of any light-speed signals to connect them, so they would always remain completely isolated from each other.

The reason, then, that such a multiverse scenario is seen as a response to the fine tuning of the physical constants comes from its possible connection to **string**

theory. String theory is the best attempt so far to unify the fundamental forces, and it suggests that, depending on the different ways the period of inflation can begin and end, the physical constants of a bubble universe could be different. We might say that the laws are constant throughout the multiverse, but they can be manifested differently in different regions. By analogy, the composition of water remains the same but it can be manifested in three different phases: liquid, solid, and gas. String theory suggests there are an enormous number of possible phases in which space-time might be manifested—as many as 10^{500}. These would correspond to 10^{500} different regions of space-time in which the physical constants are different—resulting in universes with very different properties. Among that huge number, some of those universes have combinations of physical constants that allow life to develop. In such a scenario, it is no surprise that we find ourselves in one of those universes, for they are the only ones in which we could find ourselves.

What is the evidence?

This is a short section, because there isn't any direct empirical evidence that there are multiverses of the sort just described. That doesn't mean, however, that there is no reason to think there may be multiverses out there. This was not just some ad hoc idea that appeared out of nowhere to undermine the appearance of design, as some supporters of fine tuning seem to charge. It is an implication of string theory and inflationary cosmology, neither of which is confirmed itself and yet both seem to be suggested by the mathematics of cosmology. There have been plenty of theories that were suggested first of all by the mathematics without empirical proof and only later were confirmed by experiment. Two of the more spectacular successes in this regard have been black holes and the cosmic microwave background radiation. It is certainly rash to claim we know we are part of a multiverse. But it would also be rash to claim to know we're not.

What is the significance for Christianity?

Not everyone evaluates the problem of fine tuning in the same way. Individuals' reactions to it can be understood as a function of their application of observer bias to the problem. Some have tried to reconcile the enormous odds of the one universe behaving the way it does with observer bias. Yes, they say, it is hugely improbable that the universe is hospitable for life, but we could not find it to be any other way—otherwise we wouldn't be here to observe it. Such a reaction to the evidence seems misguided and is no explanation at all. It is as though you were put before a firing squad of sharpshooters, and after the command to fire and the report of the guns, you find yourself unscathed. "You shouldn't be surprised at the outcome," someone says, "for you couldn't have observed it to be any other way." Surely this response is unsatisfactory and wrong-headed, for the relevant point remains unexplained. Why did things not go the way we expected them to go? What other factor must have been at work in the process? Was it just an extraordinary coincidence that all of the sharpshooters missed? Or did someone with an interest in my survival rig the process somehow—perhaps by loading all the guns with blanks?

If there is just our one universe with its observed laws and physical constants, this scenario seems to capture the issue and tip the scales in favor of Christians' interpretations. It is just too outlandishly improbable for things to have turned out this way unless someone who has an interest in our survival rigged the system. This is not an irrefutable proof for the existence of a creator God, but it does seem to be the most plausible explanation for a set of events that demands an explanation—just like receiving a personalized license plate or surviving the firing squad demands an explanation. The possibility of a multiverse, however, changes the story and with it the application of observer bias.

Consider the enormous odds against every one of your ancestors surviving to the point of having children. Assuming that the conditions prevailing in third-world countries today are representative of the history of our species, only two-thirds of children survive to age 5. If we multiply those odds times the hundreds of generations of human ancestors you have (let alone the thousands and millions of generations of non-human ancestors before that), the chances are practically nil that all of those people would survive to childbearing age.

But now we do seem to have a legitimate application of observer bias. Of course, you wouldn't be here if they hadn't survived, but your surprise at this situation shouldn't be the same as the surprise at surviving the firing squad. In the genealogical example, some people do survive, and through them a selection principle is at work over a vast number of people (and potential people). It is not really a surprise (and it needs no further explanation) that you find yourself as a descendent of the successful line of procreators.

If there is a multiverse with a vast number of different local bubbles, a selection process similar to the ancestor example is at work. Most of the universes would not be hospitable to life like ours, but some would be. And, of course, we find ourselves in one which is conducive to life. That fact does not need further explanation or supernatural intervention.

Conclusion

Some Christians are quick to point out that the existence of a multiverse would not end the theological implications of cosmology. It is not inconsistent with Christian theology to think that God's creation is much vaster than we once realized. Indeed, one way of telling the history of the Christian doctrine of creation is this progressive understanding from the ancient Near Eastern cosmological myths, to the Ptolemaic model of the cosmos, to the Copernican system, and to the Big Bang; multiverses are just one more step. Furthermore, Christian philosopher Robin Collins seems to have correctly noted that a multiverse only pushes the fine tuning problem back another level; now we have to ask why there is a mechanism that generates these multiverses, some of which are conducive to intelligent life (Collins 2012). Science seems to be incapable of finally answering the ultimate question, but atheist cosmologist Sean Carroll is untroubled by that inability. Perhaps it is just a brute fact that the universe exists and exhibits the kinds of regularities we find in it. The drive for metaphysical explanations is rooted in a fundamentally teleological view of the universe. Carroll thinks teleology is a human construct or an add-on to the way things really are (Carroll 2012). Christians disagree.

And so the debate continues.

Summary of main points:

1. The Big Bang is the well-confirmed scientific theory that all the matter and energy we observe today came from a point.
2. The apparent fine tuning of physical constants suggests our universe was designed with our kind of life in mind, or that we are one of vastly many universes.
3. Although there is no empirical confirmation of the existence of multiverses, the concept is consistent with what we know and provides a fascinating answer to the fine tuning evidence.

Further reading

- Carroll, Sean. 2012. "Does the Universe Need God?" In *The Blackwell Companion to Science and Christianity*, edited by J. B. Stump and Alan G. Padgett. Malden, MA: Wiley-Blackwell. A very clear exposition of the attempt to explain cosmology on a completely naturalistic basis.
- Collins, Robin. 2012. "The Fine-tuning of the Cosmos: A Fresh Look at Its Implications." In *The Blackwell Companion to Science and Christianity*, edited by J. B. Stump and Alan G. Padgett. Malden, MA: Wiley-Blackwell. A Christian philosopher surveys responses to fine tuning, including one argument not covered here.
- Craig, William Lane, and James D. Sinclair. 2009. "The *Kalam* Cosmological Argument." In *The Blackwell Companion to Natural Theology*, edited by William Lane Craig and J. P. Moreland. Malden, MA: Wiley-Blackwell. Develops the argument in significant technical detail.
- Greene, Brian. 2011. *The Hidden Reality: Parallel Universes and the Deep Laws of the Cosmos*. New York: Alfred A. Knopf. A popular science book on multiverses by one of the leaders in cosmology.
- Rees, Martin. 2000. *Just Six Numbers: The Deep Forces that Shape the Universe*. New York: Basic Books. Presents the scientific evidence behind six of the more spectacular cases of apparent fine tuning.

References

Carroll, Sean. 2012. "Does the Universe Need God?" In *The Blackwell Companion to Science and Christianity*, edited by J. B. Stump and Alan G. Padgett. Malden, MA: Wiley-Blackwell.

Christian Classics. 2016. "Whether God Exists?" http://www.ccel.org/ccel/aquinas/summa.FP_Q2_A3.html, accessed 17 February 2016.

Collins, Robin. 2009. "The Teleological Argument: An Exploration of the Fine-tuning of the Universe." In *The Blackwell Companion to Natural Theology*, edited by William Lane Craig and J. P. Moreland. Malden, MA: Wiley-Blackwell.

Collins, Robin. 2012. "The Fine-tuning of the Cosmos: A Fresh Look at Its Implications." In *The Blackwell Companion to Science and Christianity*, edited by J. B. Stump and Alan G. Padgett. Malden, MA: Wiley-Blackwell.

Craig, William Lane, and James D. Sinclair. 2009. "The *Kalam* Cosmological Argument." In *The Blackwell Companion to Natural Theology*, edited by William Lane Craig and J. P. Moreland. Malden, MA: Wiley-Blackwell.

Greene, Brian. 2011. *The Hidden Reality: Parallel Universes and the Deep Laws of the Cosmos*. New York: Alfred A. Knopf.

Hawking, Stephen, and Leonard Mlodinow. 2010. *The Grand Design*. New York: Bantam Books.

Hobson, M. P., G. P. Efstathiou, and A. N. Lasenby. 2006. *General Relativity: An Introduction for Physicists*. Cambridge: Cambridge University Press.

Hoyle, F. 1965. "Recent Developments in Cosmology." *Nature*, 208: 111–114.

Kragh, Helge. 2013. "What's in a Name: History and Meanings of the Term 'Big Bang'." arXiv:1301.0219v2 [physics.hist-ph].

Lemaître, Georges. 1931. "The Beginning of the World from the Point of View of Quantum Theory." *Nature*, 127: 706.

Penrose, Roger. 2011. *Cycles of Time: An Extraordinary New View of the Universe*. New York: Alfred A. Knopf.

Rees, Martin. 2000. *Just Six Numbers: The Deep Forces that Shape the Universe*. New York: Basic Books.

CHAPTER 9

Evolution

For more than 30 years, Gallup has asked a random sample of Americans this question:

Which of the following statements comes closest to your views on the origin and development of human beings?

1. Human beings have developed over millions of years from less advanced forms of life, but God guided this process;

2. Human beings have developed over millions of years from less advanced forms of life, but God had no part in this process; or

3. God created human beings pretty much in their present form at one time within the last 10,000 years or so.

The number of people choosing answer number three has proved to be remarkably consistent over these years, varying only slightly from 44% in 1982 to its latest value of 42% in 2014 (Gallup 2014). In this latest poll, when respondents are restricted to those who report attending church weekly, the percentage who chose the creationist answer rises to 69%. Clearly for Christians there is a perceived problem with evolution.

More complex analysis of Americans' beliefs about evolution has been conducted by Jonathan Hill. He worries that the forced choices of the Gallup poll conflate and mask more nuanced beliefs, and they give no indication of the confidence of people's beliefs. So he fielded a new, nationally representative survey of the American public in his National Study of Religion and Human Origins project (Hill 2014, and 2014a). In it he teased apart the creationist question and asked respondents whether they believed the following:

1. Humans did not evolve from other species.

2. God was involved in the creation of humans.

3. Humans were created within the last 10,000 years.

He found that only 14% affirmed all three of these, and that only 10% believed these and were certain of their beliefs. On the other side, only 6% were certain that

Science and Christianity: An Introduction to the Issues, First Edition. By J. B. Stump.
© 2017 John Wiley & Sons, Ltd. Published 2017 by John Wiley & Sons, Ltd.

humans evolved and God played no part in the process. So perhaps Hill's data suggests that Americans' views on origins are not as polarized as Gallup has led us to believe.

Still, there is widespread concern even among Christians who accept the science of evolution that there are problems fitting these two together. This chapter assumes that the findings of contemporary evolutionary science (and allied fields) are largely correct: life originated on the planet some 3.8 billion years ago and all life today (including human beings) is related through common descent. These, of course, are not unchallenged by some Christian communities, as we saw in Chapter 4. The purpose of this chapter, however, is not to rehash these arguments but to survey the implications for Christianity of the contemporary evolutionary paradigm and to explore the fruitful points of contact between evolution and Christianity.

> ### ② Questions to be addressed in this chapter:
>
> 1. Can the creation stories in the Bible be reconciled with evolution?
> 2. Would God really create through a process involving randomness and death?
> 3. Given evolution, can we still affirm that humans are created in the image of God?
> 4. Could reflecting on evolution help Christian theologians?

1. Evolution and the Bible

In Chapter 5, we consider some of the general issues related to science and the Bible for Christians. In this section, we look more specifically at why some Christians believe evolution—and human evolution in particular—presents problems for interpreting the Bible.

For Christians who take the Bible seriously as some sort of divine revelation, there are obvious difficulties with evolution. The first two chapters of Genesis appear to describe the origin of today's plant and animal species in very different terms than scientists have discovered. Also, from various parts of the Bible we seem to be able to piece together a timeline that testifies to a very recent creation. How do Christians who accept the general evolutionary framework reconcile that with their belief in the truth and trustworthiness of Scripture?

During the 20th century, one fairly popular viewpoint among Christians was **concordism**, which attempts to show that both science and the Bible give reliable information about the origin of the earth and life on it. As opposed to the Young Earth Creationists, concordists have generally accepted the conclusions of mainstream science about the age of the earth, and so their challenge has been to find suitable interpretations of the Bible that allow for this. One approach has been the Gap theory, according to which there was a very long duration of time between Genesis 1:1 "God created the heavens and earth" and Genesis 1:3 "Let there be light" (the first day of creation). The days of creation in Genesis 1 proceeded as recorded after this long gap of time. Gap theorists usually claim that fossils we have discovered are vestiges of the very ancient creation in Genesis 1:1, which was destroyed (perhaps as a result of Satan's rebellion) before the six days of creation beginning in verse 3. They say that all current life forms are descended from those created very recently. Though widespread in the first half of the 20th century, there are very few Gap theorists around today.

Another concordist approach which does have more contemporary adherents is the **Day-Age theory**. According to this interpretation of Genesis 1, the Hebrew word for day (*yom*) can also mean an indefinite period of time—like we might say today, "back in the day." In this way, they take the six days of creation as successive "ages" during which the events described on each day were accomplished over long stretches of time. The most prominent of the Day-Age theorists today is Hugh Ross, who believes that God performed millions of acts of special creation throughout these ages to bring about the variety of species we see today.

Other concordists accept that evolution occurred for plants and lower animal species. They point to the language used in Genesis, which suggests a more indirect role for God: "Then God said, 'Let the earth put forth vegetation'" (1:11), "Let the waters bring forth swarms of living creatures" (1:20), and "Let the earth bring forth living creatures of every kind" (1:24). But when God creates humans there is a change to a more direct language, "Then God said, 'Let us make humankind in our image'" (1:26). This doesn't sound like the indirect method of letting the earth bring forth. So concordists generally think that the creation of human beings must have been distinct and that God did not use pre-existing life forms to bring them about. Because of their interpretation of the Bible, these concordists have to develop an alternative interpretation of the biological evidence from what the vast majority of scientists accept today. Another more recent interpretation of Scripture seeks to avoid this conflict.

John Walton is an Old Testament professor at Wheaton College—one of the premier evangelical institutions in America. He has developed an interpretation of Genesis that removes the conflict with science today. Scientific theories are concerned with the material creation, that is where the physical stuff came from, and too often modern readers of Scripture expect it to be answering the same thing. But according to Walton, the authors of Genesis weren't addressing that question at all. Consistent with their ancient Near Eastern culture, the human authors of the creation narratives were telling the story of creation in the sense of the assignment of functions. The sun was "created" according to this ancient mindset not when there were atoms of hydrogen and helium that started fusing and giving off massive amounts of energy but when God made the sun to shine *for us* and our benefit.

Walton believes that ultimately the material too was the creation of God, but that is not what Genesis is talking about. According to his interpretation, Genesis 1:1 is the heading or chapter title of the creation account, so we find the original state of things in this chapter to be, "the earth was a formless void" (1:2). God's creative activities recorded in the six days of creation, then, consist of giving functions to the material that is already there. In this view, there simply is no biblical account of the origins of the material, and so there is no conflict with modern scientific theories about this.

On the subject of human evolution, Walton takes a similar approach. He does think that Adam and Eve were real historical people for biblical reasons, but he doesn't believe that a proper interpretation of the Bible commits Christians to thinking they were the first human beings or the ancestors of all human beings (Walton 2013, 113). Adam as portrayed in Genesis is an archetype for all humanity. He is "everyman" representing the sinfulness, mortality, and priestly role of all human beings. Again, there is ancient Near Eastern precedent for reading the Genesis narratives this way. So Walton concludes that the Bible does not give an account of the material formation of human beings as biological specimens and so does not contradict anything that the science of evolution has discovered about our material origins.

Other Christian interpreters see some validity to Walton's approach, but think it is a stretch to claim that the authors of Genesis were making no claims about the material origins of the world and human beings. Instead, they think that the Bible is divine revelation that comes packaged in the cultural concepts of the original authors and audience, and as such it reflects ancient scientific beliefs that were just wrong. For example, when the Old Testament authors speak of the "firmament," they really believed that there was a solid dome that held back the waters in the sky. And when Paul in the New Testament referred to the three-tiered universe with the heavens above the earth and an underworld below (see Philippians 2:10), he really believed that to be an accurate picture of reality. But the biblical authors were just wrong about these things. Denis Lamoureux says this does not affect the truth of Scripture, though, because we must distinguish between the inerrant spiritual truths of the Bible, and the incidental, ancient science through which those truths were communicated to its ancient audience (Lamoureux 2008, 110).

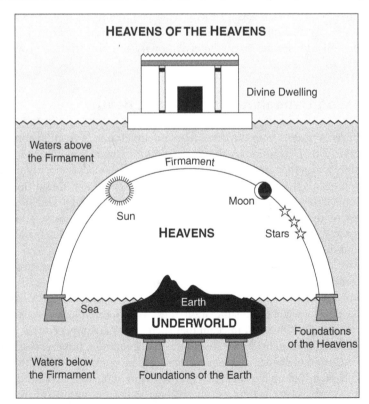

Fig. 9.1 The Three-tier Universe. Drawn by Kenneth Kully.

Bible scholar Peter Enns even claims that when the Apostle Paul referred to Adam in Romans and 1 Corinthians he undoubtedly believed that Adam was a real person and the father of the entire human race. As such, Paul used the story of Adam—which everyone in his community would have accepted—to convey the theology of sin, death, and the need for salvation in Christ. Paul's being wrong about the historical role of Adam does not take away from the theology he articulates. Enns says:

> Paul, as a first-century Jew, bore witness to God's act in Christ in the only way that he could have been expected to do so, through ancient idioms and categories known to him and his religious tradition for century upon century. One can believe that Paul is correct theologically and historically about the problem of sin and death and the solution that God provides in Christ without also needing to believe that his assumptions about human origins are accurate. The need for a savior does not require a historical Adam. (Enns 2012, 143)

Other Christians see the need to hold on to some sort of historical Adam and Eve. They accept that science does not allow for Adam and Eve to be a first ancestral couple for all humanity, but try instead to give them some representative role for all of humanity, even if they do not have a biological relationship to all of humanity. But Enns claims that this view of Adam and Eve is utterly foreign to the Adam and Eve of Scripture, so there is no good reason for holding on to it. Instead, we must reevaluate the message of Paul in the light of what we know about the world today. And, in fact, this is exactly what Paul did in his day—reevaluating the Genesis story and appropriating it for his own day. There are further concerns about the **Fall** and original sin on the evolutionary account. These are considered in Chapter 12.

2. Creation through randomness and death

Straightforward claims from the Bible about the timeframe of creation are not the only problems that evolutionary theory presents for Christianity. There are other more subtle issues that stem from the understanding of God as directly involved in creation versus the seemingly random process of evolution. Could God really have intended to create us human beings by allowing evolution to take its course? Furthermore, the evolutionary way of creating can bring about new species only at the expense of others through long processes involving lots of death and suffering. Would the Christian God really create this way?

First we should acknowledge that we humans create games that incorporate chance, and we find that the games are fairer and more interesting because of the element of chance. Whether it is the roll of a die, the shuffling of a deck of cards, or random events for a computer simulation, these are important parts of the experience of such games. This isn't to claim that such games are direct correlations (or even good analogies) of how God creates through evolution. It merely establishes that the inclusion of chance does not in itself seem incompatible with how intelligent agents might set up a system. For God, allowing some degree of randomness may be the way to give the universe an existence with some autonomy from God.

Had there been no contingency at all, the universe "would have been nothing more than an ornament attached passively to the divine being, rather than a reality in its own right" (Haught 2009, 8).

Furthermore, using randomness does not seem inconsistent even in processes for which the creator wants to guarantee some particular end. For example, governments have discovered how to design and implement a random system that reliably generates revenue without raising taxes: the lottery. It turns out that people will willingly hand over small sums of their money if given a chance to get a big payout. By controlling the odds of winning tickets, the organizers of the lottery can predict with significant accuracy how much money the system will produce over the long run. On any given day the net revenues might be very different, depending on whether someone chose the winning number. But over longer stretches of time, the random processes even out, and a predictable outcome is achieved.

> **Simon Conway Morris (b. 1951)**
>
> Paleobiologist at the university of Cambridge, best known for his work on the fossils of the Cambrian explosion. The late Stephen Jay Gould claimed that if the tape of life were rewound and played again, life would look very different. Through the documentation of numerous instances of evolutionary **convergence**, Simon Conway Morris claims that evolution tends toward (or converges on) similar solutions, and thus the re-played tape of life would be remarkably the same.

Some evolutionary thinkers today see the same sort of thing being applied to evolution because of the discovery of convergence. This is the recognition that from different starting points in the evolutionary history of life similar forms emerge again and again. Simon Conway Morris has been one of the leading expositors of this, and in his book *Life's Solution* he details numerous examples of evolutionary convergence from photosynthesis, to the camera eye, to cognition. In contrast to his rival, Stephen Jay Gould, who claimed that if we rewound the tape of life and let it play again there would be vastly different results, Conway Morris claims that we would get largely the same sorts of things. He does not claim that evolution is deterministic nor does he deny the role of contingency in evolution. But in broad strokes, he believes convergence points to an inherent predictability in evolution. He says:

> the areas open to biological occupation are much more highly constrained than is often imagined, and whilst indeed from our perspective the Tree of Life has occupied an immense area, it is an infinitesimally small fraction of all theoretical possibilities. (Conway Morris 2012, 262)

Even if we accept that evolution may in fact be more predictable than assumed by some accounts of it, there is still a question about whether this process is consistent with traditional concepts of God. Returning to the comparison with the lottery, it makes it sound like God is only concerned with the winners. But for the system to work, how many people have to lose? In evolutionary terms, it is well established that over 99% of all the species that have ever existed are now extinct. Are we suggesting that God is OK with this? The survival of the weak at the expense of the strong seems to cut against the grain of the message of Jesus. Assuming that God did intend to create the species we see today, doesn't it seem like a particularly malevolent way to go about doing that when it comes at the expense of the unfortunate losers in the evolutionary process?

One response to this challenge is to claim that the death and suffering is a necessary part of the process. Just like God can't give free will to people without the consequence that some people will use their free will for evil purposes, so too (the response goes) God can't bring about human beings through natural processes without long stretches of time during which **survival of the fittest** runs its course and produces evolutionary winners and losers. Such a response may have some truth to it, but it still seems to significantly alter the traditional conception of God.

Altering that conception isn't so bad, according to some. They think we've inherited a view of God from the Scientific Revolution in which God is conceived as a divine engineer. In that view, the system designed looks grossly inefficient and unbecoming for what should be the greatest engineer imaginable. But that is not the view of God that emerges from the theology of the Bible. There we see God as one who empties himself in becoming Jesus Christ, and who sees that suffering and death is an expression of love (Haught 2009). Such concepts perhaps enable us to understand the process of evolution differently: instead of an inefficient design, it becomes more like a dramatic narrative with tension and resolution, failure and success.

Still, it might be objected that such a story seems to suggest a callous disregard for the "losers" in the evolutionary narrative. Surely, God as revealed in Jesus Christ does not display such an attitude? Instead, Jesus gave preferential treatment to the poor and downcast. "The last shall be first, and the first last" (Matthew 20:16). There is an eschatological response to this charge which is considered in the chapter on the problem of pain and suffering (Chapter 12). Here we consider the problem from the perspective of metaphysics or, more specifically, **ontology**.

Ontology is the study of existence and the kinds of things that exist, and the specific question here is what kind of status to give to "species" in this regard. Our language cannot but use terms that refer to groups of individuals like cats, palm trees, and goldfish. But what is it that allows us to group such similar individuals together? Traditionally, the concept of species was used and implicitly understood to be a static and unchanging thing. Evolution challenges that. Of course, among individuals with significant differences we can easily put them into distinct groups: cats, palm trees, and goldfish. But when the differences are slighter, and especially when we look at a population across time, it is much more difficult.

The descendants of any particular set of parents will bear strong resemblance, but after many generations that resemblance to the ancestors is considerably smaller. On the human lineage, about 50,000 generations ago, we come to *Homo erectus*—a **hominin** species that lived around 1 million years ago, possibly living in hunter-gatherer groups using tools and fire. But was this ancestor a human being? Most biologists would say no. But there is no clear line at which *Homo erectus* becomes **Homo sapiens**. The same can be said of the other lines of descent that can be traced back from the organisms alive today. And there are other lines of descent that terminate with no further descendants. This is an "extinction," but if it is hard to define a "species," then it is hard to say what has gone extinct. All we can say is that some group of individuals had no further descendants.

The point is that when we say it is a bad thing for a species to go extinct, we are assuming that there is some entity existing above and beyond the individuals that goes out of existence when all of the individuals in that group go out of existence. But the group in question seems to be rather arbitrarily defined. It is only on the assumption of **essentialism** (that there is some particular essence of what it is to be a dog or a dodo bird) that this objection about the extinction of species in evolution carries any force. The life of an individual dog or dodo bird is not affected by its "species" going extinct some generations after it lived.

In this sense we might say that the doctrine of "survival of the fittest" which has almost become synonymous with evolution does not need to trouble Christian sensibilities. From the perspective of evolution, a "species" is not successful if it does not pass its genes on to another generation. But if there are no species, then again we can't say that they are unsuccessful. All we can say is that there are some individuals that did not procreate. And from the perspective of Christianity, such individuals have no less worth than those that did procreate. There are individual lives, and these have the same sort of life whether or not their descendants lived and prospered.

Now, of course, some of those individuals have difficult lives. Some are eaten by other individuals or suffer in other ways. There is no denying that during evolutionary time scales many, many individuals die prematurely and in gruesome ways. This is a version of the problem of evil that is distinct from the problem of species extinction. We address that problem in Chapter 12. There is another problem for traditional Christian theology more pertinent to this chapter that is a direct consequence of denying essentialism: the uniqueness of human beings.

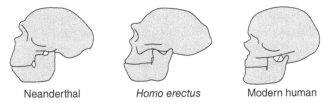

| Neanderthal | *Homo erectus* | Modern human |

Fig. 9.2 Skull shapes of *Homo* species.

3. The uniqueness of human beings

Traditional Christian theology has assigned a special place among all of creation for human beings: we bear the image of God. Evolutionary theory challenges this thought with its discovery that we have been created in continuity with all other living things. The Anglican bishop Samuel Wilberforce gave expression to the thought that accompanies evolution in the minds of many Christians still today. In 1860 (the year after the publication of Darwin's *Origin of Species*), he wrote:

> Such a notion [the evolution of human beings through natural selection] is absolutely incompatible not only with single expressions in the word of God on that subject of natural science with which it is not immediately concerned, but, which in our judgment is of far more importance, with the whole representation of that moral and spiritual condition of man which is its proper subject matter. Man's derived supremacy over the earth; man's power of articulate speech; man's gift of reason; man's free-will and responsibility; man's fall and man's redemption; the incarnation of the Eternal Son; the indwelling of the Eternal Spirit—all are equally and utterly irreconcilable with the degrading notion of the brute origin of him who was created in the image of God, and redeemed by the Eternal Son assuming to himself his nature. (Wilberforce 1874, 94)

The problem that Wilberforce felt was articulated in terms of the "brute origin" of human beings. Some people today still voice this concern, thinking it preferable and more dignified for their first ancestor to have come from dust rather than from an ancient ape. In their view, the first human being resulted from God breathing breath into that dust. But why couldn't God have breathed breath into some ancient hominids, thereby conferring humanity and the image of God upon them? It is difficult to see why one of these scenarios is preferable, other than invoking biblical literalism. And if we invoke literalism, we have to say that all people are made from dust (Psalm 103:14 and Ecclesiastes 3:20).

But some will think that invoking some mysterious breath of God to distinguish humans from non-humans is out of keeping with what we know about human biology today. Even the ancients recognized that there is "breath" in other organisms too. We could say that God gave humans "souls," but here again we go beyond what the biblical text warrants and import our own ideas. This leads some to claim that the image of God does not consist in some particular entity God put into human beings, but rather that it consists in certain capacities we have that other life forms do not. Typically, these are thought to be language, reason, and morality. Then we could solve the species problem by claiming that any individual organism that possesses these qualities is an individual who bears God's image.

Two challenges might be made to this understanding. First, it is not clear that capacities like language, reason, and morality are "all or nothing." As we look across the animal kingdom today there are hints of these capacities in "lower" animals, and more work is being done which elucidates the fact that such capacities come in degrees. Does that mean other animals bear the image of God to a degree? And in the development of *Homo sapiens* across the ages, there would be no distinct point at which these capacities suddenly appear. One way to respond to this challenge is to accept that the image of God might come in degrees and develop gradually. Even traditional Christian theology has to contend with this in the case of children: at what point does a child become morally accountable? We can give no such point except arbitrarily. So too in the evolutionary history of human beings: just as we cannot give a precise point where non-human turns into human, neither can we give a precise demarcation between those individuals who bear the image of God and those who do not.

But there is a second problem for this kind of interpretation of the image of God which causes some people to doubt it as the solution: if the image of God depends on having language, reason, and morality, then what about the isolated individual who lacks these? Does a person who goes into a coma because of an accident lose the image of God? Do young infants not have the image of God? Most Christians would not be comfortable with such implications, for then again there is a degrading of the less fortunate which stands in tension with the attitude of Jesus.

So, finally, we might understand the image of God in another sense. Instead of being found in some particular entity (like a soul) or in some particular capacity (like reason or morality), it might be claimed that we can identify human beings as image bearers because of their relationship to God. This allows that it is not because of their nature (which would cause problems on account of the difficulties with essentialism in an evolutionary understanding) that they bear the image of God. Rather, it is because God chose to enter into a special relationship with them. Perhaps at some point in the evolutionary development, God recognized a group of our ancestors as image bearers and entered into a covenant with them and their descendants. If such a relationship was begun before the line leading to **Neanderthals** and **Denisovans** split off, then these too would have had the image of God (an important question since there is evidence of interbreeding between *Homo sapiens* and these two groups). Understood in this way, the image of God is a theological concept related to election: God has chosen individuals for a particular purpose—not because of some inherent merit, but in order to serve. As with other cases of divine election, Joshua Moritz says, "The chosen person or people is elected in order to serve as God's agent in relation to a more comprehensive object of God's love" (Moritz 2014b). As such, the image of God is grounded not in our biology but in God's choice for us to be his representatives to all of creation.

Perhaps evolution has helped us come to a more accurate theological view in this case. Sometimes it is feared that evolution (and science more generally) only ever causes theology to retreat because it forces revisions to traditionally held beliefs. But as we saw in the first three chapters, the relationships between science and theology are more complex than that. We conclude this chapter by highlighting aspects of evolution which can help us recover better and more accurate theology.

4. Consonance between evolution and Christianity

It is difficult to posit a straightforward reading of Christian theology out of nature as natural theologians have sometimes tried to do. It is widely claimed that Darwin dealt a deathblow to natural theology. The apparent design we observe in nature does not point unambiguously toward a creator's intentions and providence as once assumed. We might appreciate the beauty and intricacy of nature, which could lead us to delight in God's provision for all of creation. But there is also a shadow side to creation with its pain and suffering which seems to count against the goodness of God.

Even with this picture of nature, some Christian theologians are able to hear the resonances of traditional Christian theology by adopting the perspective of a theology of nature. As opposed to natural theology, which attempts to derive theological conclusions from scientific premises, a theology of nature begins with theological commitments and seeks to interpret scientific findings in a way that is consistent with them. So if we look at the pain and suffering in nature through the lenses of Christian theology—and the theology of the cross in particular— what we see is not as troubling. Lutheran theologian George Murphy says:

> If God is willing to share in the suffering and dying of creatures in order to bring about his purpose for creation, it should not surprise us that he created a world in which from the beginning death was part of the process that would lead creation to that goal. (Murphy 2014c, 5)

We consider further aspects of the problem of evil in greater detail in Chapter 12.

Christians might also claim that coming to understand the process of evolution helps to tune our minds to see God working patiently and through paths that involve suffering in order to bring about his purposes. Even the Young Earth Creationist has to admit that creation is a process. We see that the Hawaiian Islands are still being created through volcanic processes that add to the land there. God must not have said, "Let there be the Hawaiian Islands" and they appeared fully formed. The same is true of stars which are still being formed. And, of course, we can say the same of people. The more we learn about the natural order of things, the more we see God working through natural processes. God has created natural things with the capacity to further the creative process. If omnipotent, God could have created things—including all the people in the history of the world—in one fell swoop. But God seems to delight in the process of allowing things to come to be on their own terms. The created order has a dependency on God for its very existence, but God has granted it a degree of autonomy.

And yet, this is not a deistic God who sits back uninvolved watching the whole thing happen. The reality of convergent evolution allows us to see the process as one in which God is coaxing created things toward goals he has for creation. This teleological affirmation should not be interpreted in the sense of Intelligent Design, which sees God interrupting the natural course of events to achieve his purposes. Rather, in this sense God is seen as working through the natural causes. Evolution fits with this process nicely in broad terms. As we dig deeper, though, the question arises as to how we can understand God's role and action in relation to the scientific description of natural causes. This is the topic of the next chapter.

⋮≡ Summary of main points:

1. It is difficult to take the creation stories literally, but there are a variety of hermeneutical strategies for understanding them in light of science today.

2. The negative associations with randomness and species extinction can be mitigated to a degree by moving away from understanding God as an engineer and from essentialism.

3. The image of God can be understood in several ways, perhaps most consistently with evolution as a relational concept.

4. By adopting the perspective of a theology of nature, we can see consonances in evolution with Christian theology.

Further reading

- Alexander, Denis. 2012. "Creation and Evolution." In *The Blackwell Companion to Science and Christianity*, edited by J. B. Stump and Alan G. Padgett. Malden, MA: Wiley-Blackwell. A concise summary of the central issues today.
- Conway Morris, Simon. 2003. *Life's Solution: Inevitable Humans in a Lonely Universe*. Cambridge: Cambridge University Press. A scholarly work demonstrating that evolution has converged on similar solutions many times.
- Enns, Peter. 2012. *The Evolution of Adam: What the Bible Does and Doesn't Say about Human Origins*. Grand Rapids, MI: Brazos Press. A straightforward confrontation of the implications of evolutionary science for interpreting Scripture.
- Haught, John F. 2009. "God and Evolution." In *The Oxford Handbook of Religion and Science*, edited by Philip Clayton. Oxford Handbooks Online. An insightful piece about God's use of evolution in bringing about the diversity of life on earth.

References

Conway Morris, Simon. 2012. "Creation and Evolutionary Convergence." In *The Blackwell Companion to Science and Christianity*, edited by J. B. Stump and Alan G. Padgett. Malden, MA: Wiley-Blackwell.

Enns, Peter. 2012. *The Evolution of Adam: What the Bible Does and Doesn't Say about Human Origins*. Grand Rapids, MI: Brazos Press.

Gallup. 2014. "In U.S., 42% Believe Creationist View of Human Origins," http://www.gallup.com/poll/170822/believe-creationist-view-human-origins.aspx, accessed 17 February 2016.

Haught, John F. 2009. "God and Evolution." In *The Oxford Handbook of Religion and Science*, edited by Philip Clayton. Oxford Handbooks Online.

Hill Jonathan. 2014a. "The Recipe for Creationism," http://biologos.org/blog/the-recipe-for-creationism, accessed 17 February 2016.

Hill, Jonathan. 2014. "Rethinking the Origins Debate." *Christianity Today*, February 4.

Lamoureux, Denis O. 2008. *Evolutionary Creation: A Christian Approach to Evolution*. Eugene, OR: Wipf & Stock.

Moritz Joshua. 2014b. "Chosen by God," http://biologos.org/blog/series/chosen-by-god-biblical-election-and-the-imago-dei, accessed 17 February 2016.

Murphy George. 2014c. "Human Evolution in Theological Context," http://biologos.org/uploads/projects/murphy_scholarly_essay.pdf, accessed 17 February 2016.

Walton, John H. 2013. "A Historical Adam: Archetypal Creation View." In *Four Views on the Historical Adam*, edited by Matthew Barrett and Ardel Caneday. Grand Rapids, MI: Zondervan.

Wilberforce, Samuel. 1874. "Darwin's Origin of Species." In *Essays Contributed to the Quarterly Review*. London: John Murray.

CHAPTER 10

Divine Action

W e ended the last chapter with the question of how God works in and through natural causes to achieve his goals for the created order. This problem has been particularly acute since the Scientific Revolution around the 17th century, when there was a push to explain events in terms of their efficient causes. Since Aristotle, explanations were made in terms of four different kinds of causes. These are often illustrated by talking about a statue. Consider the statue *David*. If we ask for an explanation for the statue, Aristotle would say there are four different but complementary answers:

- The **efficient** cause of the statue is Michelangelo's chiseling the block of marble into the shape that it now has.
- The **material** cause of the statue is the substance that it is made—the marble—which provides some limitation to what it could be (we couldn't make an enduring statue out of butter).
- The **formal** cause of the statue is the kind of thing that it is; according to both Plato's and Aristotle's metaphysics, there are essences of things which determine the kind of thing an object can be.
- The **final** cause of the statue is the purpose for which it was made.

Science became so extraordinarily successful, at least in part, by limiting itself to efficient causes. Scientific explanations were deemed to be complete when the history of efficient causes for some thing or event was understood. The scientific explanation for the Grand Canyon only needs to appeal to the water over time that carved out the canyon. There is no thought in the modern scientific mindset of investigating what the final cause—the purpose—of the canyon might be. This limitation to efficient causes is what makes **divine action** such a difficult problem. There is no room in scientific explanations for the purposeful action of any agents—human or divine—so once we understand the efficient causes of something, our minds today are conditioned to think there is nothing else to say.

We begin this chapter by tracing some of the history of this mindset and then explore other frameworks of thought by which we might more fruitfully understand divine action.

Science and Christianity: An Introduction to the Issues, First Edition. By J. B. Stump.
© 2017 John Wiley & Sons, Ltd. Published 2017 by John Wiley & Sons, Ltd.

Questions to be addressed in this chapter:

1. Where did deism come from?
2. What are theological objections to miracles?
3. What is **non-interventionist objective divine action**?
4. How else might Christians understand divine action?

1. The development of deism

Prior to the Scientific Revolution, it made perfect sense to people to claim God worked in and through natural causes. The giant of medieval thought Thomas Aquinas said in his *Summa Theologica*:

> Divine providence works through intermediaries. For God governs the lower through the higher, not from any impotence on his part, but from the abundance of his goodness imparting to creatures also the dignity of causing. (*Summa* I.22.3; Christian Classics 2016)

And later:

> But since things which are governed should be brought to perfection by government, this government will be so much the better in the degree the things governed are brought to perfection. Now it is a greater perfection for a thing to be good in itself and also the cause of goodness in others, than only to be good in itself. Therefore God so governs things that He makes some of them to be causes of others in government; as a master, who not only imparts knowledge to his pupils, but gives also the faculty of teaching others. (I.103.6; ibid.)

This is the doctrine of **secondary causation**, and by it, it was legitimate to say that God caused an event, as well as to say that the event came about through natural causes.

In this way, it is legitimate to ascribe causality to God for everything insofar as God is the ground of being of all things. As such, God is the primary cause of all things. But then there are also events which have secondary causes in the agency of created beings. God created things which could be genuine causes themselves. Even now we might use this form of reasoning by saying an architect built a building, even though she didn't actually pour any of the concrete, lay the plumbing, or do any of the other tasks involved in the actual construction of the building. There were other people who did those things within the parameters she laid down. And it is even intelligible to say that the building didn't turn out exactly the way she planned, if some of the workers did not carry out her plans the way she intended.

The analogy to God's action in the world is obvious. But this Thomistic way of understanding divine action fell out of favor and created the problem we face today. A very influential thinker of the next generation developed an idea that precluded Thomas's double agency view. William of Ockham (c. 1287–1347) famously claimed that we should not multiply entities or explanations unnecessarily (the principle now known as **Ockham's razor**). What this did was to promote the view that once we understand how something works naturally, then it is no longer necessary or prudent to also appeal to God as an explanation for it. So either God did it or it came about through natural causes.

> ### Ockham's razor
>
> William of Ockham (c. 1287–1347) was a Franciscan theologian and philosopher. This doctrine that bears his name is generally taken to be the principle that the simplest explanation tends to be the correct one. That is to say, the razor "shaves away" unnecessary hypotheses. The closest statement of the principle in Ockham's works is "a plurality must never be posited without necessity" (Maurer 1999, 124)

After the Protestant Reformation, a popularizer of John Calvin's theology drove home this either/or impulse. William Perkins (1558–1602) had written a book called *A Golden Chain* in 1590. In it he created a diagram that divided all of theology into the two eternal decrees of God: election and reprobation. It showed how God's causal involvement in the world issues from his eternal decrees into an unbroken chain of cause and effect. This way of dichotomizing came to be known as **casuistry**, and it permeated the climate of thought from government, to morality, to science. It was the dominant way of thinking about problems in the English-speaking world. Its application in the natural world meant that scientists were allowed only two options: (1) phenomena occurred by the direct action of God or (2) phenomena occurred as the result of the laws of nature. There was no third alternative according to which God is active in and through natural causes (Poe and Davis 2012, 87–88).

Perkins was neither an original thinker nor an outstanding literary stylist, but he was able to translate into popular works the thinking of those who were, and these had tremendous influence on the English-speaking Calvinists of his day (Merrill 1966, xviii). His thought led directly to the intellectual environment in which deism flourished. At first, there were still plenty of gaps in the scientific understanding of the world that God seemed to be significantly involved in it operation. But when more of the science was understood, God was relegated to the role of setting things up in the beginning. For those who could not accept this absentee God, the only alternative was a miracle-working God who constantly broke the natural order of things by intervening and overriding laws (**episodic deism**). We must take some care of distinguishing this latter option from the Christian commitment to the possibility of miracles. That is the next topic.

2. Miracles

In the Bible, many of the "miracles" recorded are not necessarily events that contradict the laws of nature. Indeed, the question of breaking a law of nature was not at issue in their minds, for the strict dichotomy between the natural and supernatural is an element of our modern mindset, not theirs. Rather, the biblical

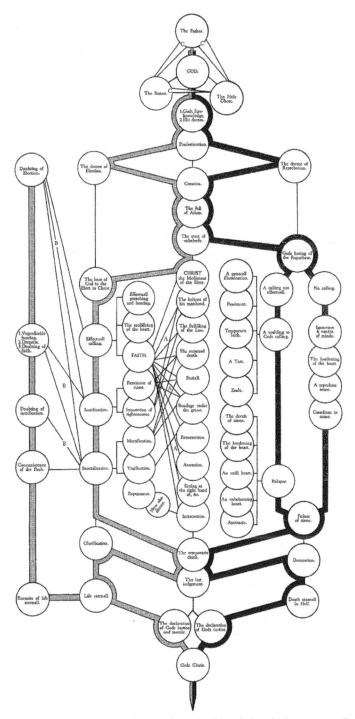

Fig. 10.1 William Perkin's diagram from *A Golden Chain*, which organizes all Christian doctrines according to Calvin's theology of election and reprobation.

authors were concerned with whether a "sign and wonder" was a true miracle or a false miracle—the former were signs of God's realm and reign; the latter were used by evil beings to lead people away from God (Matthew 24:24). So the issue for them was not breaking a law of nature, especially since that is a concept that does not map directly onto their concerns. But as we look back at their times, it is legitimate for us to consider their testimony about events that break what we know today to be laws of nature. How should Christians today think about the possibility of such occurrences?

Miracles are often thought to be incompatible with the modern scientific outlook. Twentieth-century liberal theologian Rudolf Bultmann is famous for having claimed:

> It is impossible to use electric light and the wireless and to avail ourselves of modern medical and surgical discoveries, and at the same time to believe in the New Testament world of spirits and miracles. (Bultmann 1972, 5)

The idea here is that we have come to understand the world well enough to manipulate it and produce modern technology; therefore, it would be inconsistent to think that the natural order does not always follow these laws we have discovered. More specifically, a scientific understanding of the world is thought to include the commitment that the universe is causally closed. That is to say, there is nothing external to the workings of the universe which could have effects on the objects and processes within the universe. Anglican theologian John Macquarrie explains:

> The traditional conception of miracle is irreconcilable with our modern understanding of both science and history. Science proceeds on the assumption that whatever events occur in the world can be accounted for in terms of other events that also belong within the world; and if on some occasions we are unable to give a complete account of some happening—and presumably all our accounts fall short of completeness—the scientific conviction is that further research will bring to light further factors in the situation, but factors that will turn out to be just as immanent and this-worldly as those already known. (Macquarrie 1977, 248)

So in this view, God's stepping in to the system of natural processes to perform some miracle, like changing water into wine, would constitute an intrusion and breaking of the laws of nature, and therefore is ruled out by a properly scientific outlook.

 Causal closure of the physical

An assumption of much scientific work is the causal closure of the physical. It states that every physical event has a physical explanation. That is to say, nothing from outside the physical, like supernatural intervention, can be the cause of any physical event. The usual understanding of a miracle breaks this principle.

But in Macquarrie's quotation, it is acknowledged that there is an assumption in this view: the **causal closure of the physical world**. The laws of nature as we've discovered them are descriptions of the way things go if they are not interfered with from outside the system. A person can't walk on water, and water doesn't turn to wine as we understand the properties of water. Those properties of water are determined by the nature of the molecules of H_2O. But if those molecules were manipulated somehow from outside the system of cause and effect we understand, then it is possible that water could have other properties.

By analogy, think of a chess game that progresses according to the normal rules. A player might find himself in a position where checkmate is imminent. But if someone functioning outside the rules of the game picked up his king and moved it across the board to another square, the king could be safe. The rules of chess don't allow such a thing, but obviously the rules of chess don't govern all of reality. In the same way, we might say that the rules of science don't allow water to be turned into wine, but who is to say that those rules govern all of reality? It is an assumption of science which is metaphysical or theological, and not a scientific conclusion. Perhaps God works outside of these normal rules from time to time.

There is another objection to the miraculous intervention of God based not on our understanding of science but on our moral intuitions. It is sometimes called the **Argument from Neglect** and goes something like this: there are actions we would expect a benevolent and powerful divine being to perform, like the relief of innocent suffering. But there are many instances of suffering where God does not intervene, so we conclude that either there is no God or God is incapable or unwilling to intervene in the natural order of things. Wesley Wildman compares this to a loving parent:

> When my children endanger themselves through their ignorance or willfulness, I do not hesitate as one trying to be a good father to intervene, to protect them from themselves, to teach them what they don't know, and thereby to help them become responsible people ... They do need to experience the effects of their choices, whether good or bad, but I would rightly be held negligent as a parent if I allowed them such freedom that they hurt themselves or others out of ignorance or misplaced curiosity or wickedness. (Quoted in Clayton and Knapp 2011, 45)

Wildman goes on to say that God, as traditionally understood, does not pass this test of moral responsibility. The gist of the argument is that if God can intervene sometimes, then it is reasonable for us to expect God to intervene in many other instances. Therefore, since God obviously doesn't intervene in those many other instances, it is not reasonable to think that God ever intervenes. One response to this objection is that we just don't know why God chooses to intervene in some instances and not others. We might chalk it up to the mystery of God and the claim that God's ways are not like our ways. Perhaps God has overriding reasons we don't understand now for not intervening in every instance we believe he should. We consider this line of response to the problem of evil in more detail in Chapter 12.

Another response to the Argument from Neglect is to say that if God did intervene in all of these instances then that would undermine the law-like regularity needed for the development of rational and autonomous agents like ourselves. Then it would be morally inconsistent for God to intervene just some of the time.

Using this line of reasoning, Clayton and Knapp conclude that God cannot intervene in the order of physical causality. But they remain open to God's intervention in the realm of the mind (Clayton and Knapp 2011, 44f.). We don't have space here to examine this fascinating argument, and merely conclude this section by noting that Christians do not all agree on the nature and extent of miraculous intervention. This isn't the only mode of divine action we need to consider; there is also what we might call the providential action of God, guiding the course of events in non-miraculous ways. We turn to this next.

3. Non-interventionist objective divine action

Robert Russell and John Polkinghorne are two of the major figures in the contemporary science and Christianity dialogue. Both have contributed significantly to discussions on divine action by finding a "causal joint" in the natural order within which God might act and make a difference in the outcome of events, yet without intervening in the sense of overriding natural law. Russell coined a term for this sort of action, calling it "non-interventionist, objective divine action" (NIODA). It is objective action (rather than subjective) in the sense that there are events that would not have happened the way they did if God had not acted in a special or distinct way. Divine action is non-interventionist if the events the action brings about go beyond what can be described by natural laws but do not contravene those laws (Russell 2008, 580–583).

In order for there to be NIODA, then, nature must be such that science can identify necessary conditions for some events, but not sufficient conditions. That is to say, there must be at least some natural processes that can be legitimately described as indeterminate. From the perspective of science, then, a complete description of the initial conditions of some systems and a comprehensive knowledge of the natural laws are still insufficient for us to predict with 100% accuracy later states of these kinds of systems.

For Russell, the conditions for NIODA are satisfied by nondeterministic interpretations of quantum physics. According to the Copenhagen interpretation (the most popular among physicists, but not the only interpretation), events at the quantum level are genuinely random. It is not just that we don't understand what other hidden variables there might be but that we know there cannot be any hidden variables. As such, the equations describing quantum states can give only a range of possibilities or potentials for the quantum system. There is no sufficient cause for these events from the perspective of science. God's action, then, takes the form of realizing one of these potential outcomes. This action does not break any laws of nature, because, according to the equations, the realized outcome was one of the possibilities that might occur. So God's action works within the limits of natural laws but remains hidden from scientific analysis.

One of the questions put to Russell is whether this sort of action at the quantum level has any effect on macroscopic events. Ordinarily, we understand that the probabilities at the quantum level even out on larger scales so that macroscopic events like the orbit of a comet around the sun are predictable. It wouldn't do any good for God to have influence at the quantum level if that doesn't affect the course of events on our scale. But Russell claims that events at the quantum level do account for the kind of general providence we associate with God's action in the world. He claims that it is the statistics associated with electrons, protons, photons, and other quantum level entities that give rise to the properties of matter described by physics, chemistry, and biology (ibid., 590). One of the particularly fascinating possibilities in this regard is whether the "random" mutations of DNA might be guided by God's action at the quantum level. If so, we could legitimately speak of God intentionally creating human beings (and other species) even though scientific analyses of the development of our species would only ever detect random processes.

John C. Polkinghorne (b. 1930)

One of the three "scientist theologians" (along with Ian Barbour and Arthur Peacocke) who have been among the most significant figures in turning science and religion into an academic discipline. Polkinghorne started his career as a physicist at the University of Cambridge where he researched elementary particles and contributed to the discovery of quarks. In 1979, he resigned his position and entered seminary to train as a priest in the Anglican Church, after which he wrote important books on science and Christianity. He gave the prestigious Gifford Lectures in 1993–1994, which became his book *The Faith of A Physicist* (1994), and was awarded the Templeton Prize in 2002.

Fig. 10.2 John C. Polkinghorne.

John Polkinghorne's view is similar to Russell's, but instead of locating the causal joint in nature within quantum events Polkinghorne suggests that we might find this in chaotic processes. In this technical sense, chaotic systems are those which are so sensitive to initial conditions and the slightest environmental disturbances that their future states cannot be calculated with accuracy. This phenomenon is sometimes called the **butterfly effect** because of the title of a paper in 1972 by Edward Lorenz called, "Predictability: Does the Flap of a Butterfly's Wings in Brazil Set off a Tornado in Texas?" The idea is that large-scale phenomena can be influenced by very small-scale events. An interesting example of this is the double pendulum, the motion of which turns unpredictable very quickly (YouTube 2007).

Ordinarily, chaotic processes are taken to be deterministic. We have an epistemological limitation in that we don't know with enough precision the initial conditions, and therefore we can't predict the future states of these systems. But Polkinghorne thinks there could be an ontological undeterminedness in chaotic systems. He says that the deterministic mathematics we use to describe these systems might just be an abstraction or ideal representation of what in reality is a more flexible and open structure. Then, if there really are indeterminacies in these chaotic systems, then God could fix specific outcomes that are recognized as possibilities by the physical laws without intervening and breaking those laws. And because **chaos theory** itself recognizes that subtle differences can give rise to significant effects, God can influence the course of events.

The German theologian and physicist Lydia Jaeger objects to Russell's and Polkinghorne's ways of introducing divine action into the natural order. She notes that in quantum systems, because the indeterminacy is objective—the states really are not determined—not even an omnipotent being could determine the values without violating the quantum mechanical laws (Jaeger 2012, 298). And for chaotic systems, something seems fundamentally wrong to her about using science to develop the highly successful understanding of the deterministic picture of the world, only to dismiss it in an ad hoc fashion in order to squeeze God into the picture (ibid., 298–299).

The goal of the Russell and Polkinghorne models seems correct: to give a description of God's continuous action in the world while acknowledging the law-like character of the natural order that science has discovered and described. According to Jaeger, though, these proposals continue to treat God's action as just another of the causes within the natural order—a part of the chain of efficient causality with which scientists deal. But doing this succumbs to scientism—the ideology that claims the scientific mode of explanation is the only legitimate kind of explanation. So long as we operate within this framework, Jaeger claims that there can be no solution to the problem of divine action.

Also, while there may be an appearance that this God who interacts with the world through causal joints does not intervene, this does not turn out to be the case. It is a different kind of intervention than a God who constantly breaks natural laws. But this "non-interventionist" God does in fact intervene into the causal structure of the world: the very definition of NIODA asserts that if God had not acted, then the course of things would have been different. This understanding of the situation forces us to see things in the same dichotomized way that Perkins thrust upon us: either nature is left to itself to produce a certain effect or God does something to change the way nature would have gone. This is one of the difficulties of attempting to locate God's action within the causal order discovered by science.

Furthermore, it is difficult to see how that approach does not collapse into the deist or semi-deist view of God's action. On Russell's view, does God determine the outcomes of all quantum events or just some of them? If the former, then how would we escape the implication that God completely determines every event? If the latter, then as Aubrey Moore noted in the late 19th century, "a theory of occasional intervention implies as its correlative a theory of ordinary absence" (Moore 1905, 184). That results in a form of deism. The same line of reasoning would apply to Polkinghorne's model as well.

> "The one absolutely impossible conception of God, in the present day, is that which represents him as an occasional visitor. Science has pushed the deist's God further and further away, and at the moment when it seemed as if he would be thrust out altogether Darwinism appeared, and under the disguise of a foe, did the work of a friend. It has conferred upon philosophy and religion an inestimable benefit, by showing us that we must choose between two alternatives. Either God is everywhere present in nature, or he is nowhere." (Moore 1891, 73)

It seems that any approach which aims to give a scientifically acceptable account of divine action will suffer the same difficulties. The problem with this method is that God becomes just one of the (efficient) causal factors alongside and competing with the natural causes. This is ultimately a reductionist picture of the world. If we're interested in finding a more theologically satisfying version, we need to look at divine action in a radically different way. Jaeger thinks that the problem of divine action is dissolved when we understand that descriptions of God's action belong to a different aspect of reality. We consider such an approach in the next section.

4. Alternatives for explaining divine action

Christians who accept that the natural world is God's creation have a different starting point for considering divine action. They shouldn't begin with an acceptance of the world as described by physics and then attempt to fit God's action into that picture. Instead, Jaeger claims, the starting point for Christians should be the duality of Creator and creation (Jaeger 2012, 304). In that picture of the world, the created order is entirely dependent upon, and owes its origin and continued existence to, the gracious action of God. In God's providential action, the laws of nature are seen as a description of God's continued faithful action in bringing about his will. The fact that we can use both the language of physics and the language of theology in describing God's providential action does not mean that physics and theology are one and the same (or that one is reducible to the other). Rather, it points to the fact that there are different levels or aspects of reality, and these cannot be reduced to each other.

Polkinghorne himself points to such a conception with his famous example of the boiling kettle. He asks us to consider the kinds of explanations that could be given for why a teakettle is boiling (Polkinghorne 1995). The physicist might give an explanation in terms of the closed electrical circuit with such and such resistance in the heating element of the stove, and this conveys heat to the bottom of the kettle, which in turn causes the water molecules to move more rapidly within the kettle; the increasingly rapid motion of the molecules eventually becomes sufficient to push the vapor pressure of the water higher than the atmospheric pressure, and the water boils. That is a perfectly legitimate and scientifically complete explanation. We don't have to appeal to anything outside of natural laws to explain that process.

But we might also give an explanation for the same event on another level. For it is also a correct explanation of the situation to say that the kettle is boiling because my wife wants a cup of tea! This second kind of explanation is what we might call a personal explanation. It appeals to a different sort of reality—the reality of persons who are not reducible to the laws of physics—and provides an explanation in terms more appropriate to that reality. If God is a personal being as Christian creeds attest, then it is perfectly legitimate to explore that personal aspect of reality in theological terms while at the same time encouraging others to explore the level of description more appropriate to the fundamental laws and forces of nature. And just as the two explanations for the teakettle boiling are not in conflict, neither are scientific and theological explanations of an event in conflict.

Some might criticize this approach as succumbing to the Independence thesis discussed in Chapter 1, in which science and theology have no common ground. The most popular version of this was Stephen Jay Gould's "non-overlapping magisteria" approach in which science is kept separate from theology by relegating them to studying different objects: science to the empirical world, theology to values. But there is an important difference in the approach being commended in this chapter: scientific explanations and personal (or theological) explanations are talking about the same thing, just appealing to different aspects of it.

We might also consider an artist and chemist who are both examining a portrait of a person. In describing the portrait, the artist would talk about the shading and perspective of the setting, as well as the mood and facial features of the subject. The chemist would use a very different vocabulary to describe the composition of the paint itself. There is no room in chemical analysis to refer to a person's face. Of course, the existence of a face in the portrait is certainly dependent on the chemical properties of the paint, but when talking as an artist, it is the face that is the really existing entity.

It might be objected that ultimately the artist's terms and concepts can be reduced to the chemical properties of the paint: the face is really just a certain configuration of molecules that have certain light-reflecting properties. This kind of objection is, in a nutshell, the crux of the problem of understanding the action of any agent. For if we follow the reductionist strategy, then the only real entities are those of physics; everything else we talk about is merely a convention. It is easier to say "tree" than to give the scientific description of its particles and subatomic processes. The same goes for agents (both human and divine): such words refer only to fictions that worked their way into our language through our ignorance of the real causes of things. When we understand the science, such concepts are no longer needed. That is less an argument, though, and more a restatement of the assumption that the only kind of explanation that is real is a scientific explanation, the only kind of cause that counts is the efficient cause. Still, there continues to be the challenge of describing agent causation (and in particular for this chapter, divine action) in ways that are intelligible and persuasive.

British theologian Christopher Knight thinks that the Eastern tradition of Christianity has resources more suitable to this sort of explanation. In the West, the realm of nature became separated from the realm of grace. That is to say, nature was emptied of its theological significance, and it became an independent order of natural causes which needs no divine cooperation in order to operate. The natural theologians attempted to find theological significance in that order of things (see Chapter 7), but it became increasingly possible to see only natural, regularly occurring processes and entities there which needed no divine intervention. The natural theologians attempted to ground the idea of the supernatural in this conception of nature, but neither their concept of nature nor the concept of the supernatural which emerged from it had much to do with the Judeo-Christian tradition (Dupré 1999). And so for the West there are two different realms—the natural and the supernatural—which remain unconnected except through interventions, thus the problem of divine action.

In the East, theologians saw the situation somewhat differently. There was no separation of natural from supernatural. The Logos described in John's gospel was not absent from the created order until the Incarnation. All of creation was imbued with the Logos: "all that came to be was alive with his life" (John 1:3–4). And it is not as though the coming of Christ drained the Logos out of creation. Rather, the Incarnation of the Son was the completion of a process that was begun in creation. In a sense, the Incarnation was a sign of what the created order was intended to be. It is in the West where deism is a constant threat, for God seems to stand outside of the created order, completely transcendent and unneeded for the workings of the world; and then divine action is a problem. But the theologians of the East, while still acknowledging that God is more than nature, see God as immanent or indwelling of all nature. "Creation is not something upon which God acts from the exterior, but something through which he expresses himself from within" (Ware 2004, 159).

On this view, the drama of creation is one of unfolding. God did not create the world fully formed, but it is bursting with potential. The fact that the potential is not realized right now is to recognize the created order as "fallen." Science describes the current state of creation and the way it works in laws of nature, but these are statements about the way it behaves in this less-than-mature state. When something "miraculous" happens (perhaps the origin of life and of consciousness are possible candidates for this), it might not be explainable according to these provisional natural laws. But those are not the laws of the "natural" state that is to come. Miracles are the breaking through of the age that is to come. Christopher Knight explains the view as follows:

> [The miraculous] may be seen not—as Western theologians have tended to think—as the product of some kind of divine interference with the world, but rather as the outward manifestation in this world of something that is already present but hidden within it: what we can properly call its "natural" state. The miraculous is not, in this perspective, the result of something being added to the world. It is, rather, the wiping away from that world of the grime of its fallen state, in order to reveal it in its pristine splendor. (Knight 2007, 93)

Knight's position is that God's action permeates nature, but God's desires for creation are often thwarted by its current fallen state (what he calls its "subnatural" state). Where God's kingdom is manifested—most significantly around the person of Jesus Christ, but also when his followers act according to his will—we see the "natural" state coming to the surface.

So, the miraculous aspect of divine action is resolved, according to this view, as those actions which are truly the way the created order is designed to work. And the providential aspect of divine action is understood as the way nature works. The unfolding of creation—the development of solar systems, planets, plants, animals, humans—is the doing of God. We can study this scientifically and understand lots of things about it; we can also talk about it theologically and understand other things about it. These two kinds of explanations (like the efficient and final causes, or the scientific and personal explanations) don't cancel each other out, but complement each other.

There are two further topics suggested by this discussion: the problem of evil is brought to the fore when we claim that the unfolding of creation and all its nastiness is God's doing; we'll need to examine this in more detail. But first there is another issue that science and Christianity both have relevant perspectives on, and we're not always sure how they fit together: the human person. We turn to it in the next chapter.

 Summary of main points:

1. When Ockham and Perkins popularized a way of dichotomizing things so that events could be ascribed either to nature or to God but not both, scientific explanation ruled out God's involvement.

2. It is argued by some that God should not, or even cannot, break the laws of nature.

3. Russell and Polkinghorne attempt to show how God could affect the course of nature without breaking any laws of nature.

4. Eastern theologians emphasize the immanence of God in nature and thus understand the workings of nature as what God does.

Further reading

- Harris, Mark. 2013. *The Nature of Creation: Examining the Bible and Science.* Durham: Acumen. A recent book which reads the biblical creation accounts in light of modern science.
- Knight, Christopher. 2007. *The God of Nature: Incarnation and Contemporary Science.* Minneapolis: Fortress Press. Suggests insightful ways of dealing with divine action inspired by Eastern Orthodox thinking.
- Padgett, Alan G. 2012. "God and Miracle in an Age of Science." In *The Blackwell Companion to Science and Christianity*, edited by J. B. Stump and Alan G. Padgett. Malden, MA: Wiley-Blackwell. A concise treatment of miracles and the challenge science presents to them.

References

Bultmann, Rudolf. 1972. *Kerygma and Myth: A Theological Debate*, edited by W. H. Bartsch. London: SPCK.

Christian Classics. 2016. "Summa Theologica," http://www.ccel.org/ccel/aquinas/summa.toc.html, accessed 17 February 2016.

Clayton, Philip, and Steven Knapp. 2011. *The Predicament of Belief: Science, Philosophy, Faith*. Oxford: Oxford University Press.

Dupré, Louis. 1999. "Secular Philosophy and Its Origins at the Dawn of the Modern Age." In *The Question of Christian Philosophy Today*, edited by Francis J. Ambrosio. New York: Fordham University Press.

Jaeger, Lydia. 2012. Against Physicalism-Plus-God: How Creation Accounts for Divine Action in Nature's World. *Faith and Philosophy*, 29(3): 295–312.

Knight, Christopher C. 2007. *The God of Nature: Incarnation and Contemporary Science*. Minneapolis: Fortress Press.

Lorenz Edward. 1972. "Predictability: Does the Flap of a Butterfly's Wings in Brazil Set Off a Tornado in Texas?", http://eaps4.mit.edu/research/Lorenz/Butterfly_1972.pdf, accessed 17 February 2016.

Macquarrie, John. 1977. *Principles of Christian Theology*, 2nd ed. New York: Charles Scribner's Sons.

Maurer, Armand A., ed. 1999. *The Philosophy of William of Ockham in the Light of His Principles*. Toronto: Pontifical Institute of Mediaeval Studies.

Merrill, Thomas F., ed. 1966. *William Perkins 1558–1602: English Puritanist*. Nieuwkoop: B. De Graaf.

Moore, A. L. 1891. "The Christian Doctrine of God." In *Lux Mundi*, 12th ed. edited by Charles Gore. London: John Murray.

Moore, A. L. 1905. *Science and the Faith: Essays on Apologetic Subjects*, 6th ed. London: Kegan Paul, Trench, Trübner & Co.

Poe, Harry Lee, and Jimmy H. Davis. 2012. *God and the Cosmos: Divine Activity in Space, Time and History*. Downers Grove, IL: IVP Academic.

Polkinghorne, John. 1994. *The Faith of a Physicist: Reflections of a Bottom-Up Thinker*. Princeton, NJ: Princeton University Press.

Polkinghorne, John. 1995. "Is Science Enough?" *Sewanee Theological Review*, 39: 11–26.

Russell, Robert John. 2008. "Quantum Physics and the Theology of Non-Interventionist Objective Divine Action." In *The Oxford Handbook of Religion and Science*, edited by Philip Clayton and Zachary Simpson. Oxford: Oxford University Press.

Ware, Kallistos. 2004. "God Immanent Yet Transcendent: The Divine Energies According to Saint Gregory Palamas." In *In Whom We Live and Move and Have Our Being: Panentheistic Reflections on God's Presence in a Scientific World*, edited by Philip Clayton and Arthur Peacock. Grand Rapids, MI: Eerdmans.

YouTube. 2007. "Double Pendulum," https://www.youtube.com/watch?v=U39R-MUzCjiU, accessed 17 February 2016.

CHAPTER 11

Mind, Soul, and Brain

A report from 2003 in the *Archives of Neurology* tells the case of a 40-year-old man who suddenly started collecting child pornography and having pedophiliac urges that he couldn't suppress. He even started making advances toward his stepdaughter until his wife alerted the authorities and he was arrested. The man was given the choice of going to prison or completing a rehab program for sexual predators. He desperately wanted to avoid prison, but just couldn't make it through the program without continuing his behavior. On the night before he was to be sentenced, he went to the emergency room with a severe headache. They found a large tumor growing in the orbital frontal area of his brain. Evidently, 16 years earlier he had sustained a head injury and lost consciousness for about two minutes, but without any other effects—they thought at the time. In December of 2000, they removed the tumor; he completed the rehabilitation program, and in a few months he was back living normally with his family. Then two months later he started having headaches again, and had started secretly collecting pornography again. He checked himself back into the hospital; they discovered the tumor had starting growing again. It was removed and again led to the elimination of the behavior (Burns and Swerdlow 2003).

Situations like this are troubling to us when we reflect on the nature of human beings, for they highlight two different and seemingly incompatible intuitions we have about ourselves. On the one hand, we think of human beings as something very different from the natural world. Beginning with our firsthand experience of our own mental lives, and reasonably extending that to others as well, we believe that there is something different about us from rocks, trees, frogs, and even other mammals. We are persons who are self-aware; this "self" is free and responsible; we are motivated by reasons (not just desires). But secondly, we can conceive of human beings as part of the natural world—perhaps beginning with an account like that of the unfortunate man described above, and understanding that similar issues could apply to ourselves as well. Our bodies (and brains) are composed of matter that follows natural law; it is the same matter as everything else in the world is composed of; we can influence our mental lives with drugs.

Science and Christianity: An Introduction to the Issues, First Edition. By J. B. Stump.
© 2017 John Wiley & Sons, Ltd. Published 2017 by John Wiley & Sons, Ltd.

These two images of ourselves—classically called the "manifest" image and the "scientific" image (Sellars 1963)—are very difficult to square with each other. It is easy for most people to feel some sympathy for the man described and to believe that he was not altogether responsible for his behavior. It is not as easy to see that once we start down that path we may have to put our own feelings about that man into the same category: are they too caused by material processes outside of our control? As we learn more and more about the brain, does this undermine the conception we have of ourselves as free and responsible persons? This chapter does not aim to be a thorough introduction to the discipline philosophers call the **philosophy of mind**. Instead, it aims to address a few of the relevant issues related to our view of ourselves from the perspectives of science and of Christian theology. We begin with some consideration of the classical Christian understanding of the soul and its relationship to the human person.

> **? Questions to be addressed in this chapter:**
>
> 1. What has been the traditional Christian thinking on the soul?
> 2. What is Descartes' version of dualism?
> 3. What are the challenges to dualism?
> 4. How does cognitive dualism help in thinking about persons?

1. The Christian tradition of the soul

One of the common characteristics found in most religions (though not all) is a belief in life after death. Certainly for traditional forms of Christianity there is the hope of some sort of continued conscious existence after this life is over. It is not a kind of reincarnation in which I "come back" as something different and have no recollection (or only a fuzzy memory) of my previous life. Rather, there is the expectation of continuity for my conscious awareness. Perhaps that awareness is interrupted for a time, as it is by sleeping, but nonetheless according to this expectation I should be aware of the fact that I am the same person who previously had died. How could this be? What kind of thing must I be in order to have continued conscious existence after my current life has ended? The problem here is what philosophers have called **personal identity**: what is it that makes me the same person across time? We might ask the question in a completely nonreligious context about the passage of time in this life: in what sense am I the same person now as I was when I was a toddler? But for Christians, the more urgent question concerns my transition from this life to the next: in what sense am I the same person now as I will be in the afterlife?

A typical answer to this question from the Christian tradition has been that there is a soul associated with each of us, and it is the soul that remains the same over time and across death. Just what Christians mean by "soul," however, is not always clear and consistent. Appeal to particular passages of Scripture is not always helpful, because it does not appear that all of the biblical authors (spanning several cultures and many centuries) had the same view of the soul. It is fair to say that in the Old Testament there is a more consistent picture that the soul is identified with the human person, rather than it being a separable part of us. This way of speaking was reflected in English a generation or two ago when it might have been said, "There are 27 souls in the room." But it should also be noted that in the Old Testament there was a much less pronounced expectation of survival after death or even of resurrection (Wright 2003, 85). As Judeo-Christian thinking about the afterlife developed, though, there also developed ways of thinking about how our existence now is related to it in the afterlife.

In the New Testament, Jesus tells a parable about a rich man and a beggar named Lazarus who both died. They seemed to have an immediate conscious existence after their death—the beggar was carried away by angels to be with Abraham; the rich man was buried and subsequently tormented in Hades (Luke 16:19–31). Also, as they were both dying, Jesus said to the thief on the cross who defended him, "Today you will be with me in Paradise" (Luke 23:43). Such passages give support to people who think that bodies are an inessential part of the human person, which can be discarded at death while the soul lives on. Others, however, think such an understanding of the soul is more representative of Greek thinking than "biblical" thinking. It was Plato who claimed that the body is a prison for the soul, and even though Christian Platonists like St Augustine articulated their theology in those terms, it is not representative of the scriptural witness as a whole or of all Christian tradition.

There is another important strand of the Christian tradition about the relationship between body and soul that comes through Thomas Aquinas. He was significantly influenced by Aristotle and the conception that the soul is the form of the body. That is to say, the soul is not some separately existing substance in addition to the body but rather a kind of conceptual entity that makes something what it is. As such, there are vegetable souls, animal souls, and the rational souls of humans. Aristotle famously argued against his teacher Plato that forms like these do not exist independently of the matter in which they are instantiated. Aquinas's Christian theology pushed him to admit that a soul could exist without the body—like the souls in Purgatory—by a special act of God; but these were not fully human, and that could only be a temporary state.

The weight of the New Testament witness seems to speak more in line with Aquinas's version. Most significantly, the goal of the Christian according to the Apostle Paul is not some kind of disembodied existence when the soul leaves the body but rather resurrection of the body itself. His experience on the Damascus Road (Acts 9) convinced him that Jesus had resurrected from the dead, and he argued that what had happened to Jesus would happen to all of Christ's followers at the end of times (1 Corinthians 15). Furthermore, the book of Revelation does not portray the ultimate destiny of human beings as one where we are whisked off to an ethereal existence in a heaven in the clouds; instead, the heavenly realm comes to earth and is established here in material existence (Revelation 21).

In popular culture today (which in America considers itself Christian), there is a very different understanding of the soul and the afterlife. A spate of books on after-death experiences reinforces the view that when people die they leave their bodies behind and inhabit a peaceful, immaterial world that smiles down on us who are still living. There are resonances of this view with the Platonic version mentioned above, but in the next section we'll see it has more to do with the views of René Descartes.

2. Descartes and dualism

Descartes' philosophical project was driven by the attempt to set Christian theology on firmer foundations than faith. He thought he could prove with the certainty of reason that God exists and that we humans have immortal souls. In order to do this, he began by doubting everything that could possibly be doubted, and ultimately this method of doubt concluded with the one absolute certainty, "I think, therefore I am." He claimed that even if everything else he believed was mistaken, he was still thinking and aware of his thinking, and therefore he must exist. His argument from this certain foundation to the traditional Christian doctrines of God and the soul were not widely accepted, but his formulation of the priority of our own consciousness was very influential.

There are two important implications of Descartes' work. First, he collapsed the distinctions that had been made between soul and mind (and perhaps even heart and spirit). These had been seen not so much as separable parts of the human person as aspects to a person's life. But then in Descartes' understanding, all of those aspects became functions of one thing—the mind—and its primary attribute: thinking. He claimed himself to be first and foremost a thinking thing. That was the very nature or essence of humanity. Secondly, according to Descartes, that thinking thing—the mind—was a very different thing than his body, for the nature of body was like all other matter: extended in space. So because he had such a clear and distinct idea of mind and body as different kinds of things and because he was to be identified with his mind, it must be the case that he was something distinct from his body. The famous passage from his *Meditations* is as follows:

> From the fact that I know that I exist, and at the same time I judge that obviously nothing else belongs to my nature or essence except that I am a thinking thing, I rightly conclude that my essence consists entirely in my being a thinking thing. And although perhaps (or rather, as I shall soon say, assuredly) I have a body that is very closely joined to me, nevertheless, because on the one hand I have a clear and distinct idea of myself, insofar as I am merely a thinking thing and not an extended thing, and because on the other hand I have distinct idea of a body, insofar as it is merely an extended thing and not a thinking thing, it is certain that I am really distinct from my body, and can exist without it. (*Meditation Six*; Descartes 1998, 50)

What Descartes did was not so much to set orthodox Christian theology on firmer ground as to develop and cement into public consciousness Plato's view of the body and soul. There are two different kinds of substance—mind and body—and the true self is the immaterial mind. Descartes understood that the mind and brain had to interact; there are physical substances that can affect the operation of the mind (like too much alcohol), and the mind through its choices must be able to direct the operations of the body. Descartes is often heckled for postulating that the locus of interaction between mind and brain occurred in the pineal gland of the brain—a gland that he had not detected in the brains of other animals. Of course, such a postulation solves nothing of the conceptual difficulties of how the two kinds of substances interact.

In its defense, his view gives a quick and easy resolution to the problem of the two conceptions of ourselves: our bodies (including our brains) are part of the natural world and work just like other matter does; our souls/minds are a different kind of substance: they are immaterial and account for the parts of our existence that defy material explanation. Popular culture today—in both its Christian and secular guise—seems permeated with the view that when a person dies their body decays but their true self goes off to heaven forever more.

> **Incarnation**   [in-kahr-**ney**-shuhn]
> The state of being flesh. The theological doctrine that Jesus Christ, the second person of the Trinity, became human.

There are theological considerations, though, that make the identification of the soul with the mind problematic. Consider the Incarnation: Jesus Christ is held to be fully God and fully human, and this—like the Trinity—is one of the fundamental mysteries of the Christian faith. But if we accept Descartes' substance dualist explanation of the person, the problems with understanding the Incarnation are exacerbated. In the 3rd century, the church father Tertullian held that a complete human—both body and mind—came to be inhabited by the divine Logos or mind, resulting in two distinct minds in the person of Jesus. Later fathers worried that such an explanation amounts merely to God indwelling or coming alongside a human like he had done with the prophets, rather than really becoming a human. While the **two-minds view** seems to cause a kind of psychological disunity by which Jesus would have to constantly juggle and flip-flop between his human mind and his divine mind, there are contemporary defenders of the model (e.g., Morris 2001).

The other option for explaining the human personhood of Christ on the dualist view is to follow the path of Apollinaris of Laodicea (310–390). He aimed to avoid the disunity of the two-minds view by explaining Christ's humanity and divinity as there being a divine mind put into a human body. But this **Apollinarianism** was ultimately condemned at the Council of Constantinople in 381 because it made Christ something less than fully human—he didn't have a human mind, so how could he be fully human? If the human mind is a separate substance from the body, then it becomes very difficult to see how Christ could be a complete human as well as having a divine mind.

Despite these difficulties, there are plenty of sophisticated Christian thinkers today who defend a version of **substance dualism**. In a way reminiscent of Descartes, Stuart Goetz argues that through introspection we can clearly see that we—that is our souls—are simple substances that have no parts. Material things, on the other hand, are complex things that are made of parts. So he gives what he calls the "Simple Argument" for dualism:

1. I (my soul) am (is) essentially a simple entity (I have no substantive parts).
2. My body is essentially a complex entity (my body has substantive parts).
3. If "two" entities are identical, then whatever is a property of the one is a property of the other.
4. Therefore, because I have an essential property that my body lacks, I am not identical with my body. (Goetz 2005, 44)

Given that substance dualism seems to fit with what the majority of human beings across cultures believe about themselves, Goetz thinks the burden of proof is on non-dualists to show that they have models that account better for human personhood. We turn to some of the challenges in the next section.

3. Challenges to dualism

There are some philosophical arguments against dualism. One is that positing an immaterial substance needlessly multiplies the kinds of substances there are in the world. Shouldn't the simplicity demand of Ockham's razor force us to keep from claiming there is a completely different kind of stuff in the universe than the material particles that everything else is made of? For Christians, this argument is not too powerful because they already accept that there are immaterial substances, namely God (and perhaps angels and demons). These are thought to have mental lives of some sort—they have beliefs and desires—yet are not composed of matter. So it could be argued that Ockham's razor works the other way: Christians already believe there are immaterial substances capable of rational thought, so we shouldn't posit another kind of substance that also is supposed to function that way.

Another objection against dualism is that an immaterial substance doesn't really seem capable of explaining what we want explained. Specifically, how can an immaterial substance account for our free will, capacity for using reason, and so forth any better than a material substance could? Philosopher Colin McGinn says, "Indeed, it is arguable that it is only our incapacity to form a clear idea of such a substance that induces us to suppose that locating mental phenomena in it is any advance on monism" (McGinn 1996, 25). It could be argued, though, that we see clearly that a material object is incapable of allowing for the manifest image we have of human persons. True, we can't give an explanation for how these things work for an immaterial object, but neither can we say it is obvious that they wouldn't work there.

Monism [**moh**-niz-uhm]
Any doctrine that attributes an underlying oneness to apparent multiplicity. In the philosophy of mind, monism is the theory that there is only one kind of entity that makes up human beings.

These objections might have some force, but the central conceptual problem with substance dualism is understanding how an immaterial mind could interact with the material body. Descartes' attempt at addressing this was mentioned earlier and dismissed as wrong-headed. We can't understand how this process might work by positing a special material structure as the place where interaction happens. The difficulty is that our demand for explanation typically comes in terms of how we understand material processes. We want explanations to detail the efficient causes (see discussion of causes in Chapter 10) for some event, like for what made me raise my arm when the call was made for "nay" votes. We can say that my arm went up because the relevant muscles were activated by electrical impulses coming through the nervous system, and that those electrical impulses came from the brain; but how did the brain generate them? Dualists maintain that my mind made a decision, and that is what "caused" the signals in the brain and to the arm.

Critics raise two objections: (1) How does a "decision" affect the material processes of the brain? There is no answer to that. And (2) science will push further to demand an explanation for the decision. Where did it come from? But as soon as we try to explain the decision, we're transported into a different mode of explanation: now we give reasons instead of efficient causes. I decided to vote "no" because I thought the proposal was a bad idea, etc. The **problem of interaction** between mind and brain is fundamentally a problem of how to translate between these two kinds of explanations, which is a restatement of the central problem of this chapter: we have two different views of ourselves—the scientific and the manifest.

One way of addressing this problem is through science alone. Can we show that the decision and the other elements of the manifest image are really just parts of a complicated material system in the brain? If so, then there is no interaction problem, and we can keep looking for material explanations of the decision. Science has done this kind of thing before. Thunder and lightning were once thought to be the result of angry gods fighting in the heavens, but now they are shown to be the results of weather patterns that we have come to understand and predict. If we could perform a similar reduction on the mental activities of the mind (choosing, valuing, reasoning, etc.), the interaction problem would be dissolved. Beliefs in immaterial minds would go the way of beliefs in the ancient Greek or Norse gods.

It must be acknowledged that we've made a lot of progress on this front. The advances of neuroscience in the last couple of decades are enormous. Researchers are now able to use magnetic and positron scanning to identify patterns of neural activity that are correlated with various mental tasks. Especially when compared to brain scans of stroke victims with damaged sections of the brain, such studies have been able to identify specific regions of the brain that "light up" when the people being studied do various things. Activity in one part of the cerebral cortex increases when people perform simple language tasks like supplying appropriate verbs for given nouns. Another area of the cerebral cortex is more active when a person listens to someone else talking. Different patterns of activity are displayed for mathematical problems and planning actions. The conclusion of this by researchers is that "different forms of rational thought are due to different patterns of brain activity" (Brown and Strawn 2012, 32).

For a while there was talk about a "God spot" on the brain which was correlated with spiritual experiences. The activity in Buddhist monks' brains was recorded while they were meditating, and increased activity in the front of the brain was consistently found. Subsequent studies suggest that spirituality may be linked to the decrease in brain activity in the right parietal lobe (Johnstone et al. 2012). Normally, the right parietal lobe is correlated with thoughts focused on oneself. The suggestion is that when people think less about themselves they are more open to emotional connection with the numinous or mystical.

Sometimes these kinds of discoveries are used to try to show that religious belief is a fantasy that our brains trick us into believing. If certain areas of a person's brain could be stimulated (or kept from stimulation) and this resulted in "manufactured" religious experiences, would that show that religious experience in general was just a fantasy? This doesn't seem to follow. We can also stimulate parts of the brain which results in the sensation of hearing music; does that mean that music isn't real? Of course not. We need a more sophisticated analysis of the relationship between the brain and mental experiences (including religious experience). Furthermore, in her book on the concept of the mind, author Marilynne Robinson notes the following irony:

> A nonspecialist might wonder how this locating of the soul in the deep interior of the brain differs in principle from locating the moral sense in the prefrontal cortex, as contemporary writers do, to demonstrate how free they are from the errors of Descartes. (Robinson 2010, 23)

So neuroscience right now is far from conclusive at explaining away the manifest image, but especially with stories like the one this chapter began with, it has begun to undermine the confidence some have in holding on to concepts like free will, morality, and rationality. In 2013, President Obama announced a plan to spend $100 million on brain research with the goal to "better understand how we think and how we learn and how we remember," hoping this might lead to cures for autism and Alzheimer's disease and repairs for strokes (White House 2014). It would be foolish to think we won't learn more about how the brain works, and may even come up with effective treatments for brain diseases. The question is whether any of that will completely dissolve the manifest image of human beings.

Owen Flanagan is a professor at Duke University with appointments both in the philosophy department and the graduate program in cognitive neuroscience. His 2002 book *The Problem of the Soul: Two Visions of Mind and How to Reconcile Them* acknowledges in the subtitle the central issue for the problem of understanding ourselves. His view, though, is not so much one of reconciling as eliminating the manifest image. He thinks this view of human beings has been superseded by the scientific view of human beings according to which freedom, rationality, and morality are fictions. But he understands that people would be unwilling to give up on such terms, so he suggests that the approach should be to use the same words but mean different things by them so they fit better with the scientific picture of humans (Flanagan 2002, 63, 86). So writers of his ilk may continue to use terms like free will and morality, but they do not mean the same thing as has been traditionally meant by such concepts. Some are frank about their dismissal of the traditional concepts: "ethics is an illusion fobbed off on us by our genes to get us to cooperate" (Ruse and Wilson 1993, 10). And Flanagan himself admits that in order to be consistent with the scientific image we must become existentialists about meaning in the world, emotivists about ethics, and Buddhists about religion (Flanagan 2002, 11–19). Others, though, are less overt about their dismissal of such concepts as they continue to use the same words (e.g., Harris 2010).

Existentialism [eg-zi-**sten**-shuh-liz-uhm]
The philosophical school which stresses the individual's ability and responsibility to choose ultimate meaning.

Emotivism [ee-**moh**-tiv-iz-uhm]
The philosophical school which claims that moral claims are only expressions of feeling, not statements of fact.]

Christianity has proved to be remarkably resilient over the centuries, accommodating and adjusting details of doctrine in response to scientific discoveries. But can Christians live with the dissolution of the manifest image of human beings? It doesn't seem so. Instead, they need to find a way to argue two things: (1) that the ultimate success of science will fall short of a complete explanation of everything and (2) that even the limited success of scientific explanations does not preclude thinking of ourselves as moral and rational agents. We addressed the first of these in Chapter 6; we turn to the second now.

4. Cognitive dualism

There are plenty of introductory texts to the philosophy of mind that discuss a range of non-dualist options for understanding the nature of human persons, and many of these attempt to do so from a Christian perspective. Two helpful places to start with some of these are Green and Palmer (2005) and Corcoran (2001). In the space that remains in this chapter, we consider a somewhat distinctive approach advocated by the eminent British philosopher Roger Scruton. He calls his model **cognitive dualism,** not because there is a dualism of substance involved like in Descartes' theory but because he takes both ways of thinking about the human being—the scientific and the manifest—as legitimate. In the previous chapter we discuss an approach to understanding divine action which posits different but complementary explanations for the same event. Cognitive dualism works in a similar way.

In the last chapter, we use Polkinghorne's example of two different kinds of explanation for why a teakettle is boiling: the scientific and the personal. These map onto the different images of the human being we discuss in this chapter. What Scruton does is to argue that these different kinds of explanation are rooted in very different traditions, and they are almost like different languages. The grammar of personal explanations demands reasons to be given; the grammar of scientific explanations demands physical (or efficient) causes. Both kinds of explanation can be full descriptions of a person from their perspective, but they are just perspectives. Each is like a lens through which humans are viewed. Neither of these conceptions we have of ourselves can be asserted to be the way we are in and of ourselves. Both are the products of very different ways of thinking. That doesn't mean they aren't real but rather that we can't take our "glasses" off in order to compare our conceptions against some unfiltered reality. So, the claim of cognitive dualism is that these two ways of conceptualizing the human being are both legitimate, but they are also incommensurable. That is to say, you can't translate between them, saying "Well, a desire or a free choice is really just this brain state."

Another way to think about this is that language constrains how we are able to conceptualize things. As an intriguing example, consider Ernest Vincent Wright's novel *Gadsby*, which is more than 50,000 words long, but doesn't use the letter "e" once. This is the most famous example of the genre known as "constrained writing." Wright wrote the novel as a challenge to see what might be expressed with such a severe limitation to the capabilities of English. If we can see so clearly that such writing drastically limits our ability to describe "reality," then is it so much of a leap to think that English even with the e's in it also constrains our ability to describe reality? That is not so easy to see from the inside, especially if the language we use is constitutive of our "reality" at least in some sense.

So think of the same issue in terms of our senses: for someone who was born blind, no amount of description can give him a proper idea of what the color red looks like. In his *Essay Concerning Human Understanding* John Locke speaks mockingly of a blind man who decided that red must be like the sound of a trumpet (III.IV.11; Locke 1959, 38). According to cognitive dualism, that is what it is like to try describing or reducing the terms in the manifest image to brain states or other scientific language.

So, Scruton resolves the problem of how to resolve these two conceptions into one by saying that we don't have to make them into one coherent picture.

> These two points of view are incommensurable: that is to say, we cannot derive from one of them a description of the world as seen from the other. Nor can we understand how one and the same object can be apprehended from both perspectives. Indeed, it might be more correct to say that the thing which the understanding sees as an object, reason sees as a subject, and that the mysterious identity of subject and object is something that we know to obtain, even though we cannot understand *how* it obtains, since we have no perspective that allows us to grasp both subject and object in a single mental act. (Scruton 2014, 35–36)

How does this work in practice? There are certain times when it will be more useful to use the perspective of the scientist to talk about human beings. The man with the tumor discussed at the beginning of this chapter did not need some kind of psychotherapy or lessons from an ethicist. Are there ever times, though, when it is more appropriate to speak of a person's desires, choices, values, etc., and mean something more than a reductionist version of these things? If so, then it is appropriate to adopt the manifest image. And realistically speaking, we shift back and forth between these two perspectives all the time. Cognitive dualism recognizes this fact and says it is OK that we do so.

How does cognitive dualism resolve the Christian concern of continued life after death? Here we can only offer some speculative thoughts. Perhaps we can think of the reality of persons along the lines of social realities. There are countless entities which have come into existence through culture: stop signs, philosophy conferences, football games, universities. None of these are identical to the material particles by which we locate them, because there is something else required for their existence besides the material. Think of a dollar. In the United States, a dollar can take several different forms: a collection of coins that adds up to 100 cents, a paper bill, or an electronic signification that has been certified by a bank. Scientists could examine the coins, paper, or computers, but we would not find anywhere in their explanations of those objects what the real nature of a dollar is. That comes from outside the physical natures of the objects, when a community treats those material things in a distinctive way. Then there is a whole different tradition of discourse about dollars that develops (economics) that has nothing to do with the material out of which dollars are composed. Can we say something similar about "persons"?

Philosopher Wilfred Sellars gives a classic account of the two images we have of ourselves in his essay, "Philosophy and the Scientific Image of Man." On Sellars' account, persons were "created" when we encountered human beings in a certain way. He uses the term "man" for what I've been calling "persons":

> man became man when "man came to be aware of himself as man-in-the-world" when "man first encountered himself—which is, of course, when he came to be man. For it is no merely incidental feature of man that he has a conception of himself as man-in-the-world, just as it is obvious, on reflection, that "if man had a radically different conception of himself he would be a radically different kind of man." ... I want to highlight from the very beginning what might be called the paradox of man's encounter with himself, the paradox consisting of the fact that man couldn't be man until he encountered himself. (Sellars 1963, 6)

Sellars calls this a paradox because there is a logical (not just empirical or historical) problem of circularity or "bootstrapping" here. How could humans begin to treat themselves as persons unless they were persons to begin with?

Perhaps Christian theology has further resources with which to address this problem. If human beings can create social realities, then perhaps God—or, more specifically, the Christian Trinity—can as well. Could human beings have become persons, or, to use the theological language, image bearers of God, when God began treating them as such? The historical development could have happened gradually in the same way that children become adults and morally responsible gradually. Or it could have happened more suddenly if God entered into a covenant with some hominids and thereby granted them special status, which allowed them to view themselves in a certain way and develop the "manifest image" over time.

Again, these are only speculations that can be neither confirmed nor denied by scientific or historical investigation (because, again, those belong to a different tradition of discourse). There are other points of the development of human beings and of life in general which are not as speculative. Some of these cause Christians to wonder about the goodness of God in light of the horrific consequences to life. We must address this problem in the next chapter.

 Summary of main points:

1. The Christian tradition is varied, but the New Testament witness knows little of today's popular version of a separable soul that leaves the body at death.

2. Descartes advocated a substance dualism which posits an immaterial substance as the true self and identified with the mind.

3. There are philosophical challenges to dualism, but the current brain science provides the most significant challenges to the manifest image of the human person which is rooted in dualism.

4. Cognitive dualism offers a way to affirm both the scientific and manifest image of humans, but at the expense of integrating these images into one coherent picture.

Further reading

- Brown, Warren S., and Brad D. Strawn. 2012. *The Physical Nature of Christian Life: Neuroscience, Psychology, and the Church*. Cambridge: Cambridge University Press. A Christian neuroscientist argues for a physicalist understanding of the human mind and soul.
- Green, Joel B., and Stuart L. Palmer, eds. 2005. *In Search of the Soul: Four Views of the Mind-Body Problem*. Downers Grove, IL: InterVarsity Press. Four Christians debate their positions on the mind/body problem.
- Scruton, Roger. 2014. *The Soul of the World*. Princeton: Princeton University Press. An eminent British philosopher presents the cognitive dualism position.

References

Brown, Warren S., and Brad D. Strawn. 2012. *The Physical Nature of Christian Life: Neuroscience, Psychology, and the Church*. Cambridge: Cambridge University Press.

Burns, Jeffrey M., and Russell H. Swerdlow. 2003. "Right Orbitofrontal Tumor with Pedophilia Symptom and Constructional Apraxia Sign." *Archives of Neurology*, 60(March): 437–440.

Corcoran, Kevin, ed. 2001. *Soul, Body, and Survival: Essays on the Metaphysics of Human Persons*. Ithaca, NY: Cornell University Press.

Descartes, René. 1998. *Meditations on First Philosophy*. In *Modern Philosophy: An Anthology of Primary Sources*, edited by Roger Ariew and Eric Watkins. Indianapolis: Hackett Publishing Company.

Flanagan, Owen. 2002. *The Problem of the Soul: Two Visions of Mind and How to Reconcile Them.* New York: Basic Books.

Goetz, Stewart. 2005. "Substance Dualism." In *In Search of the Soul: Four Views of the Mind-Body Problem,* edited by Joel B. Green and Stuart L. Palmer. Downers Grove, IL: InterVarsity Press.

Green, Joel B., and Stuart L. Palmer, eds. 2005. *In Search of the Soul: Four Views of the Mind-Body Problem.* Downers Grove, IL: InterVarsity Press.

Harris, Sam. 2010. *The Moral Landscape: How Science Can Determine Human Values.* New York: Free Press.

Johnstone, Brick, Angela Bodling, Dan Cohen, Shawn E. Christ, and Andrew Wegrzyn. 2012. "Right Parietal Lobe-related 'Selflessness' as the Neurophychological Basis of Spiritual Transcendence." *International Journal for the Psychology of Religion,* 22(4): 267–284.

Locke, John. 1959. *An Essay Concerning Human Understanding,* Vol 2. New York: Dover Publications.

McGinn, Colin. 1996. *The Character of Mind: An Introduction to the Philosophy of Mind,* 2nd ed. Oxford: Oxford University Press.

Morris, Thomas V. 2001. *The Logic of God Incarnate.* Eugene, OR: Wipf & Stock.

Robinson, Marilynne. 2010. *Absence of Mind.* New Haven: Yale University Press.

Ruse, Michael, and Edward O. Wilson. 1993. "The Approach of Sociobiology: The Evolution of Ethics." In *Religion and the Natural Sciences,* edited by James E. Huchingson. Fort Worth, TX: Harcourt Brace Javonovich.

Scruton, Roger. 2014. *The Soul of the World.* Princeton: Princeton University Press.

Sellars, Wilfred. 1963. "Philosophy and the Scientific Image of Man." In *Empiricism and the Philosophy of Mind.* London: Routledge & Kegan Paul.

White House. 2013. Remarks by the President on the BRAIN Initiative and AmericanInnovation,http://www.whitehouse.gov/the-press-office/2013/04/02/remarks-president-brain-initiative-and-american-innovation, accessed 17 February 2016.

Wright, N. T. 2003. *The Resurrection of the Son of God.* Minneapolis: Fortress Press.

CHAPTER 12

The Problem of Natural Evil

The problem of evil is generally encountered on two different fronts: the evils committed by human beings which cause other creatures pain and suffering, and the pain and suffering of creatures which results from natural causes like hurricanes or drought. In both of these, the problem is how to reconcile the amount of pain and suffering there is with the existence of an all-powerful and beneficent God. The former category of pain and suffering is often explained with the **free will defense**: Hitler chose to commit horrendous evils, but the world is ultimately a better place because there are free people than it would be if there were no free people in the world. Of course, there are rebuttals to the free will defense, and these are widely discussed. But our concern in this chapter is with the second version of the problem—sometimes called the **problem of natural evil**.

There are natural disasters that cause massive human suffering, like the tsunami in Japan in 2011 that caused more than 15,000 human deaths, or the Lisbon earthquake on All Saints Day of 1755 that may have been responsible for as many as 100,000 deaths. Humans have reflected on these throughout recorded history, and they are standard topics of discussion in philosophy classes. This book, though, is concerned with issues at the intersection of science and Christianity, so in this chapter we consider a version of the problem of natural evil that has become particularly acute since the discovery of the long age of the earth and the understanding of the role of suffering in the process of the development of life. There is no solution to this problem that enjoys wide support, but this chapter looks at some of the typical responses.

Questions to be addressed in this chapter:

1. What is the problem of natural evil?
2. What are some possible responses to the problem?
3. What is a stronger response?
4. How does eschatological fulfillment contribute to an adequate response?

Science and Christianity: An Introduction to the Issues, First Edition. By J. B. Stump.
© 2017 John Wiley & Sons, Ltd. Published 2017 by John Wiley & Sons, Ltd.

---

1. Articulation of the problem

Before engaging the problem of natural evil, we should acknowledge that there is also beauty and goodness in the natural world. Perhaps accounting for this causes the atheist a problem no less than the problem of natural evil for the theist. But it is the latter that is our topic here.

As evolutionary explanations became more and more understood, there developed the feeling that the suffering of creatures reflects on the nature of God. Darwin himself understood this and famously wrote to his American friend Asa Gray: "There seems to me too much misery in the world. I cannot persuade myself that a beneficent & omnipotent God would have designedly created the Ichneumonidæ with the express intention of their feeding within the living bodies of caterpillars, or that a cat should play with mice" (Darwin Project 2016). Richard Dawkins elaborates on the dark side of the natural world:

> During the minute it takes me to compose this sentence, thousands of animals are being eaten alive; others are running for their lives, whimpering with fear; others are being slowly devoured from within by rasping parasites; thousands of all kinds are dying of starvation, thirst and disease. It must be so. If there is ever a time of plenty, this very fact will automatically lead to an increase in population until the natural state of starvation and misery is restored. (Dawkins 1995, 132)

From the assertion that suffering is the natural state, Dawkins draws this conclusion: "the universe we observe has precisely the properties we should expect if there is, at bottom, no design, no purpose, no evil and no good, nothing but blind, pitiless indifference" (ibid., 133). He seems to think it obvious that a good and powerful God would not have permitted nature to take such a form. Do Christians have a way of responding to this situation? Attempts to do so are generally called **theodicy**.

Theodicy [thee-**od**-uh-see]
An explanation intended to show how traditional attributes of God, like goodness and justice, are compatible with the reality of pain and suffering in the world.

As discussed in earlier chapters, there has not been unanimity among Christians about origins for most of the history of the Church. But for many centuries there had been widespread acceptance of a traditional narrative of Christian theology that charts the course of cosmic history from creation to fall to redemption. This narrative is usually thought to provide a ready-made theodicy for all the bad stuff we find in the world today: God made everything perfect, and then all the bad things started after human beings sinned. This way of arguing is now blocked for us.

There can be no doubt now that the sort of natural world described by Darwin and Dawkins in our contemporary setting is the way the natural world has been since long before human beings were here to sin. Perhaps it is not necessary to call it the "natural state" as Dawkins does (recall Knight's "subnatural" terminology in Chapter 10), but we must acknowledge that natural history reveals that pain, suffering, and death have been constant features of the process by which life has progressed in the animal kingdom throughout its history.

About 250 million years ago, the largest extinction event in earth's history occurred. Perhaps a series of massive volcanic eruptions was the culprit (in Siberia there is a lava field two and a half miles thick for a million square miles that dates to this time). These kinds of eruptions would have caused acid rain, and the ash in the atmosphere would have caused a significant drop in the global temperature. Within 100,000 years (the blink of an eye in geologic time), almost 90% of the earth's species were gone.

Of course, the most famous extinction event is that of the dinosaurs some 65 million years ago. The rocks of that age show traces of an asteroid that struck the earth—which would have generated massive wildfires in which millions of animals (and of course plants) would have been burned alive—and signs of significant climate change that led to the slow, painful starvation of countless animals.

Extinction is one aspect of this natural history that is often invoked in describing the problem of natural evil. By most estimates today, something like 99% of all species that have ever existed are now extinct. This fact might be marshaled as an argument of extreme wastage: were all of these species "used" as a means to bring about the current life forms that we have? If so, then it is difficult to reconcile the profound loss of the many for the benefit of the (very) few.

In Chapter 9, I discuss the problem of extinction and argue that it rests on the now problematic notion of essentialism. If there is no entity corresponding to "species" then the most we can say about extinction is that some closely related individuals failed to produce viable offspring. A response to that line of argument is that when the ancestral lines of closely related individuals all die out there is something more that is lost than the fact that some individuals do not procreate. Besides the ecological interdependence with other organisms which could suffer, we might say that there is a "way of being" in the world that is lost. Christopher Southgate says: "extinction must be conceded always to be a loss of value to the biosphere as a whole. A whole strategy of being alive on the planet, a whole quality of living experience is lost when any organism becomes extinct" (Southgate 2008, 45). We might ask, though, whether "a whole strategy of being" is any less an artificial construct than is "species." Each individual varies slightly from every other individual, and so does their experience.

> **💬 Nineteenth-century reflection on animal pain**
> "The universality of pain throughout the range of the animal world, reaching back into the distant ages of geology, and involved in the very structure of the animal organism, is without doubt among the most serious problems which the Theist has to face." (Illingworth 1890, 113)

But even besides extinctions, there is no getting around the ineliminable place of pain and suffering in the struggle for life. There are remarkable examples of cooperation and perhaps even **altruism** among life forms (and this is a point to which we return below), but the law of the jungle is that the strong survive at the expense of the weak. Our existence today is possible only because of the deaths of innumerable creatures, and other innumerable creatures suffer throughout their lives. It is the history of this suffering and death that constitute the problem of natural evil. So the challenge for the Christian theist is how to reconcile this reality of the created order with a good God who declared creation to be good.

2. Some potential responses

We've already noted that we can no longer plausibly claim that creation began in a state where none of the suffering we see today was present until the first human sin occurred. There is a variation on this, though, sometimes used by **Old Earth Creationists** who are concerned to preserve the role of original sin as the cause of all pain and suffering. William Dembski claims that the sin of Adam and Eve had effects on even the deep past of the created order retroactively:

> Just as the death and Resurrection of Christ is responsible for the salvation of repentant people throughout all time, so the Fall of humanity in the Garden of Eden is responsible for every natural evil throughout all time (future, present, past, and distant past preceding the Fall. (Dembski 2009, 110)

Dembski is concerned to hold on to the view that God's creation is perfect, and the only reason we see the natural evils in it is because of human sin. Old Testament scholar Iain Provan, though, shows that such a claim has little support from the biblical passages it is usually drawn from. In Genesis, God declares that creation is "good" but that does not mean "perfect" (Provan 2014, 283). And by charging humans to multiply and to subdue the earth before the account of the Fall, it seems as though the original creation was not as God intended it to be. For Dembski, these pre-Fall statements must describe the ideal creation (even if they do not correspond to some historical time and place) which is marred because of human sin. But it is theologically unwarranted to take this as perfection. God seems to have delighted in creating the natural world in a state where there was still work to be done. We might say there was "non-order" or incompleteness that humans were to work on bringing into alignment with God's will. God must have reasons for wanting to partner with humanity in this work. The sin of humanity—no matter when it occurred—introduced "disorder" into creation, which definitely made things worse. But there doesn't seem to be a compelling theological reason for claiming that the suffering inflicted on animals by predation of dinosaurs was the result of Adam and Eve's sin 100 million years later.

Original sin

In traditional Christian theology, original sin is a term that refers both to the act of disobedience by Adam and Eve in the Garden of Eden and to the condition into which all humans were subsequently born. Even some who do not take the Adam and Eve story literally hold to the doctrine by claiming that whenever *Homo sapiens* first became morally aware they rebelled against

God and thereby put all of humanity into a condition of sin. The doctrine also plays a role in theodicy when it is claimed that before humans sinned there was no death or suffering in the animal world. The doctrine of original sin is not explicitly mentioned or developed in the Bible, but it has been part of traditional Christian theology since at least St Augustine in the 5th century. Some Christians today think the doctrine should be abandoned or significantly altered because it relies on an understanding of human origins which can no longer be scientifically maintained.

Dembski assumes there is tremendous significance to what human beings do throughout all of creation. If we find life on other planets—perhaps only bacteria which live and die—are we to conclude that the deaths there are the result of what a couple of human beings on earth did? Such a view seems bound together with the worldview in which earth is at the center of the universe and all of creation serves humanity. In Christian theology, there must always be room for a special place for humanity in the eyes of God. Humans were created in the image of God! But Dembski's view seems to make the special vocation of humanity to be the ruination of all creation. The message of Genesis 1 seems rather to be that humanity was designed to be the instrument through which creation is increasingly subdued; we are to be co-laborers with God in healing the groaning of the created order.

Dembski admits that his conclusions are entirely independent of scientific considerations. But his solution for holding on to what he calls "classical theism" and its attribution of natural evil to the first human sin also seems implausibly ad hoc. If we're going to take the classical reading of the Adam and Eve story, then it seems inconsistent to invoke a kind of backward causation to account for the natural history we've discovered. Perhaps it saves the theory, but if there are less counterintuitive responses, we should explore those.

> C. S. Lewis on a pre-human Fall
> "The origin of animal suffering could be traced, by earlier generations, to the Fall of man—the whole world was infected by the uncreating rebellion of Adam. This is now impossible, for we have good reason to believe that animals existed long before men. Carnivorousness, with all that it entails, is older than humanity. Now it is impossible at this point not to remember a certain sacred story which, though never included in the creeds, has been widely believed in the Church and seems to be implied in several Dominical, Pauline, and Johannine utterances—I mean the story that man was not the first creature to rebel against the Creator, but that some older and mightier being long since became apostate and is now the emperor of darkness and (significantly) the Lord of this world." (C. S. Lewis 1940, 137)

Another option is that the fall of Satan and his minions was responsible for the pain and suffering found in the natural order before the appearance of human beings. According to this view—often attributed to C. S. Lewis—there is still the problem with the natural history of the planet showing no evidence at all that it was ever free of pain and suffering. I suppose we might posit that very soon after creation (so soon that no traces would remain of the initial state) Satan fell into rebellion and caused the deterioration of the natural world (earthquakes, predation, etc.). But then again we're resorting to seriously ad hoc solutions for which there might be better approaches. If instead the **cosmic Fall** is posited to have happened before the beginning of the creation, then we are still left with the question of why God went ahead and created the natural world in a "fallen" state. Any answer to that question must claim it is better for there to be a fallen created order than for there not to be one at all; but this would apply equally as an answer for why the natural world is in the state it is even if there had been no cosmic Fall. So the cosmic fall option ends up doing little work.

Another of the options for dealing with the problem of natural evil is what is called **skeptical theism**. The skepticism in question is not about whether God exists, as the title might lead one to believe. Rather, it is the view that we should be skeptical of our ability to discern and understand the reasons God might have for allowing the evils we see in the world. More specifically, the skeptical theist claims that our inability to come up with good reasons for why there is the kind and amount of evil in the world does not show that God has no good reasons for allowing that evil. The basic intuition here is that our finite minds are not suited to plumbing the depths of God's infinite mind and the reasons God might have for creating the world the way it is.

Surely there is some truth to the claim that we mortals with finite minds cannot comprehend all the ways of God. There will be some point at which we fall back on our inability to fully understand why God has, for example, set up the world to work the way it does. But there are troubling consequences to taking skeptical theism to the degree needed in order to answer in full the problem of natural evil. First, if our knowledge about God is so impoverished that we can't begin to see what reasons God might have for allowing evil, then it seems that our positive knowledge about God must also be drastically limited. Are we not able to know anything about God? Second, if skeptical theism is true, can we trust any of our claims to moral knowledge? The skeptical theist claims for any instance of natural evil that, for all we know, there could be reasons why that instance is in fact a good thing (or at least better than the alternative). That seems to undermine our ability to make any sort of moral judgment that things ought not to be the way we find them to be.

Beyond these considerations against skeptical theism, there is also the commonly held intuition that we ought to be able to offer something more in the way of reasons for why the world is the way it is. In the next section, then, we consider an approach to natural evil that attempts to do just that.

3. A more robust theodicy

To restate the problem, we are considering responses to the claim that the suffering and pain of individual creatures in this created world challenges the goodness of God. One possible way of responding is to concede that God (if there is a God) must not be good. This is not an option for Christians who desire to maintain the traditional doctrine that God is wholly good and worthy of worship. There is no getting around the fact, though, that our attitude toward the created order is legitimately ambivalent—not in the sense of not caring, but in the sense of being genuinely conflicted. The created order is sublime and it is appalling. Darwin himself displays this ambivalence in this oft-quoted passage from the *Origin of Species*:

> Thus, from the war of nature, from famine and death, the most exalted object which we are capable of conceiving, namely the production of the higher animals, directly follows. There is grandeur in this view of life, with its several powers, having been originally breathed into a few forms or into one; and that, whilst this planet has gone cycling on according to the fixed law of gravity, from so simple a beginning endless forms most beautiful and most wonderful have been, and are being, evolved. (Darwin 1936, 374)

The war of nature and grandeur. Can we reconcile these with the traditional concept of God? It must be admitted that there is no easy answer to this problem. Nor will any satisfactory answer have a single focus. Rather, it will have to draw on several different insights and function as a cumulative case.

One of those insights is what is sometimes called the "only way" solution. In the version of the problem of natural evil which deals with atrocities committed by humans, the free will defense might be categorized as an "only way" solution. The explanation is that if God wanted human beings who could freely choose for themselves, then the only way for them to freely choose the good was to allow for the possibility that they might choose evil. There may be an analog of this response for the problem of natural evil, and it rests on another key insight of this cumulative case, namely that there are greater goods to be considered. Free will is considered to be a greater good that outweighs the evils caused by its misuse. For the problem of natural evil, what would those greater goods be that justify the pain and suffering in the natural world?

First, we might point to the possibility of life at all. Biological life requires a dynamic environment, and the kinds of systems that give rise to that dynamism are the same systems that give rise to earthquakes, hurricanes, and tornados. Are these sorts of natural disasters that cause so much suffering in the natural world (including, but not limited to, humans) the only way to get to the greater good of life on our planet? Possibly.

Beyond this, there are other, perhaps more subtle, goods that the evolutionary development of life gives rise to that would be absent in a different sort of world. If God is good and worthy of worship, and if the world was created in an imperfect state, then it is difficult to escape the implication that the transformation of chaos into order is good in God's sight. Otherwise, we would expect that God created things in a final, perfect form rather than creating over time. Even the Young Earth Creationist position breaks down here when we ask why God took seven days to accomplish what he could have done instantaneously. God seems to delight in the process itself—and how much more over vast stretches of time than only one week! God does not seem to be in a hurry, but instead patiently teases order out of chaos. To claim otherwise invites the question of why God even bothered with creating this order of things instead of just starting off with heaven.

 Soul-making theodicy

Irenaeus of Lyon (died c. 202) is often credited with developing the soul-making theodicy, according to which God has allowed evil and suffering in the world as a way of promoting the moral development of human beings. In the 20th century, the leading proponent of the soul-making theodicy was philosopher John Hick (1922–2012). The basic idea is that humans cannot be created as morally mature beings but must grow into that by making free choices in response to encountering evil.

Fig. 12.1 Irenaeus of Lyon.

This leads us to another aspect of the only way/greater good response: perhaps the evolutionary struggle is the only way to develop sentient, moral beings like us.

It can be argued that moral maturity is a quality that must be developed through making moral decisions. God can no more create morally mature creatures than he could create free beings who are incapable of sin. Instead, this world provides the opportunity for "soul-making." Christian philosopher Chad Meister concurs, saying: "Moral maturity requires that agents be involved in their own moral formation through the (often arduous) process of moral decision-making" (Meister 2013, 214). But then in order to have genuine moral decisions, there must be a challenging environment in which beings are subjected to the kinds of natural evils which force difficult decisions. When faced with such situations, will creatures opt for their own selfish preservation over doing what is right and good? Until recently, no one studying evolutionary history would have even considered such a question. But now there are more and more evolutionary biologists taking an interest in the role of cooperation and even altruism in the story of the development of more complex animal forms (see, for example, Deane-Drummond 2014; Coakley 2016; and Clayton and Schloss 2004). In this sense, suffering is a catalyst for greater goods, but not in a crude instrumental way. The suffering and pain is in some sense constitutive of the greater good of moral formation.

If this line of thinking has merit, we must question whether we would want a world history devoid of the kind of natural evils considered in this chapter. We need not try to force ourselves to think that evil is good, but it seems that God has structured things so that good comes from evil—and the kinds of goods that could come about no other way. Patricia Williams has developed this argument, concluding with this stunning statement:

> The source of evil is not some divine opponent of God. The source of evil is not even human sin. Rather, the sources of evil lie in attributes so valuable that we would not even consider eliminating them in order to eradicate evil. Presumably, neither would God. (Williams 2001, 139)

This sentiment is not a departure from classic Christian theology. Aquinas said: "since God, then, provides universally for all being, it belongs to His providence to permit certain defects in particular effects, that the perfect good of the universe may not be hindered, for if all evil were prevented, much good would be absent from the universe" (*Summa Theologica* 1.42.a.2; Christian Classics 2016).

Some might respond to all of this saying: "OK, these are some interesting theoretical possibilities to consider about the kind of world we live in and how to reconcile them with faith in a good God. But we're still left with the instances of countless individuals in this world—many of which were conscious—who suffered and died far short of the fulfilled lives they were intended to live." This inescapable truth forces us to reflect on one more element of theodicy.

4. Eschatological fulfillment

Focus on the individual organisms that have suffered and died without achieving anything close to fulfillment drives some Christian thinkers to claim there may be eternal rewards for animals. Keith Ward says, "Immortality, for animals as well as humans, is a necessary condition of any acceptable theodicy" (Ward 1982, 201). This is not just a post-Darwinian innovation in Christian theology. The 18th-century founder of Methodism, John Wesley, also thought there might be a place for non-human animals in the afterlife.

> May it not answer another end; namely, furnish us with a full answer to a plausible objection against the justice of God, in suffering numberless creatures that never had sinned to be so severely punished? They could not sin, for they were not moral agents. Yet how severely do they suffer!—yea, many of them beasts of burden in particular, almost the whole time of their abode on earth; so that they can have no retribution here below. But the objection vanishes away if we consider that something better remains after death for these creatures also; that these likewise shall one day be delivered from this bondage of corruption, and shall then receive an ample amends for all their present sufferings. (Wesley 1998, 251)

This is the same sort of concern that the great 18th-century philosopher Immanuel Kant used in claiming it is necessary for there to be an afterlife in which all the wrongs are righted. It is driven by our sense of justice. We might ask, though, whether our sense of justice is a reliable guide to such things. We must at least consider the response given to Job when he (rightly to our minds) complained to God that he had been treated unfairly: "Who is this that darkens counsel by words without knowledge?" (Job 38:2). Perhaps our limited perspective should call for a stronger dose of humility.

There is one other issue we must raise regarding the eschatological fulfillment of animals: our focus is too often limited to the victims—to those animals lower on the food chain. They were deprived of good long lives because they were eaten by predators. But what about the fulfillment of the lives of the predators? Many of them were deprived of good long lives according to their kind because they were not able to find prey to eat. The slow starvation of a cheetah which was not fast enough to catch the gazelle is just as much a part of the evolutionary drama as the suffering of the gazelle which was not fast enough to escape. The difficulty comes when we ask what sort of fulfillment will the predator have in the afterlife. Will there be an endless supply of prey for it to catch and devour? That doesn't seem to solve the problem.

There is an evocative image from Isaiah about the Kingdom of God:

> The wolf will live with the lamb,
>   the leopard will lie down with the goat,
> The calf and the lion and the yearling together;
>   and a little child will lead them.
> The cow will feed with the bear,
>   their young will lie down together,
>   and the lion will eat straw like the ox. (Isaiah 11:6–7)

This passage seems to suggest that the predator's fulfillment can take a significantly different form of life than what it experiences here and now. Or it might be claimed that in the eschaton God can work things out so that predators can be fulfilled in hunting prey without there being any victims who are deprived of their fulfilled lives. But if God can do that in the eschaton, we're left asking why he can't do it in the here and now. Such questions force us into the realm of speculation. We bring this book to a close in the conclusion by pushing further into that realm and considering the topic of eschatology more broadly.

 Summary of main points:

1. Christian theists must somehow reconcile the reality of pain and suffering in the natural world with a good God who created things that way.

2. Backward causation of human sin, a cosmic Fall of Satan, and skeptical theism are unpersuasive attempts at explaining natural evil.

3. "Only way" and "greater good" arguments along with soul-making considerations provide a more plausible answer to the problem of natural evil.

4. The problem of pain and suffering in sentient life is mitigated if all such beings have the possibility of fulfillment after their deaths.

Further reading

- Coakley, Sarah. 2016. *Sacrifice Regained: Evolution, Cooperation and God*. Oxford: Oxford University Press. Her 2012 Gifford Lectures exploring the role of cooperation played in developing our moral sense.
- Fretheim, Terence E. 2010. *Creation Untamed: The Bible, God, and Natural Disasters*. Grand Rapids, MI: Baker Academic. Exposes how a careful reading of the Bible's texts on creation undermine the view that natural evils are judgments of God.
- Southgate, Christopher. 2008. *The Groaning of Creation: God, Evolution, and the Problem of Evil.* Louisville, KY: Westminster John Knox Press. Provides a cumulative case theodicy drawing from different traditional responses to natural evil.

References

Christian Classics. 2016. "Summa Theologica," http://www.ccel.org/ccel/aquinas/summa.toc.html, accessed 17 February 2016.

Clayton, Philip, and Jeffrey Schloss. 2004. *Evolution and Ethics: Human Morality in Biological and Religion Perspective*. Grand Rapids, MI: Eerdmans.

Coakley, Sarah. 2016. *Sacrifice Regained: Evolution, Cooperation and God*. Oxford: Oxford University Press.

Darwin, Charles. 1936. *The Origin of Species*. New York: The Modern Library.

Darwin Project. 2016. "Letter to Asa Gray (May 22)," http://www.darwinproject.ac.uk/entry-2814, accessed 17 February 2016.

Dawkins, Richard. 1995. *River out of Eden: A Darwinian View*. New York: Basic Books.

Deane-Drummond, Celia. 2014. *The Wisdom of the Liminal: Evolution and Other Animals in Human Becoming.* Grand Rapids, MI: Eerdmans.

Dembski, William A. 2009. *The End of Christianity: Finding a Good God in an Evil World.* Nashville: B&H Publishing Group.

Illingworth, J. R. 1890. "The Problem of Pain: Its Bearing on Faith in God." In *Lux Mundi: A Series of Studies in the Religion of the Incarnation,* edited by Charles Gore. London: John Murray.

Lewis, C. S. 1996. *The Problem of Pain.* San Francisco: HarperSanFrancisco.

Meister, Chad. 2013. "God and Evil." In *Debating Christian Theism,* edited by J. P. Moreland, Chad Meister, and Khaldoun Sweis. Oxford: Oxford University Press.

Provan, Iain. 2014. *Seriously Dangerous Religion: What the Old Testament Really Says and Why It Matters.* Waco, TX: Baylor University Press.

Southgate, Christopher. 2008. *The Groaning of Creation: God, Evolution, and the Problem of Evil.* Louisville, KY: Westminster John Knox Press.

Ward, Keith. 1982. *Rational Theology and the Creativity of God.* New York: Pilgrim.

Wesley, John. 1998. "The General Deliverance." In *The Works of John Wesley,* 3rd ed. Vol. 6. Grand Rapids, MI: Baker Books.

Williams, Patricia. 2001. *Doing without Adam and Eve: Sociobiology and Original Sin.* Minneapolis: Augsburg Fortress Publishers.

CONCLUSION

The Last Things

I conclude this book with some brief thoughts about the end of all things. Eschatology is the study of the last things in theology, and for the major part of Christian history, Christian doctrine has stood in some tension with the scientific view of the natural world as eternal. Christian theology typically asserts that a different order of things is to come. The Apostle Paul said, "If for this life only we have hoped in Christ, we are of all people most to be pitied" (1 Corinthians 15:19). This new reality is not just for individuals (as discussed in Chapter 12), but for all of the created order. Before the 20th century, though, it seemed to scientists that the created order would persist indefinitely. Now we have a different understanding of things.

For example, scientists understand the workings of the sun pretty well now. It is not eternal. It has already spent about half of its hydrogen fuel, and it only has enough to burn for the next five billion years or so. Then it will become a red giant, its surface expanding out beyond the surface of Mars. That means our earth is approximately middle-aged, having been formed some four and a half billion years ago. So perhaps we should start thinking about the eventual demise of our home. Our descendants will need to find another place to live (and develop the technology that can get them there). But even that will be a temporary fix.

There will be other stars, and the early returns on the search for earth-like exoplanets suggest that many of those stars will be orbited by habitable planets. So, in theory, our descendants could migrate to a new home (as our ancestors have done so many times). But even that process can't continue forever in this universe. Stars will stop forming in our galaxy after 40 or 50 billion years, and other galaxies will be so far away after another 100 billion years that their light will never reach us. And then worst of all, in 10^{31} years (10 trillion billion billion years) all the protons and neutrons will decay, destroying all traces of anything that has ever existed (Russell 2012, 545).

The bottom line is that our physical universe is doomed. How do we reconcile this with Christian theology? Philip Clayton says: "The idea of a hope after death

Science and Christianity: An Introduction to the Issues, First Edition. By J. B. Stump.
© 2017 John Wiley & Sons, Ltd. Published 2017 by John Wiley & Sons, Ltd.

and an end that fulfills history as a whole is as intrinsic to the Christian tradition as it is foreign to the project of science" (Clayton 2005, 134). The question for the Christian who believes in this future fulfillment pertains especially to the continuity that is expected to hold between the created order and what is to come. I close the book with this topic not merely because it is fitting for the last chapter to be about the last things but because there may be a summarizing point here for understanding more general approaches to the relationship between science and theology. That is to say, how one answers the question of the relationship between this order of things and what is to come might be indicative of one's intuitions about science and theology.

Three understandings of the last things

For one strain of theology, the scientific story of the future of the universe presents absolutely no difficulty whatsoever. According to it, the future world is entirely distinct from the present. It originates from a second act of *creatio ex nihilo* and bears no relation to the present order of things. This view is often combined with rapture theology, according to which Christians will be whisked out of this world into an immaterial heaven, and all that remains here will be destroyed. In that case, the natural world today is inconsequential in the grand scheme of things. For example, Mark Driscoll, the former pastor of a large and influential church in Seattle, was reported to have said at a large conference: "I know who made the environment. He's coming back, and he's going to burn it all up. So yes, I drive an SUV" (Religion News Service 2015). Driscoll later claimed it was a joke, but even if it were, it encapsulates a prominent Christian view. That view essentially claims that theology trumps science, or at least that science is irrelevant to a proper doctrine of eschatology. It doesn't matter what the scientists say about the fate of the world (or anything else). These Christians have their doctrines and traditions that tell them everything they need to know about the eternal things that really matter; everything else is just temporary. Such a view encourages a profound distrust of science, and it ghettoizes religious thinking.

A second option for understanding the relationship between this world and the next is one of continued existence. According to this view, there is no other world. If God can be said to create a new heaven and earth, it is only through the process of *creatio continua*—the faithful processes according to which nature operates now. The only eschatology is scientific cosmology. Here science trumps theology, or at least forces theology to radically alter its views of eschatology. Before the evidence of the end of the universe was as persuasive as it is now, theologian John Macquarrie claimed: "If it were shown that the universe is indeed headed for an all-enveloping death, then this might seem to constitute a state of affairs so negative that it might be held to falsify Christian faith and abolish Christian hope" (Macquarrie 1977, 356). Such a claim could only be made by assuming that God will have no further role in the workings of the universe than preserving the path it is on now. The laws of nature as we understand them now will govern the future of all things.

Some attempt to relate this view to Christian concerns of eschatology is found in the work of theologian Kathryn Tanner. She explores the implications of eschatology for a world without a future, claiming this to be in the same vein as the theological work of Aquinas and others in understanding creation when the best science held the natural world to be eternally existing in the past (see Chapter 1). In her view, eschatology loses its predominantly future orientation. Eternal life is a quality of life and to be understood "spatially" as life in God, rather than temporally as continued existence for all time (Tanner 2000, 229–230). Whether that does justice to the hope of the Christian, it seems to indicate that the direction of influence between science and theology runs almost exclusively from the former to the latter.

One last Christian response to the dilemma of scientific eschatology is typified by John Polkinghorne and his commitment to God's *creatio ex vetere*, or creation out of the old (Polkinghorne 1994, 167). According to this view, there is continuity between this order of things and what is to come (as with the *creatio continua* model); but there is also something new that happens (as with the *creatio ex nihilo* model). The resurrection of Christ is the exemplar to be used: Christ's body was subject to the laws of nature when he suffered death, and yet his resurrected existence was in continuity with what came before—his body was not found in the tomb. There was a transformation of the old into something new. Could the same thing happen to the cosmos as a whole? Also by analogy with Christ, there is no expectation that physical existence must run its full natural course before it is transformed into something else (Christ died before what would have been the natural end of his life). That is to say, God could create the new heavens and new earth before the universe runs its natural course into utter annihilation. But also by analogy with Christ, there is some development of the present order of things required before it is transformed (if Jesus had died as an infant, it is difficult to see how he would have been transformed into the risen Christ). Perhaps the cosmos must develop to some particular state of maturity before it can be transformed into the new order of things.

Of course, all this is necessarily speculative, but the view allows for the importance of what happens here and now, yet does not limit the future possibilities to the potential of matter as we understand it now. The view also has the potential for showing how science and theology can enter into more constructive conversation. Consider the following scientifically informed theological speculation.

The fourth big bang?

Holmes Rolston III wrote a short stimulating book called *Three Big Bangs* (2010). The three big bangs are moments in the history of the universe when ontology (what there is) changed. The first is the development from nothingness to the existence of matter-energy. This is what is commonly known as the Big Bang, some fourteen billion years ago. The second was when some of that matter transformed into life. From all we can tell so far, there is an extremely small fraction of the matter in the universe that has made this transition, which happened here on earth three or four billion years ago. The third big bang was when some of that life (again, a small fraction of it) developed consciousness or mind. We don't yet have a good handle on whether to ascribe this to other animals besides ourselves, nor can we pinpoint a moment in our own evolutionary development that separates the self-aware from the brute. But there is no denying the qualitative difference between self-aware lifeforms like ourselves and mere life like bacteria, trees, or insects.

Mind depends on life just as life depends on matter-energy, and yet these higher levels are not able to be reduced to the lower. This relationship is often referred to as one of "emergence" and might provide us with a way of thinking about eschatology in which science and Christian theology are engaged in direct, productive dialogue.

At the end of his book, Rolston introduces "spirit" as another category that may be required in order to give an ultimate explanation for the complex personhood we find in the world today—distinct from merely conscious animals like dogs, chimpanzees, and our prehistoric ancestors (Rolston 2010, 114). I wonder, though, whether we might talk about spirit as a kind of fourth big bang—that which emerges from conscious existence to a new kind of being. There are obvious resonances with traditional Christian theology in the Gospel of John: "you must be born of the spirit" (John 3:5–6); and it can be seen in Paul's first letter to the Corinthians when he makes a distinction between the natural or psychical body on the one hand and the spiritual body on the other (1 Corinthians 15:44). According to that view Christ's resurrection becomes the "first fruits" of this fourth big bang (perhaps prefigured by his transfiguration in Matthew 17).

In theological language, we might see each of the big bangs as an act of *creatio ex vetere*. Some Christians hold out hope that no scientific explanations will be produced for these transitions and thus claim they are instances of God's direct intervention. It also seems possible, though, that scientific explanations could be developed without providing a complete reduction, thus preserving the emergent reality as a genuinely new kind of existence. That wouldn't mean we have to import supernatural explanations into science, but it might show the limitations of our current scientific understanding. Just as our current understanding of the laws of nature could not predict the resurrection of Christ, neither can they predict what a future eternal state of the cosmos and its matter-energy might be like. That does not, however, rule out the rational possibility of scientifically informed Christians hoping for that future state. If it does come into being, it would not signal the end of science. It seems most consistent for Christians to believe that God's *creatio ex vetere* of spirit will be at least as amenable to systematic study as life and consciousness are. Perhaps in the eschaton, science will flourish as never before as it works to understand the true laws of nature and not just those of what Christopher Knight refers to as our present "subnatural" state (Knight 2007, 95).

The discerning reader will have noticed that I've not kept my own views hidden very well in this concluding chapter. It doesn't seem to me that the models of *creatio ex nihilo* or *creatio continua* have much to offer for eschatology. I don't see how Christians can consistently think that what is to come will be completely different or just a seamless extension of what is now. Those who hold to the former see no relation between their religious beliefs and the created world, and those who hold to the latter strip down theology until there is barely anything left but some sort of general religious impulse. Since we are considering here the intersection of science with Christianity in particular, it seems that *creatio ex vetere* is the appropriate attitude for what Christian theology holds about the future. It is the model for the single most defining doctrine of Christianity: the resurrection—and not just a resurrection that resuscitates the dead, but one that transforms them into something different. If the history of the universe is any clue, we might expect that there will come a different order of being that transcends our current consciousness just as consciousness transcends life. At least that is the hope of the Christian.

Conclusion

Finally, it seems to me that the *creatio ex vetere* approach to eschatology is a token of the most productive way forward for science and Christianity in general. There will always be Christians who fear that scientific discoveries threaten the integrity of their faith, and so they retreat into an enclosed system of alternative science. And there will be others who are persuaded by scientism that religious belief is a threat to the modern world and should be expunged. These approaches are convinced that theology trumps science, or science trumps theology. Instead, I am recommending a conversation between the two without prejudging where that conversation might go. I hope the chapters of this book have provided some resources for pursuing that conversation.

References

Clayton, Philip. 2005. "Eschatology as Metaphysics under the Guise of Hope." In *World without End: Essays in Honor of Marjorie Suchocki*, edited by Joseph Bracken. Grand Rapids, MI: Eerdmans.

Knight, Christopher C. 2007. *The God of Nature: Incarnation and Contemporary Science*. Minneapolis, MN: Fortress Press.

Macquarrie, John. 1977. *Principles of Christian Theology*, 2nd ed. New York, NY: Charles Scribner's Sons.

Polkinghorne, John. 1994. *The Faith of a Physicist: Reflections from a Bottom-Up Thinker*. Princeton, NJ: Princeton University Press.

Religion News Service. 2015. "Is Mark Driscoll this Generation's Pat Robertson?" http://jonathanmerritt.religionnews.com/2013/05/13/is-mark-driscoll-this-generations-pat-robertson/, accessed 17 February 2016.

Rolston III, Holmes. 2010. *Three Big Bangs: Matter-Energy, Life, Mind*. New York: Columbia University Press.

Russell, Robert J. 2012. "Eschatology in Science and Theology." In *The Blackwell Companion to Science and Christianity*, edited by J. B.Stump and Alan G.Padgett. Malden, MA: Wiley-Blackwell.

Tanner, Kathryn. 2000. "Eschatology without a Future." In *The End of the World and the Ends of God*, edited by John Polkinghorne and Michael Welker. Harrisburg, PA: Trinity press International.

Timeline of Historical Figures Discussed

Plato	c. 429–347 BCE
Aristotle	384–322 BCE
Philo	c. 15 BCE–50 CE
Paul of Tarsus	c. 5 CE–66
Justin Martyr	c. 100–165
Ptolemy	c. 100–170
Irenaeus	d. 202
Clement of Alexandria	c. 150–215
Tertullian	c. 160–230
Origen	c. 185–254
Apollinaris of Laodicea	310–390
John Chrysostom	347–407
Augustine	354–430
John Cassian	c. 360–435
Anselm of Canterbury	1033–1109
Al-Ghazâlî	c. 1055–1111
Averroës (ibn-Rushd)	1126–1198
Roger Bacon	c. 1220–1292
Thomas Aquinas	1225–1274
Stephen Tempier	d. 1279
Siger of Brabant	c. 1240–1284
William of Ockham	c. 1287–1347
Martin Luther	1483–1546
John Calvin	1509–1564
William Perkins	1558–1602

Science and Christianity: An Introduction to the Issues, First Edition. By J. B. Stump.
© 2017 John Wiley & Sons, Ltd. Published 2017 by John Wiley & Sons, Ltd.

Galileo Galilei	1564–1642
Johannes Kepler	1571–1630
James Ussher	1581–1656
René Descartes	1596–1650
Robert Boyle	1627–1691
John Locke	1632–1704
Isaac Newton	1642–1727
Samuel Clarke	1675–1729
John Wesley	1703–1791
David Hume	1711–1776
William Paley	1743–1805
Pierre-Simon Laplace	1749–1827
Auguste Comte	1798–1857
Samuel Wilberforce	1805–1873
Charles Darwin	1809–1882
John William Draper	1811–1882
Ellen White	1827–1915
Andrew Dickson White	1832–1918
Aubrey Moore	1848–1890
Clarence Darrow	1857–1938
William Jennings Bryan	1860–1925
Pierre Duhem	1861–1916
Alfred North Whitehead	1861–1947
Max Weber	1864–1920
James Leuba	1867–1946
George McCready Price	1870–1963
Bertrand Russell	1872–1970
Pius XII	1876–1958
Albert Einstein	1879–1955
Rudolf Bultmann	1884–1976
Karl Barth	1886–1968
Edwin Hubble	1889–1953
Georges Lemaître	1894–1966
C. S. Lewis	1898–1963
Joseph Needham	1900–1995
George Gamow	1904–1968
Reijer Hooykaas	1906–1994

Willard Van Orman Quine	1908–2000
Robert Merton	1910–2003
Bernard Ramm	1916–1992
Henry Morris	1916–2006
John Paul II	1920–2005
Thomas Kuhn	1922–1996
Ian Barbour	1923–2013
Arthur Peacocke	1924–2006
John Polkinghorne	1930–

Glossary

Altruism – Unselfish regard for the well-being of others.

Analytic Proposition – Statements that are true in virtue of the relationship of terms in them. For example, "All uncles are male" is true because the term "uncle" means "male sibling of a parent." Compare with Synthetic Proposition.

Apollinarianism – The doctrine that emphasizes the unity of Christ's human and divine natures.

Argument from Design – Arguments that appeal to the observed appearance of order or purpose of natural objects or processes and conclude that God must have intervened in the natural world to make them that way.

Argument from Neglect – An argument against miraculous intervention based on the observation that there are many instances in which we would expect a loving God to intervene; since God does not intervene in these, it is concluded that God is incapable or unwilling to intervene in the natural order.

Atonement – The doctrine of how the saving work of Jesus Christ brings reconciliation between God and human beings.

Augustinian Science – Science pursued according to explicitly Christian assumptions.

Biblical Inerrancy – The doctrine that the Bible contains no errors in what it teaches.

Biblicism – The conservative evangelical application of the *sola scriptura* principle, such that one claims to adhere to the strict literal meaning of biblical passages. See *Sola Scriptura*.

Big Bang – The model for the evolution of the universe according to which the universe has expanded from a very high-density state beginning about 13.8 billion years ago.

Butterfly Effect – In chaotic systems, the incredible sensitivity to slight changes or initial conditions for the later state of the system.

Casuistry – A way of resolving the causal history of an event into one of two options: direct action of God or the result of natural causes.

Causal Closure of the Physical World – The claim that anything that happens within the material world must have been caused by objects in the material world.

Science and Christianity: An Introduction to the Issues, First Edition. By J. B. Stump.
© 2017 John Wiley & Sons, Ltd. Published 2017 by John Wiley & Sons, Ltd.

Chaos Theory – A field of study in mathematics and physical sciences which examines systems that are unpredictable because they are so sensitive to slight changes.

Cognitive Dualism – The philosophical theory that there are two very different ways that have developed for thinking about reality: the scientific and the personal.

Common Ancestry – The theory that all life on earth has descended from a single source.

Complexity Thesis – The view of the relation between science and religion according to which there is no one general description that can account for the varied ways science and religion have, in fact, interacted. John Hedley Brooke is acknowledged as the foremost defender of this view.

Concordism – The position that both science and the Bible give reliable information about the origin of the earth and of life, and these two accounts must be fit together.

Conflict Thesis – The view that science and religion offer competing accounts and cannot both be correct.

Convergence – The phenomenon in evolution that similar structures evolve multiple times independently of each other.

Cosmic Fall – The supposition that the entire cosmos was affected by the first sin of human beings (or possibly by angelic creatures). See also Fall.

Cosmic Microwave Background Radiation – The radiation from the Big Bang which has cooled into the microwave frequency.

Cosmological Argument – A family of arguments for the existence of God that appeal to facts about causation, change, or contingency of existence and conclude that a necessary Being must exist.

Cosmological Constant – A term introduced by Einstein in his equations for general relativity to counteract the gravitational pull of matter.

Cosmological Theory of Inflation – A model of the development of the early universe according to which there was a period of extremely rapid expansion.

Cosmology – The study of the origin, structure, and evolution of the universe.

Creatio Continua – Latin for "continued creation," the theistic view that God sustains the natural world.

Creatio ex Nihilo – Latin for "creation out of nothing," the theistic view that God created the original material of the universe out of nothing pre-existing.

Creatio ex Vetere – Latin for "creation out of old." The claim that God will transform the current order of things into the world that is to come.

Creation *de Novo* – The formation of objects quickly and completely without using intermediate forms.

Day-age Theory – An attempt to reconcile Genesis 1 and contemporary scientific accounts by positing that each day of the creation narrative corresponds to a long age.

Deism – The theory that God does not interact with the created world after its initial creation.

Denisovans – An extinct hominin species which lived about 40,000 years ago and interbred with humans and Neanderthals.

De Novo – See Creation *de Novo*.

Design Argument – See Argument from Design.

Divine Action – A topic in theology and philosophy which seeks to understand the relationship between God's activities and the natural world.

Double-truth – The contention, often attributed to Averroës, that natural and supernatural claims could both be true even if they clearly contradicted each other. Averroës's actual position was more complex. He believed that there may be different levels of meaning but not outright contradiction.

Duhemian Science – The attempt to preclude metaphysics and explanation from science, restricting it to reporting and classifying empirical findings.

Duhem-Quine Thesis – All knowledge claims are interdependent with a set of background beliefs.

Emotivism – The ethical theory that moral statements are merely the expression of feelings, not objective truth claims.

Empiricism – The theory that experience, rather than reason, is the foundation of knowledge. See also Rationalism.

Episodic Deism – The theory that God does interact with the world regularly, but only in sporadic instances.

Epistemology – The subdiscipline of philosophy which investigates knowledge and related concepts like rationality and the justification of beliefs.

Eschatology – The study of last things; in Christian theology it is the study of how the present order of things will come to an end and what will come after that.

Essentialism – Within biology, the position that objects and classes of objects (especially species) have a set of necessary and unchanging characteristics.

Ethics – The subdiscipline of philosophy which investigates what is good or right.

Evil, Problem of – See, Problem of Evil.

Ex Nihilo – See *Creatio ex Nihilo*.

Exclusive Humanism – The view that there is no transcendent order beyond that of human beings.

Existentialism – The philosophical school which stresses the individual's ability and responsibility to choose ultimate meaning for themselves.

Fall – The theological doctrine that the sin of human beings had a damaging effect on them (and perhaps the entire world). Traditionally ascribed to the actions of Adam and Eve. See also Cosmic Fall.

Fideism – From the Latin word *fides*, meaning faith. Now used to denote the position that beliefs can be held without justification or rational grounds.

Fine Tuning – The recognition that many of the features of the universe appear to have been designed specifically for life.

Flatness Problem – In cosmology, the difficulty explaining why there is exactly the critical density which allows space to be flat—the expansion rate eventually slowing to zero.

Free Will Defense – An attempt to explain why God would allow moral evils by claiming that it is a greater good that humans have free will, even if they sometimes use it for evil purposes.

Gap Theory – An attempt to reconcile Genesis 1 and the contemporary scientific understanding of the old age of the earth by positing millions or billions of years between Genesis 1:1 and Genesis 1:3.

General Relativity – Einstein's theory of gravitation developed in 1915.

Geocentrism – The theory that the earth is the center of the universe and all heavenly bodies orbit around it.

Geokineticism – The theory that the earth moves around the sun.

God of the Gaps – Resorting to supernatural explanation when there are no known natural explanations for some phenomenon.

Great Chain of Being – The idea that there is a continuity of existence from highest (God) to the lowest (non-existence) and an infinite series of forms that exhibit each gradation.

Handmaiden Metaphor – The claim that philosophy (or secular learning in general) should serve theology.

Heliocentrism – The theory that the sun is the center of the universe (or later, the solar system) and the earth and other planets orbit around it.

Hermeneutics – The discipline that considers interpretation, especially as it relates to the Bible.

Hominin – The group of species descending from the common ancestor of humans and chimpanzees that includes humans and other *Homo* species.

Homo Erectus – A hominin species that lived around 1 million years ago.

Homo Sapiens – The scientific classification of modern human beings.

Horizon Problem – In the standard cosmological model of the Big Bang, the difficulty explaining how temperatures could have equalized between separated parts of the universe.

Incarnation – According to Christian theology, the event when the second person of the Trinity became a human being.

Independence Thesis – The view that science and religion are completely separate and self-contained ways of knowing.

Inerrancy – See Biblical Inerrancy.

Inflationary Theory – See Cosmological Theory of Inflation.

Intelligent Design – The attempt to show that materialism is false and that life and the universe are products of a super-intelligent agent. See also Materialism.

Interaction, Problem of – See Problem of Interaction.

Irreducible Complexity – The claim by Intelligent Design theorists that some natural structures could not have developed piecemeal through natural processes but could only have been designed.

Law of Human Progress – The claim by Auguste Comte that human thinking passes through three stages: the theological, the philosophical, and the scientific.

Many Worlds Theory – An interpretation of quantum mechanics according to which all possibilities signified by the wave function are realized in alternate realities.

Materialism – The view that all that exists can ultimately be reduced to matter. There are no supernatural or immaterial substances.

Metaphysical Naturalism – See Ontological Naturalism.

Metaphysics – The most general of the subdisciplines of philosophy, inquiring into what kinds of things exist and the nature of their existence.

Methodism – The Christian movement founded by John Wesley in the 18th century which aimed to reform the Church of England.

Methodological Naturalism – The claim that science should not investigate or appeal to supernatural entities. See also Ontological Naturalism.

Middle Ages – The period in European history lasting from roughly the 5th through 15th centuries.

Modern Science – The approach to the natural world developed in the 16th and 17th centuries during the Scientific Revolution.

Monism – The theory in the Philosophy of Mind that there is only one kind of substance, and that the apparent duality of mind and body is explainable by an underlying oneness.

Multiverse Hypothesis/Theory – The supposition that our universe is only one among a huge number of universes, each of which could have different physical laws and constants.

Natural Evil, Problem of – See Problem of Natural Evil.

Natural Philosophy – A forerunner of Modern Science; the method of learning about the world through natural instead of supernatural means.

Natural Reason – The means of acquiring knowledge without the aid of super-natural revelation.

Natural Theology – The practice of arguing to theological conclusions from generally accepted premises drawn from reason or experience of the natural world.

Neanderthals – A Hominin species that went extinct about 30,000 years ago and interbred with humans.

Neo-orthodoxy Movement – A movement which arose within Protestantism in the early 20th century which opposed liberalism and sought to recover certain traditional Christian doctrines which had been rejected by liberals, including the Trinity and Christ as fully God and fully human.

NOMA – Acronym developed by Stephen Jay Gould for non-overlapping magisteria—the position which claims science and religion pertain to indepen-dent spheres of investigation. See also Independence Thesis.

Non-interventionist Objective Divine Action (NIODA) – A term coined by Robert Russell for positions that allow for God making a difference in the events of the natural world without overriding natural laws.

Ockham's Razor – Principle attributed to William of Ockham that simplicity is to be preferred in explanations, or entities should not be multiplied beyond necessity.

Old Earth Creationism – The position that accepts the dating by physicists that the earth and universe are billions of years old but denies all life (especially humans) shares common ancestry. Instead it claims that God created at least some species separately. See also Young Earth Creationism.

Ontological Argument – An argument that attempts to prove the existence of God simply from the concept of God as the most perfect being.

Ontological Naturalism – The claim that there are no supernatural entities. See also Methodological Naturalism.

Ontology – The study of being, or of what exists.

Original Sin – According to some Christian theologians, the state of humanity that resulted from the Fall.

Pauli Exclusion Principle – In quantum mechanics, the principle that two particles cannot occupy the same quantum state at the same time.

Personal Identity – The philosophical problem of how we can maintain the sameness of substance across time, particularly for human beings.

Philosophy of Mind – The subdiscipline of philosophy that considers consciousness and the possible explanations for it.

Positivism – School of philosophy in the late 19th and 20th centuries, according to which any meaningful assertion must be capable of scientific verification.

Predestination – The doctrine (usually associated with Calvinism today) that God determined who would be saved, rather than people choosing for themselves whether to accept God's offer of salvation.

Problem of Evil – The difficulty of explaining why God would allow the amount and kind of evil we observe to have taken place in the world. See also Problem of Natural Evil.

Problem of Interaction – In the philosophy of mind, the difficulty of explaining how an immaterial mind could interact with a physical body.

Problem of Natural Evil – The difficulty of explaining why a good God would allow the pain and suffering that results from events that are not caused by agents with free will. See also Natural Evil.

Protestant Reformation – The 16th-century break from the Roman Catholic Church, led by Martin Luther.

Rationalism – The theory that the foundation of knowledge is reason, rather than experience. See also Empiricism.

RNA World Hypothesis – The claim in origin of life studies that the first replicating molecule was RNA rather than DNA.

Scientific Revolution – The emergence of modern science in the 16th and 17th centuries, based on the work of Copernicus, Kepler, Galileo, Descartes, Newton, and others.

Scientism – The view that the natural sciences are the only genuine source of knowledge.

Scopes Trial – The trail of John Scopes in 1925 in Dayton, Tennessee for teaching evolution in violation of a state law.

Secondary Causation – From Aquinas, the doctrine that God can be said to cause events even though we see how those same events are the result of natural causes.

Secularization Thesis – In its cognitive guise, the claim that supernatural interpretations of reality have been steadily replaced with natural explanations because of the influence of science.

Skeptical Theism – The view that we should be skeptical of our ability to discern and understand the reasons God might have for allowing evil.

Sola Scriptura – The principle of the Protestant Reformers that the Bible, not the Church, is the final authority for doctrine and practice.

Soul-making Theodicy – God has allowed evil in the world as a way of promoting the moral development of human beings.

String Theory – In particle physics, the ultimate particles are treated as mathematical points. String theory replaces these point-particles with one-dimensional strings.

Substance Dualism – The position in the philosophy of mind which claims there are two different kinds of substances—minds and bodies—and that these are not reducible to each other.

Survival of the Fittest – The evolutionary principle that those organisms which are most capable of reproducing in their environment will tend to be most successful.

Synthetic Proposition – Statements that are true (or false) in virtue of the claims made about reality, rather than their truth being determined by the relations of terms as in Analytic Propositions.

Teleological Argument – See Argument from Design.

Theodicy – An explanation for why a good God might permit evil.

Theology – The systematic study of the nature of God.

Theory of Double-Truth – See Double-truth.

Thomistic Synthesis – The approach of Thomas Aquinas to produce one coherent system of knowledge from two separate sources: faith and reason.

Trinity – The Christian view that God exists as three distinct persons in one nature.

Two Books Metaphor – The claim that God has revealed himself in Scripture (i.e., God's word) and through nature (i.e., God's world).

Two-minds View – The view that the Incarnation is explained by supposing that Jesus possessed both a divine mind and a human mind.

Young Earth Creationism – The belief inspired by a literal reading of the Bible that God created the universe less than 10,000 years ago. See also Old Earth Creationism.

Index

Science and Christianity: An Introduction to the Issues, First Edition. By J. B. Stump.
© 2017 John Wiley & Sons, Ltd. Published 2017 by John Wiley & Sons, Ltd.